BESTSELLING
BOOK SERIES

Geocaching For Dummies®

Cheat Sheet

In Case of an Emergency

- ✔ **S/top:** Breathe deeply, compose yourself, and focus.
- ✔ **T/hink:** Always think before you take action.
- ✔ **O/bserve:** Take a look around and assess your situation.
- ✔ **P/lan:** Based on your situation, make a plan and follow it.

Geocaching Etiquette

- ✔ Respect private property and be environmentally conscious when searching for and hiding caches.
- ✔ Trade-up or replace cache items with something of equal value.
- ✔ Keep geocaching dog-friendly. Tether Fido in leash-only areas, keep a leash ready, and bring a plastic bag just in case.
- ✔ Cache In, Trash Out: If you see any litter on your way to or from a cache, pick it up and pack it out.
- ✔ After you visit a cache, send a quick thank-you by e-mail message to whomever placed the cache or acknowledge him in your cache comments when you lo...

If You Can't Find the Geocache

- ✔ Check that you entered the coordinates correctly in your receiver.
- ✔ Ensure that the coordinates' and your GPS receiver datum match.
- ✔ Check your GPS receiver for good satellite coverage.
- ✔ Use the encrypted hint shown on the cache description page.
- ✔ Use a purposeful search pattern (walk in a grid); don't wander.
- ✔ Come back another day and try again. (You'll be amazed at how easy some caches are to find the second time around.)

Essentials to Bring Geocaching

- ✔ GPS receiver, map, and compass
- ✔ Sun protection and first aid supplies
- ✔ Insulation (extra clothing)
- ✔ Illumination (flashlight/headlamp)
- ✔ Fire making equipment
- ✔ Repair kit and tools
- ✔ Nutrition and hydration (extra f... and water)
- ✔ ...ency shelter

D1010132

For Dummi... ...s for Beginners

Geocaching For Dummies®

Cheat Sheet

BESTSELLING
BOOK SERIES

Common Geocache Containers

- Surplus military ammo cans; military decontamination kit boxes
- Plastic storage containers or buckets/margarine tubs with lids
- Breath mint tins, 35mm film canisters, pill bottles
- Magnetic car key holders
- PVC piping (with end caps)

When You Find a Geocache

1. Open the container.
2. Sign the logbook.
3. Trade for some goodies.
4. Make sure that the cache container is sealed when you're done.
5. Put the cache container back exactly where you found it.
6. Check the area for any gear you've left lying on the ground.
7. Cover your tracks and don't leave too many signs of your visit.

Where Not to Place Geocaches

- Buried in holes. Covering the cache, though, is okay.
- In environmentally sensitive areas, including areas with endangered plants/animals and archaeological/historic sites.
- In national parks or designated wilderness areas.
- Within 150 feet of railroad tracks.
- Anywhere that might cause concerns about possible terrorist activities: near airports, tunnels, bridges, military facilities, municipal water supplies, and government buildings.
- Within one-tenth of a mile of another cache: This is a rule for adding a cache to the Geocaching.com database.

Wiley, the Wiley Publishing logo, For Dummies, the Dummies Man logo, the For Dummies Bestselling Book Series logo and all related trade dress are trademarks or registered trademarks of John Wiley & Sons, Inc. and/or its affiliates. All other trademarks are property of their respective owners.

Copyright © 2004 Wiley Publishing, Inc. All rights reserved.

Item 7571-6.

For more information about Wiley Publishing, call 1-800-762-2974.

For Dummies: Bestselling Book Series for Beginners

Geocaching

FOR

DUMMIES

by Joel McNamara

WILEY

Wiley Publishing, Inc.

Geocaching For Dummies®

Published by
Wiley Publishing, Inc.
111 River Street
Hoboken, NJ 07030-5774
www.wiley.com

Copyright © 2004 by Wiley Publishing, Inc., Indianapolis, Indiana

Published by Wiley Publishing, Inc., Indianapolis, Indiana

Published simultaneously in Canada

No part of this publication may be reproduced, stored in a retrieval system or transmitted in any form or by any means, electronic, mechanical, photocopying, recording, scanning or otherwise, except as permitted under Sections 107 or 108 of the 1976 United States Copyright Act, without either the prior written permission of the Publisher, or authorization through payment of the appropriate per-copy fee to the Copyright Clearance Center, 222 Rosewood Drive, Danvers, MA 01923, (978) 750-8400, fax (978) 646-8600. Requests to the Publisher for permission should be addressed to the Legal Department, Wiley Publishing, Inc., 10475 Crosspoint Blvd., Indianapolis, IN 46256, (317) 572-3447, fax (317) 572-4355, e-mail: brandreview@ wiley.com.

Trademarks: Wiley, the Wiley Publishing logo, For Dummies, the Dummies Man logo, A Reference for the Rest of Us!, The Dummies Way, Dummies Daily, The Fun and Easy Way, Dummies.com, and related trade dress are trademarks or registered trademarks of John Wiley & Sons, Inc. and/or its affiliates in the United States and other countries, and may not be used without written permission. All other trademarks are the property of their respective owners. Wiley Publishing, Inc., is not associated with any product or vendor mentioned in this book.

LIMIT OF LIABILITY/DISCLAIMER OF WARRANTY: THE PUBLISHER AND THE AUTHOR MAKE NO REPRESENTATIONS OR WARRANTIES WITH RESPECT TO THE ACCURACY OR COMPLETENESS OF THE CONTENTS OF THIS WORK AND SPECIFICALLY DISCLAIM ALL WARRANTIES, INCLUDING WITHOUT LIMITATION WARRANTIES OF FITNESS FOR A PARTICULAR PURPOSE. NO WARRANTY MAY BE CREATED OR EXTENDED BY SALES OR PROMOTIONAL MATERIALS. THE ADVICE AND STRATEGIES CONTAINED HEREIN MAY NOT BE SUITABLE FOR EVERY SITUATION. THIS WORK IS SOLD WITH THE UNDERSTANDING THAT THE PUBLISHER IS NOT ENGAGED IN RENDERING LEGAL, ACCOUNTING, OR OTHER PROFESSIONAL SERVICES. IF PROFESSIONAL ASSISTANCE IS REQUIRED, THE SERVICES OF A COMPETENT PROFESSIONAL PERSON SHOULD BE SOUGHT. NEITHER THE PUBLISHER NOR THE AUTHOR SHALL BE LIABLE FOR DAMAGES ARISING HEREFROM. THE FACT THAT AN ORGANIZATION OR WEBSITE IS REFERRED TO IN THIS WORK AS A CITATION AND/OR A POTENTIAL SOURCE OF FURTHER INFORMATION DOES NOT MEAN THAT THE AUTHOR OR THE PUBLISHER ENDORSES THE INFORMATION THE ORGANIZATION OR WEBSITE MAY PROVIDE OR RECOMMENDATIONS IT MAY MAKE. FURTHER, READERS SHOULD BE AWARE THAT INTERNET WEBSITES LISTED IN THIS WORK MAY HAVE CHANGED OR DISAPPEARED BETWEEN WHEN THIS WORK WAS WRITTEN AND WHEN IT IS READ.

For general information on our other products and services or to obtain technical support, please contact our Customer Care Department within the U.S. at 800-762-2974, outside the U.S. at 317-572-3993, or fax 317-572-4002.

Wiley also publishes its books in a variety of electronic formats. Some content that appears in print may not be available in electronic books.

Library of Congress Control Number: 2004107889

ISBN: 0-7645-7571-6

Manufactured in the United States of America

10 9 8 7 6 5 4 3 2 1

1B/SQ/QY/QU/IN

About the Author

Joel McNamara first got involved with digital maps in the early 1980s. At the time, he was studying archaeology. Instead of going out and playing Indiana Jones, he found himself in front of a computer monitor trying to predict where archeological sites were located based on LANDSAT satellite data.

The lure of computers ultimately led to his defection from academia to the software industry, where he worked as a programmer, technical writer, and manager, eventually ending up at a rather large software company based in Redmond, Washington. Joel now writes and consults on technology and other things he enjoys and finds interesting.

Over the years, he's had practical experience using GPS and maps for wildland firefighting, search and rescue, and disaster response and planning. He geocaches and is an avid user of the great outdoors (which means there's always too much gear in his garage), competes in adventure races and other endurance sports, and (so far) has always found his way back home.

This is his third book. He is the author of *GPS For Dummies* (which happens to be a good companion to this book, especially if you want to find out more about GPS and digital maps) and *Secrets of Computer Espionage: Tactics & Countermeasures,* a reference guide for computer security practitioners and anyone interested in stopping sneaky spies.

Author's Acknowledgments

I'd like to thank Katie Feltman, my acquisitions editor at Wiley, whom I've been fortunate enough to work with on all the books I've written so far. Next on the list is Kyle Looper, project editor extraordinaire, whose wit and insight made writing this book a lot of fun. I'd also like to express my gratitude to technical editor Gavin Hoban, copy editor Teresa Artman, Jason Marcuson for scintillating discussions about marketing, and all the people at Wiley whom I haven't had the pleasure of meeting (in real life or virtually) who played a role in this book's production.

Publisher's Acknowledgments

We're proud of this book; please send us your comments through our online registration form located at www.dummies.com/register/.

Some of the people who helped bring this book to market include the following:

Acquisitions, Editorial, and Media Development

Project Editor: Kyle Looper

Acquisitions Editor: Katie Feltman

Senior Copy Editor: Teresa Artman

Technical Editor: Gavin Hoban

Editorial Manager: Kevin Kirschner

Media Development Manager: Laura VanWinkle

Media Development Supervisor: Richard Graves

Editorial Assistant: Amanda Foxworth

Cartoons: Rich Tennant (www.the5thwave.com)

Composition

Project Coordinator: Courtney MacIntyre

Layout and Graphics: Karl Brandt, Andrea Dahl, Lauren Goddard, Denny Hager, Michael Kruzil, Lynsey Osborn, Heather Ryan, Brent Savage, Mary Gillot Virgin

Proofreaders: Laura Albert, Brian H. Walls, TECHBOOKS Production Services

Indexer: TECHBOOKS Production Services

Special Help: Dru Hoskins

Publishing and Editorial for Technology Dummies

 Richard Swadley, Vice President and Executive Group Publisher

 Andy Cummings, Vice President and Publisher

Mary Bednarek, Executive Acquisitions Director

 Mary C. Corder, Editorial Director

Publishing for Consumer Dummies

 Diane Graves Steele, Vice President and Publisher

 Joyce Pepple, Acquisitions Director

Composition Services

 Gerry Fahey, Vice President of Production Services

 Debbie Stailey, Director of Composition Services

Contents at a Glance

Introduction...1

Part 1: Getting Ready to Geocache 7
Chapter 1: An Introduction to Geocaching 9
Chapter 2: Selecting a GPS Receiver 21
Chapter 3: Using a GPS Receiver 43
Chapter 4: Using a Map and Compass 61

Part 11: Let's Go Geocaching 89
Chapter 5: Selecting Geocaches to Find..91
Chapter 6: Searching for a Geocache..111
Chapter 7: Discovering a Geocache 131
Chapter 8: Hiding Geocaches..143

Part 111: Advanced Geocaching.........................161
Chapter 9: Searching for Benchmarks 163
Chapter 10: Organized Geocaching Clubs and Competitions...........177
Chapter 11: GPS and Geocaching in Education 187

Part 1V: The Part of Tens...................................197
Chapter 12: Ten Internet Geocaching Resources 199
Chapter 13: Ten Geocaching Programs 203

Index...207

Table of Contents

Introduction 1

About This Book 2
What You're Not to Read...3
Foolish Assumptions 3
How This Book Is Organized...4
    Part I: Getting Ready to Geocache...........................4
    Part II: Let's Go Geocaching 4
    Part III: Advanced Geocaching...............................4
    Part IV: The Part of Tens...................................5
Icons Used in This Book..5
A Few Closing Thoughts...6

Part 1: Getting Ready to Geocache 7

Chapter 1: An Introduction to Geocaching........... 9

What Is Geocaching? 10
    Geocaching technology 10
    Geocaching explained 11
Deciding to Geocache..14
Who Geocaches? 15
What You Need to Geocache 16
Geojargon: Speaking the Lingo.....................................17

Chapter 2: Selecting a GPS Receiver 21

Understanding Basic GPS Concepts 22
    Satellites..22
    Ground stations 24
    Receivers 25
GPS Receiver Accuracy 26
Factors That Affect GPS Accuracy..................................29
Discovering GPS Receiver Features.................................30
    Shells 30
    Screen display 31
    Mapping capabilities 32
    Memory..33
    PC interface 34
    Antennas 34
    Batteries...35
    Enhanced features 36
Selecting a GPS Receiver for Geocaching 39

Chapter 3: Using a GPS Receiver 43

   Getting Familiar with Basic GPS Concepts 43

      Understanding coordinate systems 44

      Understanding datums...49

      Understanding waypoints..51

      Understanding routes 51

      Understanding tracks..52

   Using Your GPS Receiver..53

      Initializing a GPS receiver 54

      Changing receiver settings 56

      Entering a waypoint 57

      Navigating to a waypoint 59

Chapter 4: Using a Map and Compass 61

   All about Compasses 62

      Why do you need a compass?.....................................62

      How compasses work 62

      Parts of a compass 65

      Selecting a compass 68

   All about Maps 71

      Why do you need a map?...71

      Selecting the right map...72

      Understanding parts of a map 75

   Using a Map and Compass..81

      Getting familiar with basic navigation concepts 82

      Orienting the map to north 83

      Taking a bearing..84

      Setting a course 85

      Using triangulation 87

Part II: Let's Go Geocaching 89

Chapter 5: Selecting Geocaches to Find 91

   Defining the Types of Geocaches.......................................92

      Traditional cache..92

      Multicache 92

      Virtual cache 93

      Mystery cache...93

      Locationless cache 93

      Letterbox hybrid...94

      Event cache 94

      Webcam cache 94

      Caches within caches..94

   Using Geocaching.com 96

Querying the Geocaching.com Database..............................98
    Basic search techniques 98
    Detailed search techniques 101
Looking at the Search Results 103
    Viewing the list of geocaches........................103
    Getting information about a geocache................106

Chapter 6: Searching for a Geocache.............. 111

Deciding What Gear to Bring Geocaching 111
    Cache-related 112
    Food and shelter..115
    Electronic devices 117
    Safety equipment 119
Getting Close to the Geocache...................................122
Starting Your Search..125
Search Strategies as You Near the Cache 128

Chapter 7: Discovering a Geocache 131

What to Do When You Find a Geocache...............................131
    Opening the cache..132
    Signing the logbook 133
    Leaving and trading goodies 135
    Heading home 137
    Logging your find online 137
When You Can't Find a Geocache 140
    Logging a DNF 141
    Try, try again 141

Chapter 8: Hiding Geocaches..................... 143

Deciding What Type of Geocache to Create.........................144
Selecting a Container..144
    Ammo cans 145
    Household plastic storage containers 145
Selecting a Location...147
    Where to hide your cache 147
    Where not to hide your cache 148
    Hiding for seekers......................................149
    Recording the location.................................151
Stocking a Geocache...151
    Logbook and writing utensil...........................151
    Identifying information 152
    Goodies 152
Submitting a Geocache..153
Maintaining a Geocache...158
    Physical maintenance 158
    Online maintenance....................................159

Part III: Advanced Geocaching 161

Chapter 9: Searching for Benchmarks 163

Understanding Benchmarks 164
Identifying Benchmarks in Your Area...................................166
    Benchmarks from Geocaching.com 166
    Benchmarks from the National Geodetic Survey 169
Finding Benchmarks 172
    Starting your benchmark search 173
    Documenting a found benchmark 174

Chapter 10: Organized Geocaching Clubs and Competitions 177

Geocaching Clubs 177
    Why join a club?...178
    Finding a local club..179
Competitive Geocaching...184
    Geocaching stats...184
    Organized competitions......................................185

Chapter 11: GPS and Geocaching in Education 187

GPS in the Schools 188
    Geography 188
    History and sociology 189
    Ecology..189
    Mathematics...190
    Physical education 190
Incorporating GPS in a Class 191
    Developing the curriculum...................................192
    Acquiring GPS receivers 194
    Evaluating your success 194
Educational Internet Resources......................................195

Part IV: The Part of Tens 197

Chapter 12: Ten Internet Geocaching Resources 199

Geocaching.com...199
Navicache.com 200
Buxley's Geocaching Waypoint 200
GPS Visualizer..200
Today's Cacher...201
Geocacher University..201
Markwell's FAQs 201
KeenPeople.com 201
The First 100 Geocaches 202

Letterboxing North America 202
GPSInformation.net...202

Chapter 13: Ten Geocaching Programs. 203

Geocaching Swiss Army Knife (GSAK) 204
GPXSonar 204
CacheMate 204
Watcher 205
Plucker 205
GPSBabel...205
USAPhotoMaps..206
TopoFusion 206

Index *207*

Introduction

．．．

*G*eocaching is a high-tech treasure hunt where you get to play
Indiana Jones and search for hidden booty. (Wearing a fedora
and carrying a whip are completely up to you.)

Things have changed quite a lot since Indy roamed the globe looking
for rare artifacts, and the sport of geocaching relies on two modern-
day technologies:

✔ **The Internet:** Instead of translating some old piece of papyrus
   to discover the location of the lost city of Tanis, you head out
   to the Geocaching.com Web site (or other sites that maintain
   geocache databases); enter a ZIP code, state, or country; and
   you're presented with a list of caches you can search for.
   Currently, over 100,000 geocaches are located all over the
   world, so you can search for caches in your own neighborhood or hop on a Pan Am Clipper to some exotic country
   for a real adventure.

✔ **GPS receivers:** Although Jones had to figure out how to use the
   Staff of Ra to find the resting place of the Ark of the Covenant,
   searching for a geocache is usually quite a bit simpler. The list
   of geocaches that you can get from the online Geocaching.com
   database all have location coordinates associated with them.
   By entering the coordinates into a GPS receiver, you can typically get within about 30 feet of a geocache you're searching
   for (or sometimes even closer).

Dr. Jones searched for priceless artifacts like the Lost Ark, but your
hunt involves looking for containers filled with modern day memorabilia such as souvenirs, toys, and trinkets (some useful and others
not). Don't count on golden idols, but do expect to encounter some
cool and unique items in caches. You'll also usually not need to
worry about poison darts, snakes, or Nazis.

If geocaching sounds intriguing, you've come to the right place.
This book covers you everything you need to know about geocaching. You'll discover how to

✔ Select a GPS receiver to use for geocaching.

✔ Use a GPS receiver.

✔ Use a map and compass.

- Prepare yourself for geocaching trips (including what gear you'll need).
- Locate geocaches to search for on the `www.geocaching.com` Web site.
- Find geocaches.
- Hide your own geocaches and add them to the Geocaching. com database.
- Search for *benchmarks* (U.S. government survey markers).
- Use geocaching for educational purposes.
- Use Internet resources and software to enhance your geocaching experience.

About This Book

Because I have acquaintances, friends, and family who geocache, I often get lots of questions about the sport. One of the reasons why I wrote this book was to provide an easy-to-use reference that anyone could pick up; give a quick read; and within no time, be out in the fresh air enjoying geocaching.

With that in mind, this book is for several types of readers:

- **Neocachers:** In geocaching jargon, a *neocacher* is a novice geocacher; you might have just started out and have found a few caches, or you've recently read or heard about the sport and are interested in giving it a try. If you're a neocacher, you're in luck because you'll find everything you need to know to get started with geocaching.
- **Experienced geocachers:** If you're an experienced geocacher with hundreds of finds under your belt, you'll probably be familiar with a fair amount of the basic information in this book. However, in addition to the material designed for the neocachers, you're going to encounter some tips and techniques (as well as entertaining and educational stories) that apply to geocachers of all levels. Also, if you want to get a friend or family member hooked on the sport, this book makes a great birthday or Christmas present (especially wrapped together with a new GPS receiver, if your budget allows).

> ✔ **Land managers:** If you work for a federal, state, or local
> agency that manages land and have had reports of people
> wandering around the land that you're responsible for —
> staring intently at GPS receivers while looking for something,
> and you want to know what they're up to — this book is also
> for you. Geocaching is turning into an increasingly popular
> form of outdoor recreation. As a land manager, you should
> really understand what the sport is all about so you can
> develop effective policies and work together with geocaching
> groups. (The good news is that most geocachers tend to
> be responsible land users.)

What You're Not to Read

Scattered throughout this book are little anecdotes, historical notes,
and technical details. This information is definitely *not* necessary
to your understanding of geocaching; it's completely voluntary that
you read it. For this reason, I put all this information into little gray
boxes or highlight it with a Technical Stuff icon. Feel free to thumb
your nose at this information.

On the other hand, in geocaching, the journey is half the fun. I would
go ahead and read this stuff if I were you. Just keep in mind that you
don't have to.

Foolish Assumptions

If I had to make some foolish assumptions about you and other
readers of this book, here's what they'd be:

> ✔ You already have a GPS receiver (but might be a little fuzzy on
> all its features and whistles and bells).
>
> ✔ You've read my other book, *GPS For Dummies* (which has lots
> of information about GPS and digital maps and a single chap-
> ter devoted to geocaching). *Geocaching For Dummies* provides
> detailed coverage of geocaching and basic information on GPS
> and digital maps.
>
> ✔ You've got access to the Internet (home, work, school, library,
> an Internet café, wherever), and you can use a Web browser.

> ✔ You like to be outside and are looking for a good excuse to get some fresh air.
>
> ✔ You like challenges and puzzles.
>
> ✔ You always thought hunting for pirate treasure or that infamous Lost Ark would be a cool second career.

So how did I do? If I got three or four correct, you've come to the right place.

How This Book Is Organized

This book is conveniently divided into several different parts. The content in each part tends to be related, but by all means, feel free to skip around and read about what interests you the most.

Part I: Getting Ready to Geocache

Part I is all about getting to geocache. You'll find chapters devoted to general information about the sport, how to select and use a GPS receiver, and how to use a map and compass. (I know, this is a pretty old-school skill, but trust me, it comes in handy — and you'll see why.)

Part II: Let's Go Geocaching

If you can't wait to head out geocaching, this is likely the part of the book that you want to read first. Here are chapters that show you how to use the Geocaching.com database to choose geocaches to search for, how to go about finding a geocache (and most importantly, what to do when you find one), and how to hide your own cache after you get a feel for what geocaching is all about.

Part III: Advanced Geocaching

Geocaching is an evolving new sport, and variations of the basic concept are already starting to sprout up. This section of the book examines some advanced and alternative applications of geocaching. You'll find chapters on searching for benchmarks; how to use geocaching in education (with tips for teachers and parents); and how to get involved with geocaching clubs, including entering geocaching competitions.

Part IV: The Part of Tens

You can't have a *For Dummies* book without a Part of Tens section. In this part of the book, you'll find chapters on Internet geocaching resources and software programs that you can use for geocaching.

Icons Used in This Book

When you go geocaching, you'll likely be using a paper map or perhaps one that's displayed on your GPS receiver. Maps use symbols to quickly convey information, and this book does the same by using icons to help you navigate your way around. The icons that you'll encounter include the following.

 This icon represents some good insider tips — the kind of information someone might whisper in your ear (or that you eventually learn through trial and error and practical experience). Tips are designed to make your life easier so you can make sure your fun-meter is always on high while you're geocaching.

 When you see this icon, it's a gentle reminder about something of importance. Consider it similar to advice from your favorite uncle (who always seemed pretty smart and cool).

 The sport of geocaching is based on technology. When it comes to GPS, maps, and compasses, an understanding of some technical stuff is required. I try to keep the really rocket-scientist things to a bare minimum, but every now and then, technical stuff does creep in. When it does, you see this icon. I'll do my best to either give you a plain-English explanation or point you to a Web site where you can get additional details.

 The little bomb icon looks pretty scary, doesn't it? This icon means warning. It's kind of like the robot from the old *Lost in Space* TV show, saying, "Danger, Will Robinson!" It doesn't necessarily mean that you'll encounter a situation that causes your GPS receiver to melt or that you'll accidentally release evil spirits if you open up a certain geocache. What it does mean is to pay attention: Here's some worthwhile information that might save you from some mental or physical discomfort of one type or the other.

A Few Closing Thoughts

That's a brief tour of the book, but before I get started with the ins and outs of geocaching, I'd like to leave you with a few closing thoughts.

I spend some time discussing GPS receivers. One question that I often get is, *What is the best GPS receiver for geocaching?* Like any consumer electronics product, GPS receiver models are constantly changing and being updated. Instead of recommending that you buy a certain brand or model (that could possibly be replaced by something cheaper and better over the course of a few months), I tell you what questions to ask when you're shopping for a GPS receiver and give you some hints on which features are best for geocaching. You'll be able to apply these questions and selection criteria to pretty much any GPS receiver (no matter how much the marketplace changes) to pick the right model.

You'll find a fair number of references to Web sites in this book. Unfortunately, Web sites sometimes change just about as fast as the contents of a popular geocache. If a link doesn't work, you should have enough information to find what you're looking for by using a search engine such as Google.

All the information in this book should set you on your way to becoming an expert geocacher — that is, if you go out and practice. Read through the book and then head out into the great outdoors and play Indiana Jones searching for the lost geocache. Learn, experiment, and have fun!

Part I
Getting Ready to Geocache

The 5th Wave   By Rich Tennant

"...and the instructions in their cache said, 'Take a book report, leave a book report'."

In this part . . .

*B*efore you run out the door to give geocaching a try, you should have a basic understanding of the sport and some fundamental skills. That's where this part of the book comes in. Chapter 1 introduces you to geocaching and provides a general overview of what it's all about (including some good reasons to give it a try). Because GPS receivers are an essential part of geocaching, in Chapter 2, I talk about how they work and the types of features they have — and if you don't have one yet, how to choose a GPS receiver suitable for geocaching.

I follow that up with Chapter 3, where you can find basic instructions on how to use a GPS receiver. (Rest assured that no matter what the brand or model, all GPS receivers have similar features commonly used for geocaching.) In Chapter 4, I step you through the basics of using a map and a compass. I know this seems pretty old school compared with simply pushing a button on a GPS receiver to find out exactly where you are. *Trust me:* Having fundamental map and compass skills can make geocaching more enjoyable *and* save you from getting lost if you're out in the middle of nowhere and your GPS stops working (it does happen).

Chapter 1

An Introduction to Geocaching

In This Chapter

▶ Understanding geoaching

▶ Finding out how geocaching works

▶ Discovering the benefits of geocaching

▶ Minimum requirements for geocaching

*G*eocaching is a new, popular sport that relies on using a Global Positioning System (GPS) receiver, the Internet, and your powers of observation. In a nutshell, you find some stuff, take some stuff, leave some stuff, record it all in a logbook, and have fun!

To elaborate a little more, someone, somewhere, hides a container filled with goodies (toys, travel memorabilia, costume jewelry, you name it). He or she then posts the location coordinates on the Internet along with a few clues. You visit a Web site database, get the coordinates, and use your GPS receiver to zero in on the geocache location. (Your GPS receiver usually won't lead you directly to the cache, and this is where your powers of observation come into play in locating the cache's hiding place.)

 Geocaching is pronounced *GEE-oh-cash-ing*. It's not appropriate to pronounce cache as *ca-SHAY,* even if you are French. So unless you want some funny looks, stick with good ol' *cash.*

In a few short years, geocaching has grown incredibly popular. Relatively cheap and accurate GPS receivers and widespread access to the Internet have helped the sport flourish throughout the world. As of April 2004, the Geocaching.com site (www. geocaching.com; one of the first Web sites devoted to the sport and currently the largest geocaching site on the 'Net) had over 91,000 active geocaches listed in its database, spread out among 201 countries. And that number continues to grow each day. That's a lot of caches out there to find!

Although geocaching is based on a fairly simple idea, you need to understand a number of basic things — or at least be aware of them — before you get started. That's what this chapter is all about. I show you exactly what geocaching is, how the sport got started, why you should geocache, and what you'll need to get started with the sport.

What Is Geocaching?

If you're reading this book, there's a good chance you've heard about geocaching (or saw the title on a bookstore shelf, wondered what the heck it was, and started flipping through pages). The rising popularity of the sport has gotten a fair amount of media attention. Maybe you read a newspaper or magazine article about it or perhaps heard friends talking about some of their geocaching adventures.

Geocaching technology

Geocaching relies on two technologies:

- ✔ **The Internet:** Various Web sites list the coordinates of geocaches that you can search for.

- ✔ **GPS:** The satellite-based Global Positioning System (which everyone calls GPS for short) is used to help you zero in on the location of geocaches. (I discuss GPS in depth in Chapter 2. I even wrote a whole book about it: *GPS For Dummies.*)

People use these two technologies together for finding and hiding goodie-filled containers that, by now, you've probably guessed are called *geocaches.*

How geocaching got started

Until 2000, the U.S. government degraded GPS signals using something called Selective Availability (SA). SA allowed the U.S. and its allies to use special GPS receivers to get very accurate location information while preventing civilian GPS receivers from having as much precision.

In May 2000, SA was officially turned off (mostly because the U.S. government developed a way to degrade the accuracy of GPS to specific geographic regions). Suddenly, like magic, civilian GPS receivers that formerly were accurate only to about 300 feet became accurate to 30 feet. This new level of accuracy offered some interesting, creative possibilities.

Three days after SA was turned off, Dave Ulmer posted a message in the `sci.geo.satellite-nav` USENET newsgroup with coordinates of a "stash" he had hidden that contained software, videos, books, food, money, and a slingshot.

Earlier in the day, in the same newsgroup, Ulmer had proposed a worldwide "stash hunt," where people would post GPS *waypoints* (coordinates saved in a GPS receiver) on the Internet that would lead searchers to hidden goodies. While Ulmer envisioned thousands of stashes tucked in places all over the world, he had no idea how popular his idea would become.

By the end of May, in a Yahoo! Group devoted to the new sport, a member named Matt Stum suggested that the sport be called *geocaching* in order to avoid some of the negative connotations associated with drugs and the word *stash*. (A *cache* is a hidden place where goods or valuables are concealed.) Geocaching had a nice ring to it, and because it didn't sound like a bad Cheech and Chong movie, the name stuck.

The original cache is long gone, but there's a newer one at the location and even a plaque that commemorates the world's first official geocache (shown here). If you've ever in the Portland, Oregon area, think about making a pilgrimage to the shrine. (In Chapter 5, I tell you how to get there.)

Geocaching explained

Take a more detailed look at the steps that are involved in geocaching:

1. **Someone hides a geocache.**

   The cache consists of a waterproof, element-resistant container, such as a surplus ammo can or plastic tub, that's filled with small trinkets such as costume jewelry, toys, flashlights, old coins, fossils, or just about anything else you could imagine. (Chapter 8 has everything you need to know about hiding caches.) The container also contains a logbook and a pen or pencil so whoever finds a cache can record their discovery. A sample geocache with its goodies is shown in Figure 1-1.

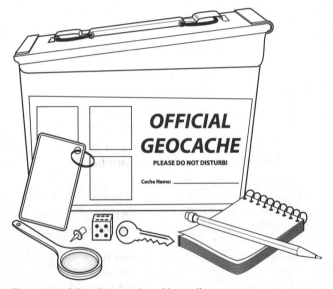

OFFICIAL GEOCACHE

PLEASE DO NOT DISTURB!

Cache Name: _____

Figure 1-1: A found geocache with goodies.

2. **The geocache hider logs the GPS coordinates of the cache and a brief description on a Web site.**

   Several different Web sites list the geocache coordinates. The largest and most popular site is www.geocaching.com. I primarily focus on this Web site throughout the book.

3. **The prospective geocache finder (that's you) is interested in searching for geocaches in a particular area and queries the Geocaching.com database.**

   You can do this by entering a ZIP code, state, country, or other search options. A list of all the geocaches in the general vicinity is displayed. (Read more about this in Chapter 5.)

4. **Look through the list of geocaches, select a few that look interesting, and enter their coordinates in your GPS receiver.**

5. **Drive as close as you can to the geocache (unless you want some additional exercise by walking or hiking a bit farther) and start your search on foot, using the GPS receiver to guide you to the cache location.**

   The GPS receiver won't take you directly to the geocache — that would be too simple. Your GPS receiver will typically get you within 50 feet or so, and then you need to use your Sherlock Holmes powers of observation and deduction to locate the hidden cache.

6. **Find the hidden container.**

   If the cache is more deviously hidden, I give you some strategies in Chapter 7.

7. **Open it up and see what's inside.**

   Whee! It's Christmas morning, and you get to pick your present.

8. **Exchange a trinket in the container that catches your eye with something you brought with you to trade.**

9. **Sign and date the logbook and carefully place the container back in its hiding place for the next geocacher to discover.**

10. **When you get home, log on to the Geocaching.com Web site, record your find, and write up a brief account of your adventures. (This is optional, but most geocachers do it.)**

That's how geocaching works. Repeat the above steps over and over again, having as much fun as possible each time you go out looking for geocaches. (I go into a lot more detail with each of these steps throughout the book.)

The original caches: Letterboxes

The whole geocaching concept isn't that new. Over 100 years ago, something similar developed in England: letterboxing. *Letterboxing* comprises placing a blank logbook and a custom-made rubber stamp in a waterproof container and then hiding it. Clues are distributed with the container's location, and searchers armed with inkpads and notebooks try to find the hidden box. If they are successful, they stamp the logbook in the box with their own personal rubber stamp and also stamp their logbook with the box's stamp. This low-tech version of geocaching is still very popular. Depending on whom you talk to, 10,000–40,000 letterboxes are hidden in England, and around 5,000 are lurking in the United States. Read more about letterboxing at www.letterboxing.org.

Deciding to Geocache

Why should you geocache? That's a fair question, and I'm going to give you a number of reasons why you should get involved in the sport. (If you're already an experienced geocacher, feel free to use some of these reasons to convince your friends and family members that they should give geocaching a try.)

- **Master your GPS receiver:** GPS receivers tend to have lots of different features and whistles and bells. Because successful geocaching depends on using a GPS receiver, the sport offers an excellent opportunity for you to get to know your receiver and how to use it. (I talk about how to use a GPS receiver in Chapter 3.)

- **See new places:** It's pretty easy to get into a rut and never go anyplace new. People tend to be creatures of habit and always visit the same places, over and over again. Geocaching breaks you out of this repetitive cycle. You've now got a good excuse to visit places you've never been before, and because new geocaches are being added all the time, it's pretty hard to get bored. Many people even incorporate geocaching into their vacations and business trips.

- **Get some exercise:** Face it; most people don't get enough exercise. For whatever reasons, it's easier just to sit on the couch and slowly (or quickly) put on the pounds. Geocaching is a great, low-impact way of increasing your fitness. It gives you a reason to get off the couch and get out in the fresh air to do some walking or hiking. Because geocaches are rated as to how difficult the terrain is and how far you'll need to walk to get to a cache, you can select outings that are based on your current level of fitness.

- **Challenge yourself:** There's scientific evidence that just like you need to exercise your body to be healthy, you also need to exercise your brain. Geocaching is a great way to do this because the sport involves a number of mental challenges. It's like doing a crossword puzzle, plus you get the extra benefit of the physical exercise. You need to use

    - *The Internet:* To find geocaches you'd like to search for

    - *Your GPS receiver:* To get to the general vicinity of a cache

    - *Your brain:* To figure out just where the cache is hidden

✔ **Hang out with friends and family:** Geocaching can be an individual or group activity, and it's a great excuse to get the family together or turn it into a social outing for a group of friends. Geocaching is even pet-friendly. Lots of geocachers take their dogs out with them on hunts. (Just remember to be considerate to others and bring a leash and a plastic bag.)

✔ **Educate kids (and adults):** Geocaching, which is starting to find its way into the classroom, is a great way to learn about history, geography, maps, and science. There are a number of ways how you can apply the basic principles of geocaching in an educational setting to make learning fun. (I discuss using GPS and geocaching in education in Chapter 11.)

✔ **Build teams:** Geocaching is also showing up as a unique tool for organizational development in building teams and developing leadership skills. Small groups are given GPS receivers and are asked to find geocaches and solve other related challenges, with effective teamwork a necessary ingredient for success.

Who Geocaches?

One of the nice things about geocaching is that just about anyone can do it; your gender, age, or economic status don't much matter. (Geocaching is a relatively inexpensive sport when it comes to required equipment.) The main requirements are a spirit of adventure, a love of puzzles and mysteries, and a good sense of fun. Here are some of the people you'll encounter in the sport:

✔ **Computer geeks:** Because geocaching involves gadgets (GPS receivers and the Internet), in the early days of the sport, a number of computer geeks were initially drawn to the activity. If you're not a geek, don't worry. You definitely don't need a computer science degree, and geocaching has become so popular that the average-Joe non-geeks currently outnumber the technology geeks.

✔ **Families and friends:** Geocaching is a very family-oriented sport; more often than not, you'll find couples, friends, and families out scouring the countryside looking for caches. Although you can certainly geocache by yourself, the social aspects of the activity and having more than one set of eyeballs to look for a well-hidden geocache are well suited to multiple-person outings.

✔ **Outdoor recreationists:** A fair number of hikers, hunters, fishers, rockhounds, and other types of recreationists have been using the outdoors long before GPS came into being. Because they typically already own a GPS receiver, many of these outdoorsmen and -women have added geocaching to their primary outside interests, getting in a little geocaching while they're biking, hiking, fishing, four-wheeling, or engaging in some other sport or pastime.

✔ **Retired folks:** Geocaching is popular with the retired set because it's a good excuse to get out of the house and do something interesting. Geocaches vary in how difficult the terrain is and how far off the beaten path they are. (Some caches aren't even off the beaten path but are in easily accessible urban areas.) You can select geocaches to search for that match your physical abilities. Geocaching is also well suited for RVers and people who like to travel because they can go geocaching where they're staying or on the way to their next destination.

What You Need to Geocache

The requirements for geocaching are fairly minimal. In fact, from a bare-bones standpoint, you need only two things:

✔ **Geocache coordinates:** If you don't know where to look, it's pretty hard to find a geocache (at least in most cases) There are numerous stories of non-geocachers accidentally stumbling onto caches, even some that were very well hidden. Geocachers turn to various Web sites on the Internet where they find tens of thousands of geocaches listed. Each of these caches has a set of coordinates associated with it, in a map grid system such as latitude and longitude or UTM (Universal Transverse Mercator). I tell you everything you need to know about how to find geocache location coordinates in Chapter 5.

✔ **GPS receiver:** With a GPS receiver, you enter the geocache coordinates, and the receiver guides you to the general vicinity of the geocache. (If you don't already have a GPS receiver, read Chapter 2 for some pointers on selecting one.) You don't need an expensive GPS unit with lots of features to geocache; a basic model priced around $100 will work just fine. (Don't forget to bring the GPS receiver user manual, especially if you just purchased your receiver and are still trying to figure out how to use it.)

Orienteering versus geocaching

One big difference between orienteering and geocaching is that in the former, the control points are marked with very visible, orange and white flags. In geocaching, the caches tend to be carefully hidden out of sight.

You can go geocaching without a GPS receiver and use only a map and compass. (My adventure racing team does this to practice our navigation skills.) This is more challenging and makes the sport more like *orienteering*, where you run around the woods trying to find control points as fast as you can, using a map and compass.

Although the geocache coordinates and a GPS receiver are the two basic requirements for geocaching, I won't kid you and say that's all you need. Geocachers also tend to carry things like maps and compasses (which you can read how to use in Chapter 4), cell-phones, food and water, and other pieces of gear. In Chapter 6, I give you a comprehensive and detailed list of other essentials that are commonly used when geocaching.

Geojargon: Speaking the Lingo

Like any sport or pastime, geocaching has its own language. Because the sport is so new, the jargon is still evolving, but here are some terms to be familiar with so when you talk to other people about geocaching, you'll sound like a pro.

- ✔ **Archived:** Caches that no longer exist but still appear in a Web site database for historical purposes. A cache can be archived because it has been stolen, is no longer maintained, or does not abide by the guidelines for where caches should be placed.

- ✔ **Cache machine:** A preplanned event in a local area, where geocachers look for caches; the event can last hours or days. This is a marathon-endurance session of geocaching, where you try to find as many caches as you can in a set amount of time. The event is named after the dedicated geocacher BruceS (a true cache machine), who found 28 caches in 24 hours, totaling 86 finds in 5 days.

✔ **DNF; Did Not Find:** As in, did not find the cache. It happens to everyone, so don't worry. If you didn't find the cache, try again on another day.

✔ **Event cache:** A formal or informal get-together of geocachers. This can be to search for caches or just sit around and have a pizza and chat.

✔ **FTF; First to Find:** Bragging rights that you were the first person to find a newly placed cache.

✔ **Geocoins:** Custom minted coins or medallions designed to place in geocaches. Quite the prize if you find one in a cache.

✔ **GPSR/GPSr:** GPS receiver. Many people drop the *R* and just call a GPS receiver a *GPS*.

✔ **Hitchhiker:** An object that moves from cache to cache. A hitchhiker is marked with some instructions, telling the finding geocacher to take it and place it in another cache.

✔ **McToys:** Cheap trinkets left in a cache, like the toys that appear in fast-food kids' meals. There are better things to leave in caches.

✔ **Muggles:** People you encounter on the trail who aren't geocachers; from the Harry Potter stories.

✔ **Neocacher:** An inexperienced or newbie geocacher.

✔ **Signature item:** Something unique that a particular geocacher always places in a cache that he or she finds.

✔ **Spoiler:** Information that might give away the location of a cache.

✔ **Swag:** Goodies that you find in a cache; from the marketing term *swag* (or *schwag*) used to describe the promotional trash and trinkets (tchotchkes) handed out at trade shows.

✔ **TNLN; Took Nothing, Left Nothing:** Just what it sounds like. Also, *TNLNSL,* which means that the geocacher additionally signed the cache log.

✔ **Travel Bug (TB):** A type of hitchhiker that you mark with a special dog tag purchased from Geocaching.com. When TBs are found, their journey is tracked on the Geocaching.com Web site. Travel Bugs can have specific goals (as in, getting from point A to point B) or are just released into the world to see how far they can travel.

Other caching pursuits

In addition to geocaching, a number of other GPS-related activities have sprung up on the Internet. A few that you might be interested in include

✔ **Geodashing:** This is a contest in which random points are selected and players need to get within 100 meters of the location. There are no caches, hints, or terrain difficulty ratings, and the points can be anywhere on Earth. In fact, some locations can be impossible to reach. A new contest takes place roughly every month. The goal of the game is for teams to collect all the points first or to get as many as they can before the contest ends. For more details, check out www.geodashing.org.

✔ **The Degree Confluence Project:** This is an interesting project in which people use their GPS receivers to visit places where latitude and longitude lines converge. They take a digital picture, which is then published on a Web site. The goal is to map all the major latitude/longitude intersections for the entire Earth. For more information, go to www.confluence.org.

✔ **Benchmark hunting:** *Benchmarks* are permanent markers installed by the government for survey purposes. Over one-half million benchmarks have been installed in the United States. The most familiar type is a small, brass disk embedded into rock or concrete. The National Geodetic Survey (www.ngs.noaa.gov) maintains a list of the benchmarks and their locations. Chapter 9 tells you everything you need to know about getting started in this sport.

✔ **GPS Drawing:** This is an interesting form of art based on using your GPS receiver to record where you've been. For some amazing examples, check out the gallery at www.gpsdrawing.com.

Chapter 2

Selecting a GPS Receiver

● ●

In This Chapter

▶ Seeing how GPS works

▶ Understanding GPS capabilities and limitations

▶ Discovering GPS receiver features

▶ Selecting a GPS receiver for geocaching

● ●

*B*ecause geocaching depends so much on GPS (Global Position-ing System), you should have a basic understanding of what GPS is. In a nutshell, by using a special radio receiver that meas-ures the distance from your location to satellites that orbit the Earth broadcasting radio signals, GPS can pinpoint your position anywhere in the world (which is essential to finding geocaches). Pretty cool, huh? Aside from buying the receiver, the system is free for anyone to use.

You can purchase an inexpensive GPS receiver, pop some batter-ies in it, turn it on, and presto! Your location appears onscreen. No map, compass, *sextant* (a traditional nautical navigation tool used to determine position by the angle of the sun or stars), or sundial is required. Enter the coordinates of a geocache, and the GPS receiver will guide you directly to the cache (at least get you pretty close to it), just like magic. It's not really magic, though, but an evolution of some great practical applications of science that have come together over the last 50 years.

In this chapter, I provide you with advice on how to select a GPS receiver to use for geocaching. But first, I want to spend a little time giving you some background on how GPS works as well as additional information on some of the capabilities and limitations of the system.

Understanding Basic GPS Concepts

I want to begin by talking about how GPS works and the different pieces that make up the system. Don't worry — although the intricacies of GPS are steeped in mathematics, physics, and engineering, you don't need to be a rocket scientist to understand how GPS works. GPS needs three components in order to work (as shown in Figure 2-1):

- ✔ **Satellites:** Transmit radio signals to Earth

- ✔ **Ground stations:** Precisely control the satellites' positions and monitor their status

- ✔ **GPS receivers:** Receive the satellite signals and determine your location based on satellites' positions and how far away they are from the receiver

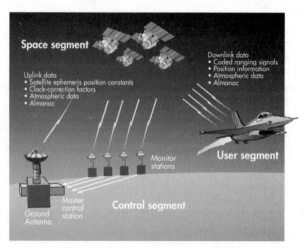

Figure 2-1: Ground stations, satellites, and receivers are all necessary for GPS to work.

Read on for a more detailed look at each of these three parts.

Satellites

In GPS jargon, a satellite is the space segment. A constellation of 24 GPS satellites (21 operational and 3 spares) orbits about 12,000 miles above the Earth (as shown in Figure 2-2). The satellites zoom through the heavens at around 7,000 miles per hour. It takes about

12 hours for a satellite to completely orbit the Earth, passing over the exact same spot approximately every 24 hours. The satellites are positioned where a GPS receiver can receive signals from at least six of the satellites at any time, at any location on Earth — that is, if nothing obstructs the signals.

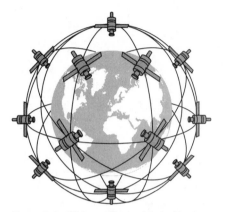

Figure 2-2: GPS satellites orbit the Earth.

Three important pieces of hardware are on each GPS satellite:

- ✔ **Computer:** An onboard computer that controls its flight and other functions

- ✔ **Atomic clock:** Keeps accurate time within 3 nanoseconds (around 3-billionths of a second)

    A super-accurate clock is required for correctly measuring the distance between the satellite and a GPS receiver based on the amount of time it takes for a satellite signal to reach the Earth.

- ✔ **Radio transmitter:** Sends signals to Earth

The solar-powered GPS satellites have a limited lifespan (around ten years). When they start to fail, spares are activated, or new satellites are sent into orbit to replace the old ones. This gives the government a chance to upgrade the GPS system by putting hardware with new features into space.

GPS satellites don't just help you stay found. All GPS satellites, starting with NAVSTAR 8 (in 1980) carry NUDET sensors. No, this isn't some high-tech, pornography-detection system. NUDET is an acronym for NUclear DETonation, and GPS satellites are equipped with sensors designed to detect nuclear-weapon explosions, assess the threat of nuclear attack, and help evaluate nuclear strike damage.

GPS radio signals

GPS satellites transmit two types of radio signals: C/A-code and P-code.

Coarse Acquisition (C/A-code) is the type of signal that consumer GPS units receive. C/A-code is sent on the L1 band at a frequency of 1575.42 MHz. C/A broadcasts are known as the Standard Positioning Service (SPS).

C/A-code is less accurate than P-code (described next) and is easier to jam and spoof (to prevent GPS units from receiving signals and to broadcast false signals to make a receiver think it's somewhere else when it's really not).

The one advantage of C/A-code is that it's quicker to use for acquiring satellites and getting an initial position fix; some military P-code receivers first track on the C/A-code and then switch over to P-code.

Precision (P-code) provides highly precise location information. P-code is difficult to jam and spoof. The U.S. military is the primary user of P-code transmissions, and it uses an encrypted form of the data (Y-code), so only special receivers can access the information. The P-code signal is broadcast on the L2 band at 1227.6 MHz. P-code broadcasts are known as the Precise Positioning Service (PPS).

Ground stations

Ground stations are the control segment of GPS. Five unmanned ground stations around the Earth monitor the satellites. Information from the stations is sent to a master control station — the Consolidated Space Operations Center (CSOC) at Schriever Air Force Base in Colorado — where the data is processed to determine each satellite's ephemeris and timing errors.

An *ephemeris* is a list of the predicted positions of astronomical bodies, such as the planets or the moon. Ephemerides (the plural of ephemeris) have been around for thousands of years because of their importance in celestial navigation. Ephemerides are compiled to track the positions of the numerous satellites orbiting the Earth.

The processed data is sent to the satellites once daily with ground antennas located around the world. This is kind of like syncing a personal digital assistant (PDA) with your personal computer to ensure that all the data is in sync between the two devices. Because the satellites have small built-in rockets, the CSOC can control them to ensure that they stay in a correct orbit.

Receivers

The last part of the GPS system is a receiver. A receiver is just like the radio in your car except that it receives GPS satellite signals instead of music. Anyone who has a GPS receiver can receive the satellite signals to determine where he or she is located.

Satellite data

GPS units receive two types of data from the NAVSTAR satellites.

- ✔ **Almanac:** Almanac data contains the approximate positions of the satellites. The data is constantly transmitted and is stored in the GPS receiver's memory.

- ✔ **Ephemeris:** Ephemeris data has the precise positions of the satellites. To get an accurate location fix, the receiver has to know how far away a satellite is. The GPS receiver calculates the distance to the satellite by using signals from the satellite.

Using the formula Distance = Velocity × Time, a GPS receiver calculates the satellite's distance. A radio signal travels at the speed of light, which is 186,000 miles per second. The GPS receiver needs to know the amount of time that the radio signal takes to travel from the satellite to the receiver in order to figure out the distance. Both the satellite and the GPS receiver generate an identical pseudo-random code sequence. When the GPS receiver receives this transmitted code, it determines how much the code needs to be shifted (by using the Doppler-shift principle) for the two code sequences to match. The shift is multiplied by the speed of light to determine the distance from the satellite to the receiver.

Both the satellite and the GPS receiver clocks must be synchronized for accurate measurements to take place. Because putting a $50,000 atomic clock in each GPS receiver wouldn't make much sense, receivers use a much cheaper quartz clock that is kept up-to-date and synchronized by the satellite signals.

Multiple satellites

The reason why so many satellites are in orbit is to provide GPS coverage all over the world. Also, a GPS receiver needs information from several satellites to tell you where you're located:

- ✔ **2-D:** A minimum of three satellite signals is required to determine your location in two dimensions: latitude and longitude.

- ✔ **3-D:** Four satellite signals are required to determine your position in three dimensions: latitude, longitude, and elevation.

A short history of GPS

Military, government, and civilian users all over the world rely on GPS for navigation and location positioning, but radio signals have been used for navigation purposes since the 1920s. LORAN (Long Range Aid to Navigation), a position-finding system that measured the time difference of arriving radio signals, was developed during World War II.

During the 1960s, several rudimentary satellite-positioning systems existed. The U.S. Army, Navy, and Air Force were all working on independent versions of radio navigation systems that could provide accurate positioning and all-weather, 24-hour coverage. In 1973, the U.S. Air Force was selected as the lead organization to consolidate all the military satellite navigation efforts into a single program. This evolved into the NAVSTAR (Navigation Satellite Timing and Ranging) Global Positioning System, which is the official name for the United States' GPS program.

The U.S. military wasn't interested in GPS for navigation purposes only. A satellite location system can be used for weapons-system targeting. Smart weapons such as the Tomahawk cruise missile use GPS in their precision guidance systems. GPS, combined with contour-matching radar and digital image-matching optics, makes a Tomahawk an extremely accurate weapon. The possibility of an enemy using GPS against the United States is one reason why civilian GPS receivers are less accurate than their restricted-use military counterparts.

The first NAVSTAR satellite was launched in 1974 to test the concept. By the mid-1980s, more satellites were put in orbit to make the system functional. In 1994, the planned full constellation of 24 satellites was in place. Soon, the military declared the system completely operational. The program has been wildly successful and is still funded through the U.S. Department of Defense.

Based on the orbits of the satellites — and if the sky is unobstructed — at any given time, your receiver should be able to get signals from at least 6 satellites (and up to 12).

GPS Receiver Accuracy

Just how accurate is a GPS receiver? According to the U.S. government and GPS receiver manufacturers, you can expect your GPS unit to be accurate within 49 feet (that's 15 meters, for metric-savvy folks). If your GPS reports that you're at a certain location, you can be reasonably sure that you're within 49 feet of that exact set of coordinates.

GPS receivers tell you how accurate your position is. Based on the quality of the satellite signals that the unit receives, the screen can display the estimated accuracy in feet or meters: The bigger the number, the less accurate the position. An example GPS receiver screen is shown in Figure 2-3. Accuracy depends on

  ✔ Receiver location

  ✔ Obstructions that block satellite signals

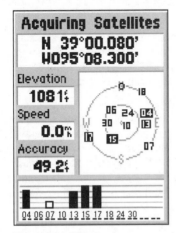

Figure 2-3: GPS receiver screen showing current position accuracy.

Generally, the more satellites you're receiving signals from, the more accuracy you'll have. Most GPS receivers display the number of satellites that you're receiving data from as well as the signal strength (also shown in Figure 2-3).

Even if you're not a U.S. government or military GPS user, you can get more accuracy by using a GPS receiver that supports corrected location data. Corrected information is broadcast over radio signals that come from non-GPS satellites that are part of the Wide Area Augmentation System (WAAS). I talk more about WAAS in the following section on GPS receiver features.

 Another technology — Differential GPS (DGPS) — uses ground-based beacons to enhance location accuracy. GPS receivers that work with DGPS require additional pieces of hardware and aren't used that often by geocachers.

Selective Availability (SA)

The average GPS user didn't always have 15-meter accuracy. In the 1970s, studies showed that the less-accurate C/A-code, designated for nonmilitary use, was more accurate than the U.S. government intended. Originally thought to provide accuracy within 100 meters, experiments showed that C/A accuracy was in the range of 20–30 meters. To degrade the accuracy of C/A-code, the U.S. government developed Selective Availability (SA). SA puts errors into data from the NAVSTAR satellites and prevents consumer GPS receivers from providing an extremely precise location fix.

Selective Availability was temporarily turned off in 1990 during the Persian Gulf War. There weren't enough U.S. and allied country military P-code GPS receivers, so the Coalition troops used thousands of civilian GPS receivers. The Gulf War marked the first time that GPS was used in large-scale combat operations.

On May 2, 2000, SA was turned off permanently. Overnight, the accuracy of civilian GPS users all over the world went from 100 meters to 15 meters, and the sport of geocaching was almost immediately born. Turning off SA on a global scale was directly related to the U.S. military's ability to degrade the C/A-code on a regional basis. For example, during the invasion of Afghanistan, the American military jammed GPS signals in Afghanistan to prevent the Taliban from using consumer receivers in operations against American forces.

Table 2-1 shows what type of accuracy you can expect from a GPS receiver. These numbers are guidelines; at times, you might get slightly more or less accuracy.

Table 2-1	GPS Accuracy	
GPS Mode	*Distance in Feet*	*Distance in Meters*
GPS without SA	49	15
GPS with DGPS	10–16	3–5
GPS with WAAS	10	3

Although survey-grade GPS receivers can provide accuracy of less than two centimeters, they are very specialized and expensive, require a lot of training, and aren't very portable. Their accuracy is achieved with DGPS and post-processing collected data to reduce location errors. The average geocacher doesn't need this level of precision (although at times, it might be nice trying to locate hard-to-find caches).

Factors That Affect GPS Accuracy

A number of conditions can reduce the accuracy of a GPS receiver. From a top-down perspective (that is, from orbit down to ground level), the possible sources of trouble look like this:

- **Ephemeris errors:** Ephemeris errors occur when the satellite doesn't correctly transmit its exact position in orbit.

- **Ionosphere conditions:** The *ionosphere* starts at about 43–50 miles above the Earth and continues for hundreds of miles. Satellite signals traveling through the ionosphere are slowed down because of *plasma* (a low-density gas). Although GPS receivers attempt account for this delay, unexpected plasma activity can cause calculation errors.

- **Troposphere conditions:** The *troposphere* is the lowest region in the Earth's atmosphere and goes up from ground level to about 11 miles. Variations in temperature, pressure, and humidity all can cause variations in how fast radio waves travel, resulting in relatively small accuracy errors.

- **Timing errors:** Because placing an atomic clock in every GPS receiver is impractical, timing errors from the receiver's less precise clock can cause slight position inaccuracies.

- **Multipath errors:** When a satellite signal bounces off a hard surface (such as a building or canyon wall) before it reaches the receiver, a delay in the travel time occurs, which causes an inaccurate distance calculation. An example of a multipath error is shown in Figure 2-4.

- **Poor satellite coverage:** When a significant part of the sky is blocked, your GPS unit has difficulty receiving satellite data. Unfortunately, you can't say that if 50 percent (or some other percentage) of the sky is blocked, you'll have poor satellite reception because the GPS satellites are constantly moving in orbit. A satellite that provides a good signal one day might provide a poor signal at the exact same location on another day because its position has changed and is now being blocked by a tree. The more open sky you have, the better your chances of not having satellite signals blocked. Building interiors, streets surrounded by tall buildings, dense tree canopies, canyons, and mountainous areas are typical problem areas.

If satellite coverage is poor, try moving to a different location to see whether you get any improvement.

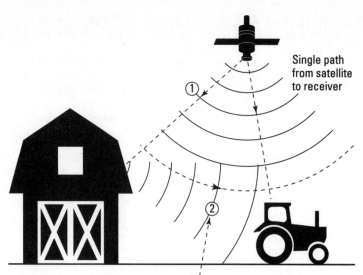

Single path from satellite to receiver

Multipath signal reaches receiver later and causes errors

Figure 2-4: Multipath errors are caused by bounced satellite signals.

Clouds, rain, snow, and weather don't reduce the strength of GPS signals enough to reduce accuracy. The only way that weather can weaken signals is when a significant amount of rain or snow accumulates on the GPS receiver antenna or on an overhead tree canopy.

Discovering GPS Receiver Features

A number of different types of GPS receivers are available, including precision surveying receivers, car navigation systems, restricted-use government and military models, and handheld consumer models designed for outdoor recreational use.

Because most geocachers use handheld GPS receivers, I want to describe some of the common features that you'll find in these electronic products. Lots of GPS receiver models are on the market, and they all vary, depending on the features they have.

Shells

The outer shells of handheld GPS receivers come in all sorts of different sizes, shapes, weights, and colors. (Figure 2-5 shows a variety of GPS models.) You have lots of options to select a model that's both aesthetically pleasing (such as color and shape) as well as functional (whether the size and the layout of the buttons work for you).

Figure 2-5: GPS receivers come in many sizes and shapes.

Although a GPS receiver that's yellow or a garish fluorescent green isn't the most fashionable, it's a lot easier to find when you set it down on the ground or on a rock.

Although most GPS receivers are designed to be fairly robust, they aren't meant to survive extreme abuse, such as dropping them from a height down onto rocks. The majority of receivers are waterproof, though, so you don't need to worry about operating them in the rain and snow. Some models even float.

Screen display

GPS receivers have two choices for information display:

- **Monochrome LCD screen:** Most GPS receivers have a monochrome liquid crystal display (LCD) screen.

- **Color screen:** Newer GPS models are starting to incorporate color screens. These are especially useful for displaying maps.

A GPS receiver's screen size depends on the receiver's size. Smaller, lighter models have small screens; larger units sport bigger screens.

Generally, a bigger screen is easier to read. Different models of GPS receiver also have different pixel resolutions. The higher the screen resolution, the more crisp the display will be. For night use, all screens can be backlit.

GPS receiver screens can get scratched fairly easily. You can protect them by using a carrying case or by purchasing plastic screen protectors sold for PDAs, cutting them to fit the size of the receiver screen.

Mapping capabilities

Every GPS receiver has a map page (as shown in Figure 2-6) that shows waypoints and tracks. (*Waypoints* are marked locations, and tracks are a record of where you've been. I discuss these fully in Chapter 3.) The page is a simple map that plots travel and locations. It doesn't show roads, geographic features, or man-made structures.

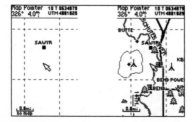

Figure 2-6: Simple and sophisticated GPS receiver screens.

Some GPS receivers do display maps that show roads, rivers, cities, and other features on their screens. You can zoom in and out to show different levels of detail. The two types of mapping GPS receivers are

✔ **Basemap:** These GPS units have a basemap loaded into read-only memory that contains roads, highways, water bodies, cities, airports, railroads, and interstate exits. Basemap GPS receivers aren't expandable, and you can't load more-detailed maps to the unit to supplement the existing basemap.

Basemaps might not be up-to-date and sometimes show features that don't exist.

> ✔ **Uploadable map:** More-detailed maps can be added to this type of unit (in either internal memory or an external memory card). You can install road maps, topographic maps, and nautical charts. Many of these maps also have built-in databases, so your GPS receiver can display restaurants, gas stations, or attractions near a certain location.

Refer to Figure 2-6 to see screens from a GPS receiver with a simple plot map and another GPS unit with an uploadable map.

GPS receivers that display maps use *proprietary* map data and software developed by the receiver manufacturer. You can't load another manufacturer's or software company's maps onto a GPS receiver. (For example, you can't load a Garmin or DeLorme map onto a Magellan receiver.) Many new users think they can load any old map onto their receiver, but this isn't the case. Check a GPS receiver manufacturer's Web site for information on the types of maps a certain model can use.

All mapping GPS receivers aren't created equal. Some units have faster processors that refresh the map quicker when it scrolls.

A handheld GPS receiver's screen is only a few inches across. The limitations of such a small display certainly don't make the devices a replacement for traditional paper maps. Also, don't expect to get the quality and detail of a paper map on an electronic map that you can upload to a GPS receiver.

Memory

A GPS receiver's internal memory holds data such as waypoints, track logs, routes, and uploadable digital maps (if the model supports them). The more memory the receiver has, the more data you can store in it. Just like PDAs and cellphones, all the data that's been stored in the GPS receiver is retained when the device is turned off.

GPS receivers have different amounts of internal memory. Unlike personal computers, however, you can't add new memory chips to a GPS unit to expand its internal memory.

Some GPS receivers aren't limited to internal memory for storage, instead using memory cards (such as MMC and SD cards) that are plugged into the receiver to store data. These receivers are very versatile.

PC interface

Most, although not all, GPS receivers support the ability to inter-
face with a PC. A cable is used to connect the GPS receiver to a
PC's serial port (and with a few receivers, to the PC's USB port).
With a PC interface, you can

- ✔ Upload firmware revisions to the receiver.

- ✔ Exchange waypoints, routes, and tracks between the PC and
  GPS receiver.

- ✔ Upload maps from the PC to the receiver (if it supports this
  capability).

- ✔ Connect your GPS receiver to a laptop running mapping software to provide real-time navigation.

If the GPS receiver supports an external memory card, you can
also use it to move data between the PC and receiver.

Antennas

Well, yes, a GPS unit has to have an antenna to receive radio signals if it's going to do you any good. Several types are available,
each with its advantages.

Internal antennas

All GPS receivers have one of two kinds of built-in antennas. One
antenna design isn't superior to the other. Performance is related
to the receiver's antenna design and size. (Cough . . . bigger sometimes *is* better.)

Patch

An internal *patch antenna* is a square conductor mounted over
a groundplane (another square piece of metal). Patch antenna
models reacquire satellites faster after losing the signal.

For best performance with an internal patch antenna, hold the
receiver face up and parallel with the ground.

Quad helix

An internal *quadrifilar helix* (quad helix) antenna is a circular tube
wrapped with wire. Quad helix antennas are more sensitive and
tend to work better under tree cover than other types.

For best performance with an internal quad helix antenna, hold the receiver so that the top is pointing up to the sky.

External antennas

Some GPS receivers have connectors for attaching external antennas. An external antenna is useful if the GPS receiver's view of the sky is otherwise blocked, like in a boat, a car, an airplane, or a backpack.

Reradiating antennas

If a GPS receiver doesn't have a jack for connecting an external antenna, you can improve the reception with a reradiating antenna. These antennas work just as well as conventional external antennas that plug into a GPS receiver.

A reradiating antenna combines two GPS antennas:

- ✔ One antenna receives the GPS signal from the satellites.
- ✔ The other antenna is connected to the first and positioned next to the GPS unit's internal antenna.

Here are a couple of sources for reradiating antennas:

- ✔ **Roll your own:** If you're handy with a soldering iron, search Google for *reradiating antenna GPS* to get tips on how to make one yourself.
- ✔ **Buy one:** Purchase an assembled reradiating antenna from Pc-Mobile at `www.pc-mobile.net/gpsant.htm`.

External and reradiating antennas aren't used that often for geocaching but can be useful if you're using your GPS receiver for other activities.

Batteries

Depending on the model, GPS receivers use two to four AA or AAA batteries. Garmin has recently introduced receiver models that have internal, rechargeable lithium-ion (Li-Ion) batteries. Battery life depends on the model and what features you're using. For example, leaving the backlight turned on drains batteries quite rapidly. With the smaller GPS receivers that use AAA batteries, you can expect roughly 6–10 hours of battery life. Receivers that use AA batteries will typically last between 10–20 hours, again depending on the model. I've personally found manufacturer battery-life claims to be relatively optimistic.

Invest in one or two sets of nickel metal-hydride (NiMH) batteries and a battery charger. These reusable batteries are cheaper in the long run than using conventional alkaline batteries and are also much more environmentally friendly because you can recharge them hundreds of times before throwing them away.

Some GPS receivers feature a battery saver mode that turns off various functions to conserve battery life.

Enhanced features

In addition to cases, screen displays, batteries, antennas, and common features that all GPS receivers share, some models have enhanced features that further differentiate themselves from other receivers. Some of these features can be especially useful for geocaching.

Compass

All GPS receivers can tell you which direction you're heading — that is, as long as you're moving. The minute you stop, the receiver stops acting as a compass. To address this limitation, some GPS receivers incorporate an electronic compass that doesn't rely on the GPS satellites. This can be handy because some geocaches require that you follow a certain compass heading to successfully find the cache.

Operation

Like with an old-fashioned compass, you can stand still and see which direction your GPS receiver is pointing toward. The only difference is that you see a digital display onscreen instead of a floating needle.

On some GPS receivers, you need to hold the unit flat and level for the compass to work correctly. Other models have a three-axis compass that allows the receiver to be tilted.

Paying attention to these factors can improve the performance and convenience of an electronic compass:

- **Magnetic fields:** Metal objects, cars, and other electronic devices reduce the accuracy of any electronic or magnetic compass.

- **Battery life:** Using an electronic compass can affect battery life. Some GPS receivers have settings that turn off the compass or use it only when the receiver can't determine a direction from satellite data.

Calibration

Electronic compasses need to be calibrated whenever you change batteries. If your GPS unit has an electronic compass, follow your user guide's instructions to calibrate it. Usually, this requires being outside, holding the GPS unit flat and level, and slowly turning in a circle twice.

Altimeter

The elevation or altitude calculated by a GPS receiver from satellite data isn't very accurate. Because of this, some GPS units have *altimeters,* which provide the elevation, ascent/descent rates, change in elevation over distance or time, and the change of barometric pressure over time. (The rough-and-ready rule is that if barometric pressure is falling, bad weather is on the way — if it's rising, good weather is coming.) If calibrated and used correctly, barometric altimeters can be accurate within ten feet of the actual elevation. Knowing your altitude is useful if you have something to reference it to, such as a topographic map (which you can read lots more about in Chapter 4).

On GPS units with an electronic altimeter/barometer, calibrating the altimeter to ensure accuracy is important. To do so, visit a physical location with a known elevation and enter the elevation according to the directions in your user's guide.

Airports are good places to calibrate your altimeter or get an initial base reading; their elevation is posted for pilots to use while calibrating their airplanes' altimeters. If you're relying on the altimeter/barometer for outdoor recreation use, I recommend always calibrating it before you head out on a trip.

WAAS

Wide Area Augmentation System (WAAS) combines satellites and ground stations to improve GPS position accuracy to potentially better than three meters. Vertical accuracy is also improved to 3–7 meters. Obviously, this puts you closer to the geocache location.

WAAS is a U.S. Federal Aviation Administration (FAA) system, designed so GPS can be used for airplane flight approaches. The system has a series of ground-reference stations throughout the United States. These monitor GPS satellite data and then send the data to two master stations — one on the west coast and the other on the east coast. These master stations create a GPS message that corrects for position inaccuracies caused by satellite orbital drift and atmospheric conditions. The corrected messages are sent to non-NAVSTAR satellites in stationary orbit over the equator. The satellites then broadcast the data to GPS receivers that are WAAS-enabled. (Just about all GPS receivers manufactured in the past several years support WAAS.)

GPS units that support WAAS have a built-in receiver to process the WAAS signals, which means that you don't need to purchase additional hardware as you would if you were using DGPS to get better accuracy. Some GPS receivers support turning WAAS on and off. If WAAS is on, battery life is shorter (although not as significantly as it is when using the backlight). In fact, on these models, you can't use WAAS if the receiver's battery-saver mode is activated. Whether you turn WAAS on or off depends on your needs. Unless you need a higher level of accuracy, you can leave WAAS turned off if your GPS receiver supports toggling it on and off. WAAS is ideally suited for aviation as well as for open land and marine use. The system might not, however, provide any benefits in areas where trees or mountains obstruct the view of the horizon.

If your GPS receiver is WAAS-compatible, it will let you know when it is receiving WAAS information that makes its position reporting more accurate.

Under certain conditions — say, when weak WAAS satellite signals are being received or the GPS receiver is a long way from a ground station — accuracy can actually worsen when WAAS is enabled. If your GPS receiver allows you to turn off WAAS, check whether the EPE (Estimated Position Error) gets better or worse. Check your receiver user guide for information on EPE and how to view it.

WAAS is available only in North America. Other governments are establishing similar systems that use the same format radio signals such as

- ✔ European Euro Geostationary Navigation Overlay Service (EGNOS)
- ✔ Japanese Multi-Functional Satellite Augmentation System (MSAS)

Autorouting

Some handheld GPS receivers support an autorouting feature. You enter a street address, and the GPS receiver plots a route for you, providing you with turn-by-turn street directions on how to reach your destination. A street map appears on the receiver's screen showing the route and your current travel path. GPS receivers that support autorouting are handy because you can use them for off-road outdoor activities as well as for paved-road navigation.

Accessory programs

Many GPS receivers have built-in accessory programs that display various handy features such as

- ✔ Calendars with the best times to hunt and fish
- ✔ Sunrise, moonrise, sunset, and moonset tables
- ✔ Tide tables
- ✔ Calculators
- ✔ Games

Garmin has even included a geocaching logbook program on some of its newer models of GPS receivers.

Selecting a GPS Receiver for Geocaching

Before you purchase a GPS receiver, you should spend some time kicking the proverbial tires. Don't rush out and buy a receiver based on one or two good Internet reviews without having a chance to hold that very GPS receiver in your hands to see how it works. Spend some time comparing different brands and models to determine which one works best for you. Because GPS units are sold in most sporting goods stores and many large retail chains, you shouldn't have to buy a receiver sight unseen.

The three largest manufacturers of consumer GPS receivers in the United States are Garmin, Magellan (a part of Thales Navigation), and Lowrance. All these manufacturers have extensive Web sites that provide detailed information about their products (including the types of maps you can upload to certain receivers). If you're in the market for a GPS receiver, definitely spend some time browsing through product literature. The Web site addresses for these manufacturers are

- ✔ **Garmin:** www.garmin.com
- ✔ **Magellan:** www.magellangps.com
- ✔ **Lowrance:** www.lowrance.com

"The Big Three" all make great GPS receivers, and it's pretty hard to go wrong with one of their models.

All GPS receiver manufacturers offer free Adobe Acrobat PDF versions of their product user manuals on their respective Web sites. If you're in the market for a GPS receiver, these are excellent resources for comparing features and seeing what the user interface is like, because the manuals have instructions as well as screenshots.

Friends with GPS receivers are also a good source of information; ask to take their different brands and models out for a test drive. Attending a geocaching club get-together is another way to get the lowdown on what people think about different models. (Chapter 10 has a list of the geocaching club Web sites, organized by state.)

Here are the two big questions that you should ask yourself before you begin your GPS receiver search:

- ✓ **What am I going to use it for?** It's a given that you're going to use the GPS receiver for geocaching, but is there anything else you plan on using it for? Maybe you also want to use it for navigating streets and roads, or for boating, or for making maps. Think about what activities you'll be doing with your GPS receiver. When you get specific with your answers, you start to identify those features that a GPS receiver should have to meet your needs.

- ✓ **How much do I want to spend?** How much money you've got in your wallet or purse is obviously going to influence which models you end up considering. The more features a GPS receiver has, the more it's going to cost. If you can figure out exactly what you're going to use the receiver for (see the previous bullet) as well as which features you really need (versus those that are nice to have), you'll end up saving some money. Generally, figure on spending anywhere from a little under $100–$500 for a handheld GPS receiver that you can use for geocaching.

Although your budget will narrow down your choices, you're likely still going to be faced with a number of models to choose from. The next step is to further narrow the list of candidates with some more questions and things to consider, including

- ✓ **Map display:** Do you want to view maps on your GPS receiver? If so, you definitely need a *mapping model* — a GPS receiver that displays maps. See the sidebar, "To map or not to map."

- ✓ **Accessories:** Does your budget include accessories such as a carrying case, PC interface cable, vehicle and bike mounting bracket, rechargeable batteries, and uploadable maps?

To map or not to map

In terms of features, probably the biggest decision you'll need to make is whether to get a GPS receiver that displays maps. Quite honestly, no matter what a salesperson might tell you, a GPS receiver that uses built-in or uploaded maps isn't required for geocaching or other outdoor activities such as hiking, fishing, bird watching, or kayaking. Using waypoints and tracks (see Chapter 3) are all you need to navigate and successfully stay found. Also, even though your GPS receiver doesn't display maps, if it can interface with a PC, you can still download information on where you've been and have it show up in a digital mapping program on your PC.

That said, mapping GPS receivers are pretty handy because they give you a quick, big-picture view of where you're located in relation to other features such as mountain peaks, rivers, and roads. And just the sight of a map, even though it's tiny and lacks a lot of detail, can be pretty reassuring at times if you get turned around, which eventually happens to everyone.

Although I'm a firm believer that a mapping GPS receiver should never take the place of a paper map and compass, if your budget allows a receiver that supports maps (along with the software and digital maps to load with it), I'd say to buy it. I personally use a mapping model for geocaching and other outdoor activities, treating the map feature as just another tool in my bag of navigation tricks.

✔ **Battery needs:** Consider the following questions:

- How many hours does the GPS receiver run on a set of batteries, and how long do you plan to be out geocaching? Remember two things: Different models (and their features) have different battery diets, and different battery types have varying lifespans.

- Will you need to carry spare batteries (always a good idea), and if so, how many? I recommend always carrying at least one fresh set of spare batteries.

- Will you be using a cigarette lighter power adapter as an alternative to using batteries?

✔ **Memory:** How much memory does the GPS receiver have, and is it expandable? This is a critical question if you're interested in a GPS receiver that supports uploadable maps. Visit the GPS receiver manufacturers' Web sites to get an idea of how much memory the maps can take up.

✔ **Display screen:** Find out the following:

- How big is the screen, and how well can you read it? Make sure to consider visibility at night, in bright sunlight, and in poor weather conditions. The size of the screen is directly related to the overall size of the GPS receiver; so if you want a larger, more readable screen, expect a larger GPS receiver to go with it.

- Do you really need a color screen? A color screen makes reading maps easier because different colors are associated with map features, but this is more of a personal preference than a requirement.

✔ **User interface:** Does operating the GPS receiver make sense to you? Sure, some learning is required to come up to speed, but using a GPS receiver should mostly be intuitive. Be sure to compare different brands and models because user interfaces are far from standardized.

✔ **External controls:** Look at different designs:

- Are the buttons and controls on the GPS receiver easy to use? Naturally, this is also related to the user interface.

- Are the controls difficult to operate while wearing gloves or mittens? You're not planning on being a fair-weather geocacher, are you?

✔ **Weight, size, and case:** Do you want absolutely the smallest package you can get? Note that there's only about a 7-ounce weight difference between the lightest and heaviest handheld GPS receivers. How rugged does the case construction seem?

✔ **Computer interface:** Do you plan to connect your GPS receiver to a computer to download and upload data? If so, make sure that the receiver can interface with a computer to exchange data; I personally think this feature is a must so you can upgrade the GPS receiver's firmware.

Geocachers, and GPS users in general, tend to be very brand-loyal when it comes to their receivers. You'll encounter lots of online (and in-person) discussions where the various merits of brands and models are argued. Keep in mind, though, that you can successfully use just about any modern GPS receiver for geocaching.

One of the best Internet GPS information resources is Joe Mehaffey, Jack Yeazel, and Dale DePriest's gpsinformation.net Web site. You'll find a variety of up-to-date product reviews and both general and technical GPS information there. The address is www.gpsinformation.net.

Chapter 3

Using a GPS Receiver

· ·

In This Chapter

▶ Discovering coordinate systems

▶ Understanding datums

▶ Getting a handle on waypoints, routes, and tracks

▶ Initializing your GPS receiver

▶ Setting and navigating to waypoints

· ·

*I*n this chapter, I cover the fundamentals of what you need to know to use a GPS receiver for geocaching. I start out by discussing some basic yet important concepts like coordinate systems, datums, waypoints, and tracks. Understanding these concepts is essential for successful and enjoyable geocaching. Then I get practical and talk about how to initialize your GPS receiver, change settings, and enter and navigate to a waypoint, which is an important skill for finding geocaches.

 Although all GPS receivers provide location, speed, and distance information and use coordinate systems, datums, and waypoints, how the information is displayed and how you operate the receiver vary from model to model. Considering this, I try to keep the discussion in this chapter fairly general so it applies to all GPS receivers. As you read through the sections, keep your receiver user guide handy so you can see how basic concepts specifically apply to your model.

Getting Familiar with Basic GPS Concepts

The sport of geocaching relies on using a GPS receiver. A receiver displays your current location and provides information about how to get from where you're currently located to some other place (like a geocache). Although that sounds fairly straightforward, you need to understand a number of underlying principles to effectively use your GPS receiver. If you don't have a good grasp of these basic concepts, your geocaching adventures will likely end up being frustrating instead of fun.

Understanding coordinate systems

A *coordinate system* is a way to locate places on a map, usually some type of imaginary grid laid over a map. Grid systems are a whole lot easier to use and more accurate than, "Well, all ya gotta do is take the old dirt road by the broken fence for a mile, then turn right at the dump, and you'll find the geocache when the road starts getting bumpy."

A simple coordinate system can consist of a vertical row of letters (A, B, C) on the left side of a map and a horizontal row of numbers (1, 2, 3) at the bottom of a map. To tell someone where a known location of a geocache is (for example), you put your finger on the geocache and then move it in a straight line to the left until you hit the row of letters. Then put your finger on the geocache again, but this time move down until you reach the row of numbers. You now can say confidently that the geocache is located at A12. (Remember the kids' game Battleship? It's the same idea.)

A number of coordinate systems are in use. For the purpose of GPS receivers and geocaching, you need to be aware of only two systems: latitude and longitude, and UTM. When a Web site lists a geocache's location (or someone e-mails you the coordinates), it will be in one or both of these coordinate systems.

Latitude and longitude

Latitude and longitude is the oldest map-coordinate system for plotting locations on the earth. The Roman scholar Ptolemy devised it almost 2,000 years ago. Ptolemy wrote about the difficulties of accurately representing the earth on a flat piece of paper and created latitude and longitude as a way of solving the problem. That's pretty impressive for a time way before the age of computers and satellites.

Latitude and longitude are based on math, but they're not really complicated. Angles are measured in degrees, and they're used for measuring circles and spheres. Spheres can be divided into 360 degrees; because the Earth is basically a sphere, it can also be measured in degrees. This is the basis of latitude and longitude, which use imaginary degree lines to divide the surface of the Earth, as shown in Figure 3-1.

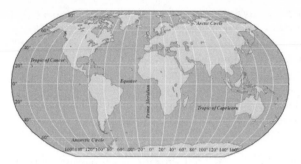

Figure 3-1: Latitude and longitude are imaginary lines.

The *equator* is an imaginary circle around the Earth — an equal distance from the north and south poles and perpendicular to the Earth's axis of rotation. The equator divides the Earth into the Northern Hemisphere (everything north of the equator) and the Southern Hemisphere (everything south of the equator).

Latitude

Latitude is the angular distance measured north and south of the equator (which is 0 degrees of latitude).

As you go north from the equator, the north latitude increases to 90 degrees when you arrive at the north pole.

As you go south of the equator, the south latitude increases to 90 degrees at the south pole.

In the Northern Hemisphere, the latitude is always given in degrees north; in the Southern Hemisphere, it's given in degrees south.

Longitude

Longitude works the same way as latitude, but the angular distances are measured east and west of the *prime meridian* (which marks the 0° longitude line that passes through Greenwich, England without even disturbing traffic).

When you travel east from the prime meridian, the longitude increases to 180 degrees.

As you go west from the prime meridian, longitude also increases to 180 degrees. (The place where the two 180° longitudes meet is the *International Date Line.*)

In the Eastern Hemisphere (which is east of the prime meridian to 180 degrees east), the longitude is given in *degrees east*.

In the Western Hemisphere (which is west of the prime meridian to 180 degrees west), longitude is expressed in *degrees west*.

If you see a longitude coordinate preceded by a minus sign, the coordinate is in the Western Hemisphere. If the coordinate has a plus sign in front of it, the location is in the Eastern Hemisphere.

Suppose that you're using latitude and longitude to locate the very first recorded geocache (which happens to be outside of Estacada, Oregon). Its coordinates are

45° 17' 27.6" N 122° 24' 47.99" W

A matter of degree

One degree is actually a pretty big unit of measure. One degree of latitude or longitude is roughly equal to 70 miles. As my technical editor astutely points out, this is a ballpark number. The distance associated with a degree of latitude remains fairly constant no matter where you are, but the distance of a degree of longitude decreases as you head from the equator toward either of the poles.

Degrees are composed of smaller, fractional amounts that sound like you're telling time.

✔ **Degree:** A *degree* is composed of 60 minutes.

   One *minute* is about 1.2 miles.

✔ **Minute:** A *minute* is composed of 60 seconds.

   One *second* is around .02 mile.

If you use minutes and seconds in conjunction with degrees, you can describe a very accurate location.

Latitude and longitude measurement units are abbreviated with the following symbols:

✔ **Degree:** °

✔ **Minute:** '

✔ **Second:** "

That means that the historical, first cache is

- ✔ 45 degrees, 17 minutes, and 27.6 seconds north of the equator
- ✔ 122 degrees, 24 minutes, 47.99 seconds west of the prime meridian

Lots of latitude

Latitude and longitude are pretty straightforward and logical if you think about it. Unfortunately, over the years, people have muddied things a bit by coming up with different ways to represent latitude and longitude coordinates.

Latitude and longitude coordinates can be written as

- ✔ **Degrees, minutes, and seconds:** This is the traditional way, with the preceding example of the first recorded geocache expressed as 45° 17' 27.6" N 122° 24' 47.99" W.

- ✔ **Degrees and decimal minutes:** Seconds are dropped, and the decimal version of minutes is used along with degrees, so now the cache is at 45° 17.46" N –122° 24.8". (The minus sign, in the middle, indicates west.) This is probably the most common format used for listing geocache coordinates.

- ✔ **Decimal degrees:** Minutes and seconds are both dropped, and only the decimal representation of degrees is used, which puts the cache at 45.291° N –122.413333°. (Once again, the conjoining minus sign implies west.)

Although they look different, all these coordinate notations point to the same location. The math is pretty straightforward if you want to convert the coordinates from one format to another, but it's a heck of a lot easier to point your Web browser to `http://jeeep.com/details/coord` for a handy online conversion calculator if you need to.

UTM

UTM, which stands for Universal Transverse Mercator, is a modern coordinate system developed in the 1940s. It's similar to latitude and longitude, but it uses meters instead of degrees, minutes, and seconds. UTM coordinates are very accurate, and the system is pretty easy to use and understand.

Although the United States hasn't moved to the metric system, the system is widely used by GPS receivers. UTM coordinates are much easier than latitude and longitude to plot on paper maps. The two key values to convert metric measurements are

✔ **Meter:** 1 meter = 3.28 feet = 1.09 yards.

   For ballpark measurements, a *meter* is a bit over a yard.

✔ **Kilometer:** 1 kilometer = 1,000 meters = 3,280 feet = 1,094 yards = 0.62 mile.

   For ballpark measurements, a *kilometer* is a bit more than half a mile.

The UTM system is based on the simple A, B, C – 1, 2, 3 grid system, with the world divided into zones. C'mon, c'mon, c'mon, let me tell you what it's all about:

✔ Sixty primary zones run north and south: Numbers identify the zones that run north and south.

✔ Twenty optional zones run east to west:

   • These zones indicate whether a coordinate is in the Northern or Southern Hemisphere.

   • Letters designate the east/west zones.

Often, the letter is dropped from a UTM coordinate, and only the zone is used to make things simpler. For example, because most of Florida is in Zone 17R, if you were plotting geocache locations in the state, you could just use Zone 17 in your UTM coordinates. Figure 3-2 shows the UTM zone map.

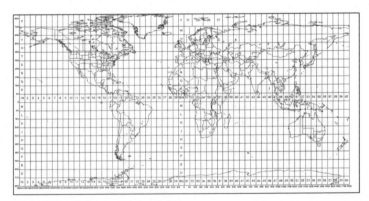

Figure 3-2: UTM zones of the world.

To provide a precise location, UTM uses two units:

✔ **Easting:** The distance in meters to the east from the start of a UTM zone line

The letter *E* follows Easting values.

✔ **Northing:** The distance in meters from the equator

The letter *N* follows Northing values.

There's no such thing as a *Southing.* Northing is used in the Southern Hemisphere to describe the distance away from the equator, even though a location is south of the equator. (Is that weird, or what?)

Continuing with my example of the location of the very first recorded geocache, if you want to use UTM to locate the cache, the coordinates look like this:

10T 0546003 E 5015445 N

That means the cache is in Zone 10T, which is 5,015,445 meters north of the equator and 546,003 meters east of where the zone line starts. (For those of you without a calculator in front of you, that's about 3,116 miles north of the equator, and about 339 miles east of where the number 10 zone line starts out in the Pacific Ocean.)

Sometimes, you'll see UTM coordinates written with the *E* and *N* respectively placed before the Easting and Northing numbers (notably with geocache coordinates listed at the Geocaching.com site). Don't panic; this is just another way of stating the coordinates, and you should still be able to figure out which value is which.

Understanding datums

A *datum* is a frame of reference for mapping. Because the Earth isn't flat, geographic coordinate systems use *ellipsoids* (think of a sphere that's not perfectly spherical, much like the shape of the Earth) to calculate positions on our third planet from the sun. A *datum* is the position of the ellipsoid relative to the center of the Earth.

If that makes your brain hurt, don't worry. Here are the only two important and simple things that you need to know about datums when it comes to geocaching:

> ✔ **All maps have a datum.**
>
> Hundreds of different datums are in use throughout the world, with cool names such as the Kerguelen Island, Djakarta, Hu-Tzu-Shan, or Qornoq datums. Most good maps used for navigation — and highway maps don't count — usually state which datum was used in making the map.
>
> ✔ **You can set what datum your GPS receiver uses.**

The default datum for GPS receivers is WGS 84, more formally known as the World Geodetic System 1984. WGS 84 was adopted as a world standard and is derived from a datum called the North American Datum of 1983, or NAD 83.

Most United States Geological Survey (USGS) topographic maps that you use for hiking or serious geocaching are based on an earlier datum called the North American Datum of 1927, or NAD 27. This datum is divided up into different geographic areas, so if you're in the United States — at least in the lower 48 states — use a version of NAD 27 that mentions the continental U.S.

Why is all this datum stuff so important? Suppose that the coordinates of a geocache use the WGS 84 datum, but your GPS receiver is set to use the NAD 27 datum. When you go out looking for the cache, the location can be off as much as 200 meters, and there's a good chance you'll never find the cache. The latitude and longitude or UTM coordinates will be identical, but the location is going to end up in two different spots because of the different datums. (The same would hold true if you were trying to find a set of WGS 84 coordinates you recorded on your GPS receiver on a map that's based on the NAD 27 datum.)

The moral of the story is to make sure that the datum on your GPS receiver matches the datum associated with the geocache coordinates. The good news is that geocache coordinates almost always tell you the datum used, so you won't end up getting confused.

 If you want to find out more about datums and map projections, check out Peter Dana's excellent Geographer's Craft Web site `www.colorado.edu/geography/gcraft/notes/notes.html`.

Understanding waypoints

A *waypoint* is GPS lingo for a location or point that you store in your GPS receiver. (Some manufacturers also call them *marks* or *landmarks*.) A waypoint consists of the following information:

- ✔ **Location:** The location of the waypoint in whichever coordinate system the GPS receiver is currently using. Some receivers also store the elevation of the location.

- ✔ **Name:** The name of the waypoint. You get to choose your own name, but the length varies between GPS receiver models from six characters on up.

- ✔ **Date and time:** The date and time when the waypoint was created.

- ✔ **Optional icon or symbol:** An optional icon or symbol associated with the waypoint that appears on the GPS receiver's map page when the area around the waypoint is displayed. This could be a tent for a campground, a boat for a boat launch, or a fish for a favorite fishing spot.

All GPS receivers can store waypoints, but the maximum number that you can save varies from model to model. As a general rule, as the price of a GPS receiver price goes up, so does the number of waypoints that can be stored. Lower-end consumer GPS receivers store from 100–250 waypoints, and top-of-the-line models can store 1,000 or more.

Waypoints are important for geocaching because you'll create a waypoint on your GPS receiver for each geocache you're looking for. After a waypoint is set, your GPS receiver has several features that help guide you to that waypoint. (I talk more about this in the upcoming section.)

Understanding routes

A *route* is a course that you're currently traveling or plan to take. In GPS terms, a route is the straight-line course between one or more waypoints. If multiple waypoints are in a route, the course between two waypoints is called a *leg.* A single route can be made up of a number of legs.

After you create your route, the GPS receiver tells you how long each of the legs will be and also the total distance of the route. When you *activate* the route (tell the GPS receiver you're ready to use it), the following information is displayed:

✔ The direction you need to travel in order to reach the next waypoint in the route

✔ How far away the next waypoint is

✔ How much time it's going to take to get there

After you reach a waypoint in the route, the GPS receiver automatically starts calculating the information for the next leg. This continues until you reach your final destination.

If you're trying to find a series of geocaches in the same general area, you could create a route to guide you to the caches in a certain order.

A fair number of geocachers don't use routes and find them to be an overrated feature. (I happen to fall into that camp.) After all, when you reach your first cache, you can easily select the next cache location waypoint and be on your way.

Understanding tracks

Remember the story of Hansel and Gretel, the kids who dropped breadcrumbs in the forest to try to find their way back home? Their story would've had a different ending if they had a GPS receiver because all newer GPS receivers leave electronic breadcrumbs — *tracks* or *trails,* which are different names for the same thing — as you travel. (Of course, in today's tale, a little Pac-Man could still leave little Hansel and Gretel stranded at the gingerbread house.) Every so often, the GPS receiver saves the coordinates of the current position to memory. This series of tracks is a *track log* or *track history.* (Because various GPS models handle tracks differently, check your user manual for specific details.)

Note these differences between tracks and waypoints:

✔ **Names and symbols:** Although tracks and waypoints are both location data points, tracks don't have names or symbols associated with them and can't be edited in the GPS receiver.

✔ **Autocreation:** Unlike waypoints — which you need to manually enter — tracks are automatically created whenever a GPS receiver is turned on (that is, if you have the Track feature enabled).

If track logging is enabled, tracks are shown on the GPS receiver's map page while you move, just like a trail of breadcrumbs following you. Because the GPS receiver constantly collects tracks while it's powered on, you need to clear the current track log before you start a new trip. Some receivers also allow you to save the current track log.

If you turn your GPS receiver off or if you lose satellite reception, the GPS receiver stops recording tracks. When it's turned back on again or good satellite coverage resumes, the GPS receiver continues recording tracks, but it assumes that you traveled in a straight line between the last track location saved before satellite reception was lost and your current position.

Some GPS receivers allow you to set how often tracks are saved, either by time or distance intervals. For example, you could specify that a track be saved every minute or each time that you travel a tenth of a mile. Leaving the default, automatic setting for track collection should work for most occasions.

When you reach your final destination, your GPS receiver can optionally use the track log to help you navigate back to your starting point by using the track data to guide you in retracing your steps. Check your user manual for model-specific instructions on how to do this.

Tracks are probably one of the most useful GPS receiver features if you're working with digital maps. From a number of free and commercial mapping programs, you can overlay your tracks on top of a map to see exactly where you've been. Check out Chapters 12 and 13 for some mapping Web sites and programs you can use with your recorded tracks.

Depending on the model, GPS receivers can store between 1,000–10,000 tracks and up to 10 track logs. If you exceed the maximum number of tracks, the GPS receiver will either stop collecting tracks or begin overwriting the oldest tracks that were collected first with the most current ones. (Some GPS receivers let you define what action to take.) The number of tracks collected over time depends completely on your activity, speed, GPS coverage, and the GPS receiver's track settings.

Using Your GPS Receiver

After you have a basic understanding of coordinate systems, datums, waypoints, routes, and tracks, you're ready to start using your GPS receiver.

Initializing a GPS receiver

If you just bought a GPS receiver for geocaching, you'll need to *initialize* it first (get an initial location fix and setting variables such as your time zone). The type of initialization and the amount of time that this takes depend on what information the GPS receiver has received from the satellites and when.

The process is mostly all automatic, and you don't need to do much as your GPS receiver starts up and begins to acquire satellites. Your GPS user manual might contain model-specific initialization information.

To initialize a new GPS receiver, take it outside to someplace that has an unobstructed view of the sky (such as a large field or a park) and turn on the power. (You did install the batteries first, right?) After the start-up screen displays, the receiver will begin trying to acquire satellites.

It can take anywhere from 5–30 minutes for the GPS receiver to gather enough satellite data to get a position fix for the first time (usually more toward the 5 minutes end of the scale). Don't worry; your GPS receiver isn't going to be this slow all the time. After the receiver is first initialized, it usually only takes 15–45 seconds to lock on to the satellites when you turn it on in the future (if no obstructions block the view of the sky).

GPS receiver initialization nitty-gritty

You really don't need to know this technical information to operate your GPS receiver, but to start acquiring satellites to get an accurate location fix, a GPS receiver needs the following satellite data:

✔ A current almanac (rough positions of all the satellites in orbit)

✔ The GPS receiver's current location

✔ The date and time

✔ Ephemeris data (precise position of individual satellites)

If some or all of the data is missing or out-of-date, the GPS receiver needs to get updated information from the satellites before it can accurately fix a current position. The types of data that are out-of-date or missing determine how long the GPS receiver takes to initialize. If the GPS receiver is brand-new, has moved several hundred miles away from where it was last used, or has been stored for a prolonged period of time, initialization will take longer.

In order to speed up the location fix for the first time, or when the GPS receiver has been moved hundreds of miles since it was last turned on, many GPS receivers have an option where you move a cursor on an onscreen map of the United States or world to show your general location. Providing a general location helps the GPS receiver narrow its search for satellites that are visible from your present location, thus speeding up the initialization process.

Most GPS receivers have a satellite status page that's displayed while the receiver is acquiring satellites; see an example status page in Figure 3-3. This page typically consists of two circles that represent a dome of sky above your head. The outer circle is the horizon, the inner circle is 45 degrees above the horizon, and the center of the inner circle is directly overhead. The *N* on the page represents north.

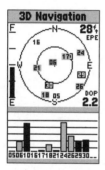

Figure 3-3: A GPS receiver satellite status page.

Based on the almanac information, the GPS receiver shows the position of satellites within the circles, representing them with unique numbers. As a signal from a satellite is acquired, the number is highlighted or bolded.

Underneath the circles are a series of bar graphs with numbers underneath them that represent signal strength. The numbers correspond to the satellites the GPS receiver has located. The more a bar is filled in, the stronger the GPS receiver is receiving signals from that particular satellite.

Try moving your GPS receiver around to watch the satellite signal strength change. If the signals are weak or you get a message about poor satellite coverage, move to a different location and change the position of the receiver to better align it with the satellites that are shown onscreen. If you're successful, you'll see new satellites acquired, the signal strength increase, or both. The more satellites you acquire and the stronger the signals, the more accurate your receiver will be.

Depending on your GPS receiver's antenna type, holding the receiver properly will optimize signal reception. If your GPS receiver has a patch antenna, hold it face up, parallel to the ground. If your GPS receiver has a quad helix antenna, hold it straight up so that the top of the receiver is pointing toward the sky. To see the differences between patch and quad helix antennas, check out Chapter 2.

After the GPS receiver gets enough information from the satellites to fix your location, the screen typically displays an Estimated Position Error (EPE) number. Based on the satellite data received, this is the estimated error for the current position. The smaller the number displayed, which will either be in feet or meters, the more accurate your position.

Estimated Position Error is a bit confusing. If you see an EPE of 20 feet, it doesn't mean that you're within 20 feet of the actual coordinates. You're actually within up to two times the distance of the EPE (or even more) from the actual location. For example, if you have an EPE of 50, your location could be 1–100 feet of the actual coordinates. EPE is not a maximum distance away from the actual location; it's only a measurement estimate based on available satellite data. To complicate things even further, different GPS receiver manufacturers use different formulas for determining EPE. If you set three different GPS receiver brands next to each other, they'll all display different EPE numbers. Some manufacturers are conservative with their numbers, and others are optimistic. Don't get too caught up with EPE numbers; just treat them as ballpark estimates — and remember, the smaller the number, the better.

Changing receiver settings

After you initialize your GPS receiver for the first time, you should change a few of the receiver's default system settings. You only need to do this once. A few GPS receivers will prompt you to make some of these changes as part of the initialization process; these changes mostly customize settings based on your location and needs. Check your user manual for specific information on how to change the system settings described here.

Although GPS receivers have a number of system settings that you can change, here are some of the important settings you'll want to initially adjust:

- **Time:** Your GPS receiver gets very precise time data from atomic clocks aboard the satellites, but it's up to you how the time will be displayed. You need to specify

    - Whether to use 24-hour (military time) or 12-hour (AM and PM) time

    - Whether Daylight Savings Time is automatically turned on and off

    - What your time zone is (or your offset from UTC, which stands for Universal Coordinated Time, the world time standard)

- **Units of measure:** Your GPS receiver can display distance information in statute (such as feet and miles), nautical (knots), or metric (meters and kilometers) formats. The default setting for GPS units sold in the United States is statute, so unless you want to use the more logical metric system, leave the setting as-is.

- **Coordinate system:** By default, your GPS receiver displays positions in latitude and longitude. If you want to use UTM coordinates for geocaching, now's the time to change the setting.

- **Datum:** The default datum for all GPS receivers is WGS 84. Unless you're planning on using your receiver with maps that have a different datum, leave the default setting.

- **Battery type:** The default battery setting on most GPS receivers is alkaline. If you're using another type of battery, be sure to select the correct type. The battery type setting doesn't affect the GPS receiver's operation; it only ensures that the battery life is correctly displayed onscreen because different types of batteries have different power characteristics.

- **Language:** Most GPS receivers are multilingual, so if you'd rather view the user interface in a language other than English, it's as simple as selecting a different language from a menu.

Entering a waypoint

Remember that a waypoint is simply a location you mark in your GPS receiver. The two types of waypoints that you can enter and save to your GPS receiver are either a

✔ **Known location:** If you know the coordinates of a location that you want to save as a waypoint (like a geocache, hint, hint), you can manually enter it in the GPS receiver. (In Chapter 5, I show you how to get geocache coordinates from the Geocaching.com Web site that you can enter as waypoints.) Again, check your user manual for directions on how to manually enter a waypoint for your GPS receiver.

or a

✔ **Current location:** GPS receivers have a button on the case or an onscreen command for marking the current location as a waypoint. (Check your user manual for details about how waypoints are marked for your unit.) After the waypoint is marked, the GPS receiver screen displays a waypoint information page where you can name the waypoint and associate an icon with it. A good example of using a current location waypoint is creating a waypoint for where your car is parked while you're geocaching so you can find your way back to it.

Power to the people

All batteries are not created equal, and using different types can increase the amount of time between battery changes on your GPS receiver. Here are some good Internet resources to get you up to speed on batteries:

✔ **Battery drain for selected GPS receivers:** `www.gpsinformation.net/main/bat-5.txt`. This site offers the lowdown on just how much juice different GPS receiver models consume.

✔ **The Great Battery Shootout!:** `www.imaging-resource.com/ACCS/BATTS/BATTS.HTM`. This site is more oriented to digital cameras (not GPS receiver-specific), but you'll find some good data on how different types of batteries perform.

✔ **Battery University:** `www.batteryuniversity.com/index.htm`. This is an educational Web site with lots of information on rechargeable battery technology.

✔ **Newsgroups:** `sci.geo.satellite-nav`. Do a Google Groups search in this USENET newsgroup for batteries and be prepared to spend a couple of hours reading through educational (and sometimes controversial) posts.

When you check out some of these sources, you'll probably run into a reference to mAh (milliampere-hours). Most rechargeable batteries like NiMH have the mAh rating printed on their label. This rating refers to the battery capacity; typically, the higher the mAh number, the longer the battery will last.

Always use meaningful names when you save a waypoint. GPS receivers typically assign a sequential number as the default waypoint name. Although numbers and cryptic codes might make sense when you enter them, I guarantee you that you probably won't remember what they mean a couple of weeks down the road. *Note:* Some GPS receivers support waypoint names only in uppercase characters, but others allow you to use both uppercase and lowercase characters.

All the geocaches listed in the Geocaching.com database conveniently have six-character waypoint names that start with *GC* that you can use when you enter the coordinates in your GPS receiver. Using these waypoint names makes it easy to reference exactly which geocache you're searching for.

GPS receivers have a number of features that can help you navigate to a waypoint that you've entered, which is a good segue to the next section.

Navigating to a waypoint

Here's where your GPS receiver plays a very important role in geocaching. All receivers have an information page that lists the waypoints that you've created and stored. (Again, check your user manual for information on how to access and use this list.) The waypoints can be listed by name or those closest to your current location, and any of the waypoints in the list can be deleted or edited. An example waypoint list page is shown in Figure 3-4.

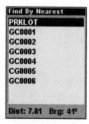

Figure 3-4: GPS receiver waypoint list page.

By selecting a waypoint, no matter where you are, you can find your way to it.

✔ The distance to the waypoint is shown and decreases or increases as you get closer to or farther away from the waypoint.

✔ The compass direction in degrees that you'll need to head to get to the waypoint is also shown. In Figure 3-4, the distance and compass bearing to the first waypoint in a list, which is selected, is shown.

GPS receivers designed for outdoor use always assume a straight line as the route between your current location and a waypoint (GPS receivers that support autorouting for street navigation are an exception). That might be convenient for airplanes and boats, but it doesn't take into account cliffs, rivers, streams, private property, and other obstacles on land that you might encounter while trying to locate a geocache. That's one of the reasons why a topographic or other useful type of map is a good thing to have with you.

Depending on the GPS receiver model, other waypoint-related information that you might be able to display includes

✔ **Travel time:** The amount of time it will take you to reach the waypoint based on your current speed.

✔ **Compass:** A picture of a compass that displays the waypoint direction heading.

✔ **Directional arrow:** An arrow that points in the correct direction that you should be heading.

✔ **Navigational hints:** A picture of a road that moves as you travel. If the road is centered onscreen, your destination is straight ahead. If the road veers to the right or the left, you need to correct your course so that the road is centered. A symbol associated with the waypoint will grow larger as you get closer to it.

Most GPS receivers support simple *plot displays,* which are map pages that show waypoint symbols, tracks, and your current position. More advanced (and expensive) GPS receivers support more sophisticated maps, and your waypoints and tracks appear along with roads, rivers, bodies of water, and whatever features the map shows. When the map page is displayed, you can zoom in, zoom out, and move around the map with an onscreen cursor that you control with buttons on the GPS receiver.

After you enter a waypoint for a geocache's location, all these features can be used in helping you get close to (or sometimes even right on top of) the cache you're looking for.

Chapter 4

Using a Map and Compass

In This Chapter

▶ Discovering how compasses work

▶ Differentiating between true and magnetic north

▶ Understanding declination

▶ Selecting a compass for geocaching

▶ Choosing maps to use for geocaching

▶ Dissecting the parts of a map

▶ Using a map and compass together

▶ Reading how to take bearings, set courses, and triangulate

Compared with GPS technology, traditional maps and compasses seem like musty old relics from a bygone era. After all, a GPS receiver can easily tell you exactly where you are with a few button presses and one glance at the screen. There are even models available that support digital maps that can show you the surrounding terrain.

However, I think of maps, compasses, and GPS receivers the same way I view basic math skills and electronic calculators. You should know how to add, subtract, multiply, and divide without a calculator just in case you don't have one or for some reason it's not working. Knowing the fundamentals of using a map and compass is like being able to do basic math on paper (or by counting your fingers).

When you're geocaching, having a map and compass with you — and knowing how to use them — serves two important purposes:

✔ Provides a navigation insurance policy in case you lose your GPS receiver or it stops working.

✔ Helps you plan appropriate routes to get to a geocache. (Sometimes the straight-line route that the GPS receiver displays isn't the best.)

In this chapter, I introduce you to the fundamentals of maps and compasses. You discover how to select maps and compasses that are well suited for geocaching, and I also present the fundamentals of basic land navigation.

All about Compasses

Magnetic compasses are among the oldest navigation tools for getting around on either land or water. In this section, I tell you why you should carry a compass while you're geocaching, explain how compasses work, describe the parts of a compass, and provide some tips on selecting a compass to use for geocaching.

Why do you need a compass?

You're probably wondering that if you already have a GPS receiver (especially if it has an electronic compass), why you should bother carrying a compass while you're geocaching. I'm glad you asked because here are some good reasons why:

- ✔ **Compasses don't need batteries to tell you which direction you're going.**
- ✔ **Compasses work in deep canyons and under thick tree canopies.** GPS receivers sometimes don't work under these conditions.
- ✔ **Water or extreme temperatures don't affect compasses.** In general, compasses are far less fragile compared with GPS receivers.
- ✔ **Some geocaches require you to take compass bearings to successfully find a cache.**
- ✔ **Compasses are relatively inexpensive.** This makes them a cheap, backup insurance policy just in case something bad happens to your GPS receiver.

How compasses work

Compasses rely on the Earth's magnetic field. The earliest compasses can be traced back to around 2500 B.C. During this time, the Chinese discovered that the mineral we now call magnetite (also known as *lodestone*) had magnetic properties and would align itself in a north-south direction. Spoon-shaped pieces of crafted magnetite — *south-pointers* — were used for divination.

A long time went by until magnetite started to be used for navigation. By the 7th century, Chinese scholars discovered they could magnetize iron needles with lodestones. These magnetic needles could be suspended in water on a piece of wood or hung from a silk thread and orient to a north-south direction. By the 15th century, trading ships from China were actively using early compasses during their voyages.

In addition to magnetic compasses, there are also other types of compasses, such as gyroscopic and electronic flux gate. In this chapter, I stick to talking about handheld magnetic compasses, which is what you'll be using when you're geocaching.

Not much has really changed in terms of how a compass works since the Chinese discovered the properties of magnetite. Modern materials are used for production, but the basic principle of a magnetized needle pointing north remains unchanged.

Magnetic and true north

If you haven't had much experience with maps and compasses, you might think that there's only one north. However, there are actually two norths, and here is where things can get muddled up if you don't know the difference:

- ✔ **True north:** This is the location of the Earth's axis of rotation and the basis for lines of latitude and longitude. True north is also known as *geographic north*. Most maps are oriented so that the top of the map is always pointing toward true north.

- ✔ **Magnetic north:** This is the north that's shown on a compass, which is determined by the Earth's internal magnetic field. The magnetic north pole is currently about 800 miles south of the true north pole.

In most places, when your compass points north, you need to either add or subtract from the magnetic north setting to get true north, and vice versa if you're going from true north to magnetic north.

When someone gives you a compass direction heading, it will either be true or magnetic (and ideally, he or she will have told you which one). If not, I would usually guess magnetic — but understand that I might end up off course because of the declination, which is a perfect introduction to the next section.

Understanding declination

Declination is a very important concept when you're using a compass. Although a compass' magnetic needle does indeed point north, the Earth's magnetic field varies from place to place. Thus, if you're converting between true and magnetic north, the number of degrees that you need to add or subtract to get the correct value depends on your location and how you're using the map and compass. (See the sidebar, "Declination dissected.") This number is *declination*. Figure 4-1 shows a declination map of the United States to give you an idea of the different declination values throughout the country.

In the United States, the line of zero declination (the *agonic line*) runs from Wisconsin down through Alabama and across the Florida panhandle. If you're located along the imaginary agonic line, true and magnetic north will be the same. The farther east or west you move, the greater the distance between true and magnetic north.

Most topographic maps have the declination printed at the bottom of the map so you can correctly adjust your compass. However, the magnetic fields on the Earth do change over time, so the declination on older maps might no longer be accurate. For example I have a United States Geological Survey (USGS) map of Bend, Oregon that states that the magnetic declination to use with the map is 19° east. That was the declination recorded in 1981. The USGS hasn't revised the map yet, so this particular map is still being sold. In the spring of 2004, when I was writing this book, the declination for Bend has changed — it's now a little less than 17° east.

Declination dissected

Declination values are stated in degrees (either east or west, depending on which side of the zero declination line you're on), such as 20° east. Whether you subtract or add the degrees depends on your location and how you're using the map and compass.

✔ **Field compass to map:** This means you're reading a compass direction (a *bearing*) and want to transfer that bearing (based on magnetic north) to a map that is oriented to true north. If the declination is east, add the declination value to the bearing. If the declination is west, subtract the declination value from the bearing.

✔ **Map to field compass:** You've got a compass direction plotted on a map (based on true north) and want to correctly transfer the bearing to a compass (which is using magnetic north). If the declination is east, subtract the declination value from the bearing. If the declination is west, add the declination value to the bearing.

By the way, you can interchange the words *outside* and *field*. Surveyors, foresters, and other folks use *field* to describe where they are; *in the field* means doing work *outside* instead of work inside the office.

Magnetic Declination of the U.S., 2004

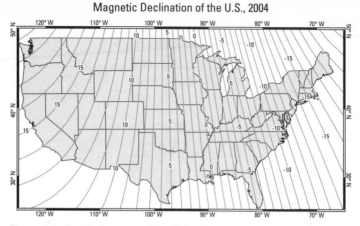

Figure 4-1: Declination map of the United States.

Even if the declination has changed only a few degrees, it can have a big impact on navigation. For each degree your compass heading is not correct, your position will be off 92 feet each mile. For example, if the declination were 2 degrees off, over the course of 5 miles, you'd end up 920 feet away from where you thought you'd be. The farther you travel, the more impact an incorrect declination makes in successfully reaching your destination.

To find out the current declination for any location, visit www. ngdc.noaa.gov/cgi-bin/seg/gmag/declination1.pl.

Parts of a compass

Unlike a GPS receiver, a compass doesn't have an LCD screen, buttons, and lots of electronic circuitry. Despite its rather simple design, you still need to know about the different parts of a compass and what they do. Take a look at the basic components of a compass that you'll use for geocaching (as shown in Figure 4-2).

Base plate

The *base plate* is a transparent piece of plastic on which the magnetic needle and dial are mounted. It has a direction of travel arrow that you point in the direction you're heading (or of which you want to take a bearing, which I talk about more in the "Using a Map and Compass" section later in this chapter). Many compasses also have rulers with different scales printed on the base plate, which is handy for measuring distances on maps. The base plate has a lanyard hole through which you can thread a piece of small cord and then wear the compass around your neck or on your wrist.

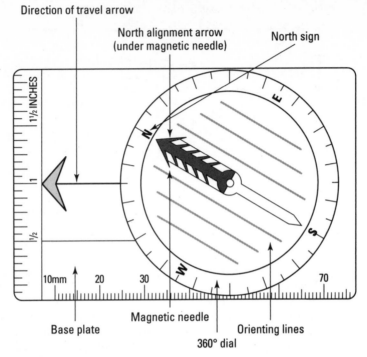

Figure 4-2: Parts of a compass.

Magnetic needle

The magnetic needle is the brains of the compass and points to magnetic north. The needle is suspended on a frictionless pivot point (typically a sapphire bearing). One end of the needle is colored red, which indicates north.

The compass can be dampened or undampened.

- **Dampened:** The needle is suspended in a liquid. Liquid-dampened compasses are preferred because they absorb shock better and there isn't as much needle bounce.

  The fluid inside a compass is usually a mixture of 55 percent distilled water and 45 percent ethyl alcohol, glycerin, or a refined petroleum product. This prevents the liquid from freezing in cold temperatures.

- **Undampened:** Air surrounds the compass needle, and no liquid is present for dampening. These compasses are typically cheaper than dampened compasses but are less rugged.

Dial

The *dial* (also known as a *bezel*) is a round housing that is attached to the base plate and encloses the needle. A series of numbers from 0–360, with marks between the numbers, is printed on the outside of the dial. These numbers and marks are compass directions, which are expressed in degrees.

- ✔ **North:** 360 degrees
- ✔ **East:** 90 degrees
- ✔ **South:** 180 degrees
- ✔ **West:** 270 degrees

The numeric value of the degree marks on a compass varies depending on the compass model. On more precise compasses, a single mark represents one or two degrees. With lower-end compasses, each mark can equal up to 10 degrees. A smaller increment means the compass is potentially more accurate, but a lot of accuracy depends on the user.

Compass scales come marked 0–360 degrees *(azimuth),* and 0–90 degrees *(quadrant,* with 0–90 degree marks repeated four times). Although some surveyors favor the quadrant compasses, the average compass user can easily become confused by the scale. Before you purchase a new compass, check the scale. For ease of use, I recommend a 360° azimuth model.

In addition to the numbers and marks, there are also letters. *N* (north), *E* (east), *S* (south), and *W* (west) are printed next to their representative degree settings. Some compasses might also show *SE* for southeast, *SW* for southwest, and so on.

You can rotate the compass dial by turning it clockwise or counter-clockwise. This is how you take a compass bearing, which I talk more about in the "Using a Map and Compass" section later in this chapter.

The transparent bottom of the dial, just below the compass needle, has a red outlined north alignment arrow printed on it as well as several north-south orienting lines. When you rotate the dial, the alignment arrow and the orienting lines move. I discuss how to use these features when I talk about bearings and courses.

Optional features

In addition to these basic parts of a compass, some models might have additional features, including

✔ **Adjustable declination:** By turning a small screw, you can set the correct magnetic declination for your location by moving the north alignment arrow. With one of these types of compasses, you won't need to manually add or subtract to get true north.

✔ **Luminous markings:** Many compasses feature glow-in-the-dark marks on the magnetic needle, dial, and direction of travel arrow so you can use the compass in the dark or low light.

✔ **Magnifying glass:** Some models have an area of the base plate that serves as a magnifying glass. This is handy for reading tiny detail on maps.

✔ **Inclinometer:** A few compasses, mostly designed for professional use, have a built-in *inclinometer* that allows you to measure the degree of a slope.

✔ **Global compasses:** If you use a compass sold in the Northern Hemisphere in the Southern Hemisphere (the other side of the equator), the compass' magnetic needle will dip down and affect accuracy, and the dip is greater as you get closer to the South Pole. Some compasses are specifically designed to work in both hemispheres to avoid this problem.

None of these optional features are absolutely necessary for geocaching, and you end up paying a little more for them compared with the cost of a basic compass.

The one optional figure that I would recommend is adjustable declination. You just set the declination for your part of the world and forget about it — no pesky math formulas to remember. Just remember to change the declination to the correct value if you're traveling someplace else that has a different declination from home.

Selecting a compass

If you visit a sporting goods store or an online retailer, you'll find all sorts of compasses in different sizes and shapes, with a variety of features. In this section, I briefly talk you through how to choose a compass that you can use for geocaching and other outdoor pursuits.

Types of compasses

Three types of compasses are suitable for geocaching: base plate, sighting, and pocket. (Examples of these compasses are shown in Figure 4-3.)

Figure 4-3: A base plate, sighting, and pocket compass.

Base plate compasses

As its name suggests, a *base plate compass* has a rectangular base that's a bit larger than the round housing that surrounds the compass. You can lay the transparent base plate over a map and use the markings and edges of the compass to help you navigate. Base plate compasses are perfect for geocaching. These compasses are priced in the $10–$35 price range.

Base plate compasses are also known as *orienteering compasses* because the design was originally intended for the sport of orienteering. The versatility and usefulness of these compasses soon spread outside the orienteering world, and the base plate compass is popular for all outdoor pursuits. There are specialized compasses for orienteering, such as thumb compasses and competition models with magnetic needles that settle faster than a standard compass.

Sighting compasses

A *sighting compass* is a base plate compass that's designed so you can make eye contact with whatever object or terrain feature you're pointing the compass toward. Usually, this is accomplished with a case with a mirror inside that surrounds the dial and flips up and down. The mirror allows you to see the compass needle and dial while you're looking directly at the feature you have sighted. Sighting compasses are among the most accurate hand-held compasses and are designed for people who take their compass work seriously. They range in price between $20 to over $100.

If you've served in the military, you're probably familiar with a *lensatic* compass. These compasses are favored by armed forces for their ruggedness and precision (especially important if you're calling in an artillery strike). Quite honestly, lensatic compasses are overkill for geocaching and hiking; you're better off with a base plate compass designed for orienteering because they're lighter, easier to use, and more versatile. Expect to pay around $100 for a military-issue lensatic compass; cheaper knock-off models are available on the market, but their quality is far below that of the real thing.

Pocket compasses

These are small compasses that often only have the *cardinal* compass points (north, south, east, west) or have marks in anywhere from 10–90° increments. You'll sometimes find these under-$10 compasses mounted on a thermometer or zipper pull. They're fine for giving you a general sense of direction but aren't well suited for navigation. Because they're small and lightweight, they make good back-up compasses.

Although compasses are very rarely wrong, sometimes outdoors users mistakenly put trust in their own intuition. "The compass must be broken because there's no way that can be north!" Oops. From my experience in search and rescue, I've seen this happen with both novice and experienced hikers when their compass is indeed showing the correct direction. If you don't trust your compass, try carrying two. When both are saying the same thing, it's a little harder to rationalize that your intuition is right and both compasses are wrong (although I've seen that happen on a few occasions, too).

Compass manufacturers

The three main manufacturers of compasses are

- ✔ **Brunton:** www.brunton.com
- ✔ **Silva:** www.silvacompass.com
- ✔ **Suunto:** www.suunto.com

All these companies make excellent compasses that you can't go wrong with.

I recommend that you stay away from cheaper, off-brand compasses. A compass is something that you should be able to depend on, and the quality, durability, and dependability of bargain compasses are considerably less than those of the models produced by any of the major compass manufacturers listed here.

The bottom line

To sum up my geocaching compass recommendations:

✔ Get a Brunton, Silva, or Suunto brand base plate or sighting compass.

✔ Spend a few extra dollars to get a model with adjustable declination.

✔ Choose a model with markings in 2° intervals (never more than 5 degrees unless it's a back-up pocket compass).

✔ Select an azimuth model with 0–360 degrees marked on the dial.

✔ Select a model that has easy-to-read numbers and marks on the dial.

Because a compass relies on the Earth's magnetic field to work, be sure when you use it that you keep it away from any metal objects (like a car hood) or electronic devices that generate an electromagnetic field (such as a GPS receiver or handheld radio).

All about Maps

Call me old school, but I'm a firm believer that anyone who geocaches should know how to use maps. Although some geocachers head out on their adventures armed with only a GPS receiver, a map can help you find the best route to a cache as well as keep you from getting lost if for some reason your GPS receiver stops working and you've wandered too far off the beaten path.

In this section, I tell you why maps are important, discuss how to select the right types of maps for geocaching, and finish up with some basic pointers on how to read a map.

Why do you need a map?

If you wondered why you need a compass while you're geocaching, you're probably asking yourself the same question about maps — and I'm talking about maps printed on paper, not the digital maps displayed on the screen of a GPS receiver. Guess what? I just happen to have a list of reasons why maps are important, and here they are:

✔ Paper maps can give you the "big picture" (unlike the maps displayed on the small screen of a GPS receiver) and let you plan the best route for finding a geocache.

When you enter the coordinates of a geocache in your GPS receiver, the receiver will give you a straight-line route for getting to the cache. That could be over rivers, down cliffs, and on top of mountains. With a map, you can plan a potentially easier and more enjoyable route.

✔ Many paper maps provide you with considerably more detail about the terrain than can a map displayed on a GPS receiver screen.

✔ Paper maps are easy to read in the bright sunlight, unlike many GPS receiver screens.

✔ Paper maps don't need batteries, and they work in places that GPS receivers have trouble with, such as under tree canopies or both natural and urban (tall buildings) canyons.

✔ Paper maps are lightweight, can be folded, and are easy to store.

With some urban geocaches or caches that are close to major roads and trails, taking a map with you probably isn't required. Based on the cache description, you should apply some common sense as to whether you should bring a map with you.

Selecting the right map

Because you spend most of your time with your feet or tires on the ground while geocaching, land maps are important to know how to about. In general, the two types of land maps are

✔ **Topographic:** These maps show natural land features such as lakes, rivers, and mountain peaks as well as man-made features like roads, railroad tracks, and canals. These maps (see an example in Figure 4-4) also have contour lines that trace the outline of the terrain and show elevation. *Contour lines* suggest what the land looks like in three dimensions (3-D).

✔ **Planimetric:** These maps don't provide much information about the terrain. Lakes, rivers, and mountain pass elevations might be shown, but there isn't any detailed land information. A classic example of a planimetric map is a state highway map or a road atlas. Planimetric maps are perfect in cities or on highways, but they're not suited for backcountry use. Figure 4-5 is a planimetric map of The Dalles, Oregon area.

When you're dealing with planimetric maps, you'll often encounter the terms *atlas* and *gazetter*.

- **Atlas:** A collection of maps, usually in a book

- **Gazetteer:** A geographical dictionary or a book that gives the names and descriptions of places

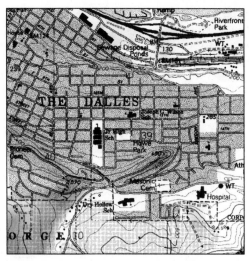

Figure 4-4: A topographic map showing contour lines and other features.

Figure 4-5: A planimetric map lacks terrain features and contours.

An important point to consider is there's no single universal map type for geocaching. Different map types display different features and details that are suited for a particular use — or user. A skilled map user always selects a map that meets his or her specific needs.

USGS topographic maps

The most popular topographic maps for use within the U.S. are made by the USGS. These maps cover different sizes of area; the smaller the area, the greater the detail. Topographic maps are often called *topo maps*.

The topo maps that show the most detail are sometimes called *quad sheets* or *7.5 minute maps* because they map just one *quadrangle* (geographer-speak for a rectangular piece of land) that covers 7.5 minutes of longitude and latitude. Figure 4-4, for example, is a topographic map of The Dalles, Oregon.

Topo maps are perfect when your geocaching adventures involve off-road hikes and treks. The maps are available in sporting goods stores that cater to hikers, map retailers, and through online map stores.

Topo maps can be pretty unwieldy while you're out geocaching, so here's a helpful link on how to fold a large map: www.backpacker. com/article/0,2646,6927,00.html.

Street maps

Topographic maps are great for when you get off the beaten path, but when you're geocaching, you usually end up driving on a paved road up to some point before you head off on foot. That's when a good street map comes in handy. Street maps are also essential if you're looking for geocaches hidden in more urban areas (or letter-boxing). A good source of street maps for an area is through the local Chamber of Commerce or visitor center.

Digital maps

PCs and the Internet have revolutionized the world of maps. Instead of heading down to the local map store to buy a map, you can visit a free Web site or purchase a reasonably priced map software package from companies such as DeLorme (www.delorme.com) or Maptech (www.maptech.com) and create your own topographic or street maps.

Two of my favorite, free Web sites for creating geocaching maps are

✔ **MapQuest (www.mapquest.com):** Displays street maps for locations in the United States based on addresses or ZIP codes.

Here's a sneaky way to get MapQuest to display a street map near a geocache's location. Enter this link in your browser:

```
www.mapquest.com/maps/map.adp?latlongtype=
decimal&latitude=44.032817&longitude=-121.330283
```

Replace the latitude and longitude values with the coordinates for a geocache. The new values will need to be in decimal degrees, so check out Chapter 3 for information on how to convert from other coordinate formats.

✔ **TerraServer-USA (www.terraserver-usa.com):** Displays USGS topographic maps and aerial photos (which can be extremely useful in pinpointing geocache locations). You can enter the coordinates of a cache, and the Web site will generate a map of the surrounding area that you can print out.

If you want to read more detailed information about the many digital map programs and Web sites that are available, check out *GPS For Dummies* (Wiley), written by yours truly.

If you're geocaching outside the United States and are looking for digital maps, pay a visit to oddens.geog.uu.nl/index.html. Odden's Bookmarks is one of the most comprehensive collection of map links on the Internet. This European Web site has over 20,000 links to maps and map sites all over the world. You can spend hours browsing through links to international map sources.

Understanding parts of a map

Having a map with you while you're geocaching is a one thing, but being able to effectively use it is another. In this section, I bring you up to speed on the types of information that you'll find on maps and how to interpret what some of the numbers, symbols, and squiggly lines mean.

Maps are almost always oriented so the top of the map is facing north. If a map doesn't follow this convention, a good mapmaker places an arrow on the map that points north.

Scale

Most maps have a *scale,* which is the ratio of the horizontal distance on the map to the corresponding horizontal distance on the ground. For example, 1 inch on a map can represent 1 mile on the ground.

Anatomy of a map

Most maps have basic elements in common. Here are some, along with the terms that *cartographers* (mapmakers) use to describe them:

- **Citation:** This is information about data sources used in making the map and when the map was made.

- **Collar:** This is the white space that surrounds the neatline (see the upcoming bullet) and the mapped area.

- **Compass rose:** A map has either a simple arrow that shows north or a full compass rose (an image that indicates all four cardinal points: North, East, South, and West) so the user can correctly orient the map to a compass.

- **Coordinates:** Maps usually have either letters and numbers or coordinates, such as latitude and longitude values, marked along the borders so users can locate positions on the map.

- **Legend:** This is a box that shows an explanation of symbols used on the map. Some maps show all the symbols; others rely on a separate symbol guide.

- **Mapped area:** This is the main part of the map, displaying the geographic area.

- **Neatline:** This is the line that surrounds the mapped area.

- **Scale:** This distance-equivalence information (such as *one inch = one mile*) helps you estimate distances on a map and is typically found at the bottom of a map.

- **Title:** This is usually the name of the map, but it also tells you which area it's mapping.

The map scale is usually shown at the bottom of the map in the legend. Often, rulers with the scale mark specific distances for you. A scale from a USGS topographic map is shown in Figure 4-6.

Figure 4-6: Scale information in on a USGS 7.5 minute topographic map.

Many maps use a representative fraction to describe scale. This is the ratio of the map distance to the ground distance in the same units of measure. For example, a map that's 1:24,000-scale means that 1 inch measured on the map is equivalent to 24,000 inches on the ground. The number can be inches, feet, millimeters, centimeters, or some other unit of measure.

The units on the top and bottom of the representative fraction must be the same. You can't mix measurement units.

When you're dealing with scale, keep these guidelines in mind:

- ✔ **The smaller the number to the right of the 1, the more detail the map has.**

   A 1:24,000 map has much more detail than a 1:100,000-scale map. A 1:24,000 map is a large-scale map, showing a small area.

- ✔ **The smaller the number to the right of the 1, the smaller the area the map displays.**

   In Figure 4-7, the 1:100,000-scale map shows a much larger area than the 1:24,000-scale map. A 1:100,000 map is a small-scale map and shows a large area.

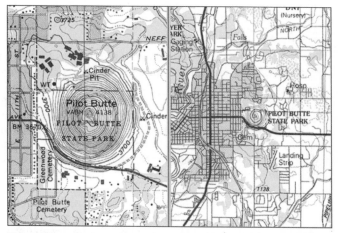

Figure 4-7: 1:100,000 and 1:24,000 scale maps show different details and areas.

Coordinate marks

Any map that's suitable for navigation will have coordinate system marks printed. For topographic maps, these marks are typically in latitude and longitude, UTM, or both. (For more about the latitude and longitude and UTM coordinate systems, see Chapter 3.) The marks are usually found on the map collar with the major intervals numbered. For example, the top corner of a topographic map might show the latitude and longitude.

The coordinate marks help you identify specific locations on a map. For example, if you had the coordinates of a geocache, you could find its location on a map by lining up the coordinate marks on the side of the map.

Transparent overlay rulers and grids make plotting positions and measuring distances on maps a piece of cake. Check out www.maptools.com for some free PDF files with rulers and grids that you can print out on transparency sheets. You can also purchase already made rulers and grids.

Citations

A *citation* contains information about when the map was made and what datum was used in making the map, although not all maps have this data. (Check out Chapter 3 for the scoop on datums and why they're critical for successful geocaching.) These two bits of information are important because they give you an idea of how accurate the map will represent the current terrain (especially in areas that have experienced a lot of change, such as development) and which datum you should set your GPS receiver for if you're using it with that particular map. The citation usually appears at the bottom of the map.

Symbols

Symbols — icons, lines, and colored shading, as well as circles, squares, and other shapes — are important parts of a map's language. They give the map more detailed meaning without cluttering up the picture with too many words. They represent roads, rivers, railroads, buildings, cities, and just about any natural or man-made feature you can think of. Symbols definitions are either shown on the map or are compiled in a separate map symbol guide. Some common symbols found on USGS topographic maps are shown in Figure 4-8.

Whether you're using a paper or a digital map, always familiarize yourself with its symbols. The more symbols you know, the better decisions you'll make when you're relying on a map for navigation.

Map symbols aren't universal. A symbol can have different meanings on different maps. For example, the symbol for a secondary highway on a USGS topographic map is a railroad on a Swiss map.

You can get a small booklet that contains the full list of USGS symbols at most places that sell topographic maps, or you can view all of the symbols online at http://mac.usgs.gov/mac/isb/pubs/booklets/symbols.

Contours

Contour lines are continuous lines found on topographic maps that provide information about elevation. Each line represents a specific elevation; all locations along that line have the exact same elevation. On USGS topographic maps, contour lines are brown.

Color my world

USGS topographic maps use colors for map symbols and features to make them easier to identify and to provide a natural appearance to the maps. The colors include

✔ **Black:** Boundaries and most cultural or man-made features

✔ **Blue:** Water features such as lakes, rivers, and swamps

✔ **Green:** Vegetation such as woods, orchards, and vineyards

✔ **Brown:** Relief features such as contours, cuts, and fills

✔ **Purple:** Updated information

✔ **Red:** Main roads, built-up areas, boundaries, and special features

If you're making a copy of a colored map, always opt for color instead of black and white so its features are easier to identify.

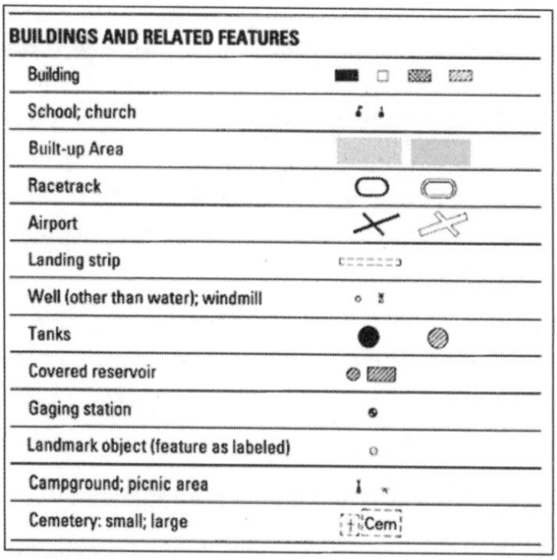

BUILDINGS AND RELATED FEATURES	
Building	■ □ ▨ ▨
School; church	⌇ ⌇
Built-up Area	
Racetrack	◯ ◯
Airport	✕ ✈
Landing strip	[⁻ ⁻ ⁻ ⁻]
Well (other than water); windmill	○ ⚡
Tanks	● ◎
Covered reservoir	◎ ▨
Gaging station	⊙
Landmark object (feature as labeled)	○
Campground; picnic area	⌇ ⌐
Cemetery: small; large	⌐†⌐Cem⌐

Figure 4-8: Selected USGS topographic map symbols.

To make the contour lines easier to read, every fifth line — an *index contour* — is printed darker. If you follow the index contour line, you'll eventually find the elevation associated with the line printed. The thinner or lighter-colored contour lines are *intermediate contours* and don't have printed elevations associated with them.

The *contour interval* is the difference in elevation between two adjacent contour lines. Usually, the contour interval is printed on the legend or collar of a map. For example, if a map reads *Contour*

Interval 20 Feet, the elevation change between contour lines is 20 feet.

Another way to determine elevation on a USGS topographic map is to use *spot elevation.* If you see an *X* printed with a number next to it, this is the elevation of the spot marked that's with the *X*.

By looking at how closely contour lines are spaced on a map, you can get a good sense of what the elevation change is going to be like. If the lines are widely spaced, the elevation doesn't change much, and the terrain is mostly flat. If the contour lines are close together, the elevation change will be greater. In a nutshell, the more contour lines that are grouped close together, the steeper the terrain.

In addition to getting a sense of elevation change, contour lines can also clue you as to what the terrain looks like. Think of contour lines like a layer cake, with each contour elevation defining the height and shape of the cake layer. Figure 4-9 shows different contour lines that appear on a map and how the landforms associated with the contours would appear in real life.

Contour clues

How contour lines appear on a map can give you some important clues as to what kind of terrain you might be traversing to reach a geocache. Here are some general guidelines for interpreting contour lines on maps:

- Contour lines are V-shaped in streambeds and narrow valleys (stretches of low land between hills or mountains). The point of the V points uphill or upstream.

- Contour lines are U-shaped on ridges (long narrow sections of land, often located on a mountainside), with the bottom of the U pointing down the ridge.

- Contour lines form an M or a W shape just before a stream junction.

- Closely spaced contour lines mean steep terrain. Very narrowly spaced contour lines mean a cliff.

- Equally spaced contour lines means that the terrain has a uniform slope.

- A small, closed contour line indicates a depression (a low place in the ground with no outlet for surface drainage) or a summit. If there are hash marks inside the circle, it's a depression.

- Contour lines are typically smooth. When they're not, it could mean large rock outcrops, cliffs, or fractured areas of the Earth's surface.

- The larger the contour intervals, the more difficult it is to figure out what the terrain is like.

Map contour   Terrain appearance

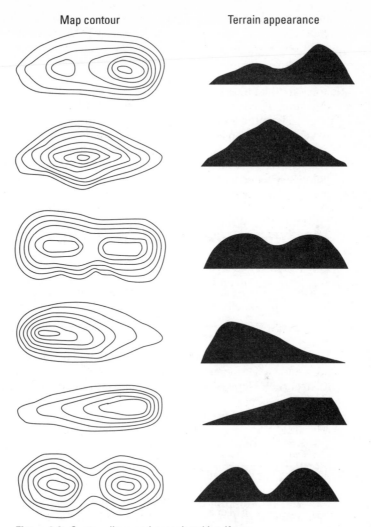

Figure 4-9: Contour lines and associated landforms.

Using a Map and Compass

Maps and compasses go together like bread and butter (or steak and eggs if you're on a low-carb diet). Although each can be used by itself to a certain degree, to get the most out of these two navigation tools, you should use them together. By using a map and compass in tandem, you can determine your location even when your GPS receiver can't.

In this section, I introduce you to some basic land navigation concepts, including how to orient a map, how to take a bearing and set a course, and how to use triangulation to determine where you're located.

You can't just a read a book, even this one, and immediately develop good map and compass skills. It takes time and experience to become an outstanding land navigator. If you want to fully develop your map and compass skills, you need to practice. You might also consider getting involved with a local orienteering club or taking a community college course. In both cases, you'll get some field experience with someone standing over your shoulder showing you the ropes.

Getting familiar with basic navigation concepts

Before you start using maps and a compass together, you should be aware of some basic land navigation concepts and terminology.

Holding the compass

Many people new to land navigation think you just look at a compass and go. However, holding a compass incorrectly can affect its accuracy. Here are some tips to maximize your accuracy:

- **Always hold the compass level so that the needle swings freely.** You don't want the needle moving or tipped down toward the base plate.

- **Bend your elbows close to your sides.** This keeps the compass steady and prevents the needle from bouncing around.

- **You should hold the compass at a height that lets you take a line of sight reading, matching up the direction of travel arrow with the degree marks on the compass dial.** You should be able to turn the dial without causing the needle to move around too much.

- **When you look at the compass, raise and lower your eyes instead of moving your head.**

- **Keep the compass away from metal objects and electronic devices (such as GPS receivers).** Both can cause inaccurate readings because of their magnetic fields.

Never, ever use a map and a compass on a car hood. I've seen it happen a couple of times, and the errors caused by the metal hood weren't too pretty.

Understanding degrees

Whenever you use a compass, you need to visualize that you're standing in the center of a big imaginary pie (the flavor is up to you) that's been divided up into 360 equal pieces. In navigation terms, each one of these pie slices equals one degree.

A circle that's divided into 360 degrees allows you to accurately state a direction of anything that surrounds you, no matter where it is. (The technical map-speak term for such a direction is an *azimuth*.)

The degrees are numbered clockwise and start with 0 degrees (the same as 360 degrees), which is north, followed by 90 degrees (east), 180 degrees (south), and 270 degrees (west).

Understanding bearings and courses

A *bearing* is simply a direction to some object or terrain feature from your current position, expressed in degrees. (I'll show you how to take a bearing with your compass coming up shortly.)

A *course* is a set direction that you're traveling. For example, if you want to head to a geocache that you know is under a radio tower on a hill, you'd take a bearing to the radio tower. The compass direction would be the course you would follow to reach the tower.

When you're using a map and compass, always take magnetic declination into account. Most topographic maps have the declination printed at the bottom of the map as an aid to compass users. However, keep in mind that the declination might have changed since the map was originally made.

Orienting the map to north

Orienting the map north means positioning the map so that you, the map, and the compass all are facing north. Doing so lets you readily recognize terrain features on the map. For example, if there were a river fork on your right, by orienting the map to the north, you could estimate your position by looking for any river forks on the map that appeared to the east. To orient a map, follow these steps:

1. **Rotate the compass dial so that north is lined up with the direction of travel arrow.**

2. **Take the compass and map in your hand and place the edge of the compass on the margin of the map or on any line that runs north and south.**

> The top of the map is almost always north.

3. **Turn your body (while still holding the map and compass) until the magnetic needle is lined up with north on the compass dial.**

   The map is now oriented to the north.

Taking a bearing

Bearings (the compass direction of an object or terrain feature) are pretty straightforward to take. Here's how:

1. **Point the compass's direction of travel arrow at an object or terrain feature.**

2. **Rotate the compass dial until the magnetic needle lines up with the red, north alignment arrow.**

3. **Read the degree mark that lines up with the direction of travel arrow.**

   Those degrees are your magnetic bearing. (If you want to transfer that bearing to a map, you'll need to account for declination, which I describe in the "Declination dissected" sidebar earlier in the chapter.)

Topographic orientation

Another way to orient a map is by using two prominent landmarks. Let me give you an example. Suppose you're out geocaching and see a *mesa* (a table-shaped mountain) off to your right. To your left is a fork in a river. You'd locate these two features on the map and then turn the map until the features on the map matched the general direction in which the actual landmarks appeared.

Congratulations, your map is now oriented so that the top of the map is pointing north. The technique is *terrain association,* which is simply associating the map to fit the terrain. (Check out: www.online-orienteering.net/elevation_relief/48 for descriptions and illustrations of major terrain features such as hills, valleys, saddles and ridges.)

Terrain association can also be used for figuring out your current position. By looking for features you see around you and then matching them to features on the map, you can zero in on your location. This takes some practice and skill in reading the terrain on a map and then translating it into what it would look like in real life. Even skilled navigators sometimes "bend the map" — that is, compare the terrain and map features and force the map to erroneously validate where they think they are.

An old memory jogger for this process is *Put Red Fred in the shed* — *Red Fred* being the magnetic needle, and the *shed* being the outlined, red north alignment arrow that moves when you turn the compass dial.

Sometimes it's useful to know the compass direction from some object or feature back to your current position. This is a *back bearing*.

Here are the two ways to get a back bearing:

✔ **Find the bearing to the object or feature from your current position and then add or subtract 180.**

The number you get must be between 0 and 360.

or

✔ **Take a bearing to the object or feature, and instead of putting Red Fred in the shed, rotate the compass dial so that the red magnetic north needle lines the black, opposite side of the north alignment arrow.**

The most common mistake I've seen people make when taking a bearing is to rotate the compass dial so the magnetic needle is aligned south instead of north. Doing so will give you a bearing that is off by 180°. Always double-check your alignment and remember to account for declination.

Setting a course

Sometimes you'll encounter a geocache that tells you to walk a set distance (such as 20 paces) following a certain compass bearing before you can get to the cache. To find the cache, you'll need to set a course. Here's how:

1. **Turn the compass dial so that the direction you want to head in degrees lines up with the direction of travel arrow.**

2. **Turn your entire body until the red, magnetic north needle lines up with the red north alignment arrow.**

   Put Red Fred in the shed.

The direction of travel arrow now points to your course heading, which you can follow to the cache.

Breaking a course into legs

If you're following a fairly long compass course, break the course up into straight-line legs. A *leg* is simply a collection of shorter segments of a single course. To break up a course into legs, follow these steps (bad pun intended):

1. **Find some readily distinguishable, stationary object on the course's compass bearing.**

   It might be a uniquely shaped tree, rock, or any feature or object that stands out from the rest of the terrain. After you select an object, burn it into your memory just in case something temporarily obscures the object while you're walking toward it.

2. **Walk to that object or feature.**

   You don't need to be looking at your compass or even walking in a straight line because you know that the feature is on your course's compass bearing.

3. **When you get to the feature, go through the steps described earlier for setting a course, using the same compass bearing you started with.**

4. **Identify another unique feature (or a readily recognizable map terrain feature) on the bearing and head toward it.**

   Repeat these steps until you reach your destination.

Using your compass as a protractor

Say you want to set a course between two known points on a map. You're at point A and want to get to point B but need to figure out the correct compass bearing to set your course. You can easily do this by using your compass as a protractor. To do so, follow along:

1. **Lay your compass flat on a map, placing the back edge of the base plate on point A.**

   The back of the compass is the part of the base plate that doesn't have the direction of travel arrow.

2. **Use the edge of the compass to make a straight line between point A and point B.**

   If the edge isn't long enough, lay a ruler along the compass edge to extend the edge until it reaches point B.

3. **Rotate the compass dial so that the north-south orienting lines are parallel with the map's margins.**

   The north alignment arrow should be facing up. Don't pay any attention to the magnetic needle; you don't need it when you're using your compass as a protractor.

The degree value on the compass dial that lines up with the direction of travel arrow is the bearing between point A and B.

You did remember declination, didn't you?

Another navigational skill you might want to develop is pacing. *Pacing* is simply counting the number of steps it takes to cover a certain distance. Use your GPS receiver to measure a set distance and then count each step you take. Do this several times to come up with an average. Your pace count will change depending on the terrain (smooth or rugged, flat, uphill, or downhill).

Using triangulation

Even with a GPS receiver, there are times when you're going to ask yourself, "Just where the heck am I?" Triangulation is one way of using a map and compass to determine your current location. (This is an especially good skill to have if your GPS receiver stops working and you end up lost.) It involves identifying at least three prominent and distinct features you can see (such as a mountain summit, radio tower, or fork in a river), finding them on your map, and then using your compass to plot your position. Here's the process:

1. **Locate three prominent features you can see that aren't close to one another.**

   You'll get the most accuracy if the three points are around 120 degrees apart.

   Triangulation can also be done with two known landmarks (technically called *biangulation*), but three or more points give you a higher level of accuracy in plotting your location.

2. **Use a compass to take a bearing from your current location to the first feature.**

3. **Rotate the compass dial so the bearing to the feature lines up with the direction of travel arrow.**

4. **Lay your map flat and locate the feature on the map.**

5. **Put the compass on the map so that the edge of the compass points towards and is on the feature.**

6. **While keeping the edge on the feature, rotate the entire compass so that the north-south orienting lines point north.**

7. **Draw a line down the edge of the compass toward your position. (The edge of the compass should still be on the feature.)**

   This line passes through all the locations that have the bearing you recorded when viewing the feature.

8. **Repeat Steps 2–7 for the other two features.**

You're probably getting tired of me saying this by now, but you did remember declination, didn't you? If not, cruise to the "Declination dissected" sidebar elsewhere in the chapter.

The three lines will intersect and form a triangle. Your approximate position should be somewhere within that triangle. Figure 4-10 shows a located position by using triangulation.

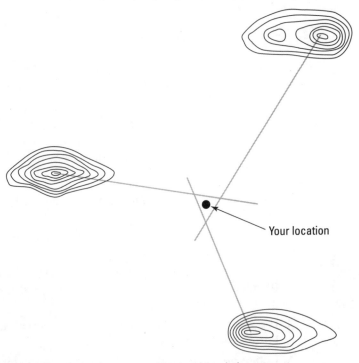

Your location

Figure 4-10: Determine your position by triangulation.

This chapter gives you some basic map and compass skills you can use while you're geocaching. It really only scratches the surface when it comes to land navigation, though. To find out more about this topic, I suggest you pick up a copy of the classic book, *Be Expert with Map and Compass,* by Björn Kjellström.

Part II
Let's Go Geocaching

The 5th Wave   By Rich Tennant

"It's just another stupid McToy that says
'hello' in 25 different languages."

In this part . . .

This part of the book gives you the nitty-gritty details on going geocaching. In Chapter 5, I describe the different types of geocaches that you can look for and show you how to use the Geocaching.com Web site database to list geocaches that are in your own neighborhood or anywhere in the world. You'll read about what information is associated with a geocache, and how to use it to help narrow your search. Chapter 6 gets into the nuts and bolts of searching for a geocache. I talk about what you should bring with you and how to search, starting from driving to a location nearby the cache to setting out on foot — you'll also find some hints and tips for discovering elusive caches.

With any luck, you'll soon locate the hidden cache — and in Chapter 7, you can read what to do when you do, including leaving goodies and logging your find both in the cache's logbook and online. After you've geocached for a while, you might decide you want to hide your own cache. You'll find everything you need to know about hiding and maintaining caches in Chapter 8, including what types of containers to use, clever hiding places, where and where not to hide caches, and how to list your cache in the Geocaching.com database.

Chapter 5

Selecting Geocaches to Find

● ●

In This Chapter

▶ Discovering the different types of geocaches

▶ Getting a Geocaching.com account

▶ Querying the Geocaching.com database

▶ Listing geocaches

▶ Viewing information about a geocache

● ●

*I*f you were searching for the lost treasure of Captain Jack Sparrow, you certainly wouldn't just wander around aimlessly, looking in every nook and cranny for its hiding place. No, you'd get yourself a genuine pirate treasure map first, and then proceed to where *X* marks the sport. Spot. Whatever. Savvy?

The same holds true for geocaching, but instead of using a faded sheet of parchment to start your quest for a geocache, you'll go much more high-tech with a Web browser and an Internet connection. Your first port of call is the Geocaching.com Web site (www. geocaching.com), the 'Net's largest collection of geocache information. There, you specify where you'd like to go treasure hunting, and a list of nearby geocaches, with descriptions and coordinates, is displayed. With this in hand, you can start looking for the booty. (I describe how to go about the actual searching in Chapter 6.)

In this chapter, you discover the different types of geocaches that you can look for. Then you take a whirlwind tour of the Geocaching.com Web site, finding out how to use basic and advanced search features to list geocaches. You also discover all the descriptive information you can get for a geocache — which is critical when you set out on foot searching for a cache.

Defining the Types of Geocaches

Before you start searching for geocaches, knowing what types of caches you might encounter is a good idea (although you needn't worry about turning up cursed Aztec gold). In this section, I briefly describe the different types of caches that the Geocaching.com database contains. When you view a list of geocaches (which I talk about later in the chapter), each of the caches has an icon associated with it so you can easily tell what type of cache it is.

The two main types of geocachers are those who search for all types of caches and those who primarily focus on certain type of caches. If you're just getting started in the sport, I suggest that you initially try to find all different types to caches to increase your experience and skills. After you put a number of cache notches in your GPS receiver, you can start specializing if you're so inclined.

Traditional cache

A *traditional* geocache hearkens back to the very first cache that Dave Ulmer hid back in May, 2000: some type of container (such as a surplus ammo can, bucket, or plastic food storage container), a logbook for people to sign, and a collection of trinkets that cache finders can exchange. Look for the single-container icon, as shown in the margin.

Multicache

A *multicache* (as in multiple) is a geocache with more than one location. The two types of these caches are

- ✔ **Offset caches:** An *offset cache* has a series of hidden containers or markers. (These types of caches can also incorporate historical monuments, plaques, or benchmarks. When you find the first location, there are directions to the next one, and so on, until you locate the final cache, which has the logbook and the goodies.

- ✔ **Clue caches:** *Clue caches* have questions and clues posted in their description that you must resolve to reach your final destination. For example, *Count the number of rusted bolts on the post.* The latitude coordinate is N 43 degrees, with correct number of minutes equal to 19 times the number of bolts. So if you count 28 bolts and multiply that number by 19, you get 532 — and thus you need to head to 43 degrees, 532 minutes north.

The multicache icon shows two containers, as shown in the margin here.

Traditional geocaches and multicaches make up the majority of caches listed in the Geocaching.com database.

Virtual cache

A *virtual cache* doesn't have a hidden container, logbook, or goodies. The coordinates point to a location with a gorgeous view, an interesting historical spot, or someplace that catches a geocacher's fancy that he or she wants to share. Usually it's a location where you couldn't place a conventional cache, for practical (a paved scenic overlook where there's nowhere to really place a cache) or legal (such as a U.S. National Park site where hiding caches is prohibited) reasons.

The ghost icon for a virtual geocache doesn't mean that it is a haunted geocache. A *haunted geocache* is a cache purposely placed in a spooky or creepy place — think *Blair Witch Project*. No icons are associated with haunted caches, but the description will clue you in . . . and you can visit them if you dare.

Mystery cache

A *mystery* or *puzzle geocache* contains clues on the cache information page that you must solve before you can find the cache. Often, the coordinates of a starting point are given, and you must figure out the puzzle or puzzle pieces to start out. (**Note:** Many multicaches formally fall into the mystery cache category but are still labeled as multicaches.) Mystery caches carry a question mark icon, as shown in the margin.

Locationless cache

When you go geocaching, you normally start with a set of coordinates and try to find a hidden container at that location. A *locationless cache* works in reverse. You're asked to locate a specific object and feature and then post the coordinates (and usually a digital photo) to the Geocaching.com site. You might be asked to locate a certain type of neon sign, an aircraft navigation aid, or a building with a unique architectural style. There aren't as many locationless geocaches as conventional caches, but they are kind of fun.

The icon for a locationless cache is a globe with a flag at the top, as shown in the margin.

Letterbox hybrid

Geocaching has its roots in the old British pastime of *letterboxing* (see www.letterboxing.org), which uses hidden containers, log-books, and rubber ink stamps. Some hidden sites are both modern geocaches and traditional letterboxes. A sealed envelope icon points you to a letterbox cache, as shown in the margin.

Event cache

An *event cache* is a posted notice of a geocaching get-together. It contains the date, time, place and description of an event. The event could be a group geocaching outing or an informal meeting at a local pizza place to talk about geocaching. Event caches *expire* — that is, after they take place, they're removed from the Geocaching.com database just in case someone misreads the date and shows up wondering where everyone is. If you see a grayed-out event listing in the site database, the event has already taken place.

Event caches are denoted by a speech bubble icon, as shown in the margin.

Webcam cache

Webcam caches aren't really hidden caches per se but rather the locations of outdoors Web cams. The cache hider provides the coordinates of the Web cam and a link to its Web site. Your quest is to find the Web camera; when you do, you pose for a picture as your proof. When you then log your find on Geocaching.com, you're usually asked to submit a screen capture from the Web cam site of you posing. This means that you need a cellphone so you can call someone to go to the Web cam's site and save the screen image.

The icon for a Webcam cache looks like . . . um, a Web cam, sort of. See the margin.

Caches within caches

A few other types of geocaches don't fall into one of the primary cache types. These geocaches might be traditional, multicache, or mystery caches with a unique flavor of their own.

Theme caches

Some geocaches have specific themes, such as a TV show (*Star Trek*), book (Harry Potter), or a certain type of animal (penguins, for example). The cache hider is a fan of the theme and stuffs his or her cache with associated goodies. Theme caches are identified in the geocache description. If you visit the cache, you're asked to bring something that relates to the theme.

Travel Bugs

A *Travel Bug* is a trinket placed in a cache that has a special dog tag attached to it. Key chains, toy cars, and small dolls are examples of items that have become Travel Bugs. As their name suggests, Travel Bugs are meant for traveling. If a geocacher finds one in a cache, he or she is supposed to move it to another cache. Each of the Travel Bug dog tags has a unique number stamped on it, and their journeys can be tracked on the Geocaching.com Web site.

For example, a Star Wars Darth Vader action figure Travel Bug started his travels in an Arkansas geocache in February, 2002. By the time he was returned to his owner nine months later, he had journeyed 17,534.64 miles, including tagging along on aerial combat missions in Afghanistan, pub-hopping in England, and working on his tan in Florida. At last report, Darth was getting some well-deserved R&R in Texas.

When you view a list of geocaches, caches that contain Travel Bugs have an icon that looks like the bug on the special dog tag pictured here. I tell you more about Travel Bugs, including how to set your own loose, in Chapter 8.

Microcaches

Microcaches are very small caches that contain only a log or a single piece of paper that identifies it as a geocache. Microcaches can be some of the most challenging geocaches to find because of their small size and large number of possible hiding places. You'll typically find microcaches in miniscule containers such as plastic 35mm film canisters or candy tins. Microcache hiders can get devilishly clever; microcaches have been discovered on the back of plastic-coated leaves and in hollowed-out bolts. Microcaches tend to be located in more urban versus rural areas, and the hider will warn you ahead of time in the online description that you'll be looking for one of these itsy, bitsy caches.

Log caches

Log caches have nothing to do with timber or Paul Bunyan. They contain only a logbook, which you're asked to sign. There are no goodies to take, and you're asked not to leave anything. As with the other cache types, log caches are identified in the cache description.

Using Geocaching.com

The Geocaching.com Web site (www.geocaching.com) is where all the action takes place on the Internet. Anyone can visit the site and get free, up-to-date information about geocaches all over the world. You have lots of caches to choose from, too. In April, 2004, over 91,000 active geocaches were listed in its database, in 201 different countries — and the number grows on a daily basis.

In the remainder of this chapter, I talk about how you can use Geocaching.com to search for geocaches — online, that is. Read Chapter 6 for the scoop on searching in the real world. Before I get into the nitty-gritty of gathering information about geocaches, I want to talk a little about Geocaching.com and accounts.

Here are the three levels of access to the Geocaching.com site, each associated with different types of accounts:

✔ **No account:** As I mention earlier, the Geocaching.com site can be used freely by anyone interested in searching for geocaches. All you need are a Web browser and an Internet connection to view geocache coordinates and information.

✔ **Basic account:** The next level of access is a free, basic account. By registering with your name and e-mail address, you can log online geocaches that you find, submit your own hidden caches to be included in the database, automatically be notified when new caches are added in your area, use interactive maps, and participate in online forums devoted to the sport. This is kind of a no-brainer. You should sign up for a basic account if you geocache more than once or twice.

 ✔ **Premium account:** Geocaching.com also offers premium accounts (Groundspeak Premium Membership). These nominally priced accounts ($3 a month or $30 a year) give you access to the Pocket Queries feature (you can bulk-download cache information to use with PDA and PC software and GPS receivers), enhanced forum features, and member-only caches (see the icon in the margin). Getting a premium account is a nice way to support the Geocaching.com site, and all it's done for the sport.

 If you don't have an account, I suggest that you get one. (Basic or premium is your choice.) Some of the Web site features that I talk about in the book (such as logging finds and adding your own geocaches to the database) require an account.

Getting an account is fast and easy. You can sign up for one and get additional information on the Geocaching.com home page. Just click the Create an account now link and then fill in some basic information.

After you have an account, you can log in at the top of the home page by clicking the log in link. The Web site supports the use of Web browser cookies, so if you have cookies enabled, you'll automatically be logged in on subsequent visits to the site.

Geocaching aliases

Most people who geocache use an alias that's the same as their Geocaching.com account username. They use the alias instead of their real name when they sign cache logs and make Internet posts. The aliases are cool-sounding names like Navdog, Wiley Cacher, or Moun10Bike. Be imaginative and come up with an alias that fits who you are. ***Note:*** Aliases must be unique. If you try to register a new account on Geocaching.com and someone else already has registered that username/alias, you'll need to select another one.

Querying the Geocaching.com Database

The Geocaching.com Web site provides a simple, easy-to-use interface to a large database containing information on close to 100,000 geocaches. (Just like the number of hamburgers served, this number increases every day.) The Web site is where you'll start your search for a geocache, gathering a variety of information before you step outside with your GPS receiver and start your hunt.

In this section, I describe how to use the Geocaching.com site to search for geocache information. You'll see how to perform basic and advanced searches, view lists of geocaches that meet your search criteria, and zero in on a single cache to get detailed information you'll use to find that cache.

Basic search techniques

When you visit the Geocaching.com home page, you can immediately start searching for caches.

In the upper-right corner of the home page are three basic search commands (as shown in Figure 5-1). Look at each one of these search options individually.

Web site designs always change, and the location of the basic Geocaching.com search commands and their appearance might change. If Figure 5-1 doesn't match the current Geocaching.com Web page, you still should be smart enough to search for caches (after reading this section). Think of it as good practice for honing your Sherlock skills.

Searching by ZIP code

The topmost search command on the Geocaching.com site allows you to search for geocaches by ZIP code. Actually, this is really by postal code — this option works for caches located in the United States, the United Kingdom, Canada, and Australia.

Enter a valid postal code and then click the Submit button. A list of geocaches within 100 miles of the approximate center of the postal code is displayed. (To display the distance in miles or kilometers, click the Switch link at the bottom of the results page.)

If you enter a postal code that doesn't exist in the database, you'll be taken to the advanced search options page.

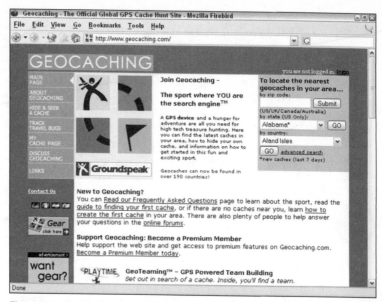

Figure 5-1: Begin with the basic search options.

To find a ZIP code for any city or town in the United States, visit
www.usps.com/zip4/citytown_zip.htm.

Searching by state

If you're looking for geocaches within the U.S., you can search the
Geocaching.com database by state. This option has a drop-down
list box containing all the states. Select the state you're interested
in, and then click the GO button. A new Web page appears (like
Figure 5-2) that has geocache information for the state you selected.

The following categories are shown:

✔ **Select a local city:** A drop-down list box contains all cities
   in the state that have populations greater than 20,000 people.
   Choose the city (or town), and then click the Get Caches
   button to display a list of geocaches within 100 miles of
   the city.

   Click the Other search options link to further narrow your
   search by using keywords, waypoints, and U.S. area codes.

✔ **Events, Past and Present:** Upcoming geocaching get-togethers
   in the state are listed here; click them to get more information.
   Recent past events are colored gray so you don't get confused
   and try to attend them.

✔ **Latest Caches Hidden:** This is a list of new caches in the state that have been added to the database within the past few days. The date, cache name (click its name to get detailed information about it), and the cache hider are displayed.

✔ **Latest Travel Bugs:** This is a list of recent Travel Bug sightings in the state. Click the Travel Bug link to get information about the bug or click the geocache name to get information about where the bug is currently residing.

✔ **Local Organizations:** These are Web site links for geocaching clubs, and organizations in that state are shown.

The organization links are not the be-all, do-all lists of geocaching clubs. Do a Google search for *geocaching* and your state or local area to check for other geocaching organization Web sites that might not be listed.

Searching by country

If you want to look for international caches in the Geocaching.com database, use the drop-down list box of countries on the site's home page. (However, not all countries shown might have geocaches present.) Select a country and then click the GO button. You're taken to the advanced search page, which I discuss more in detail in the following section. Click the Seek button to display a list of geocaches in the selected country.

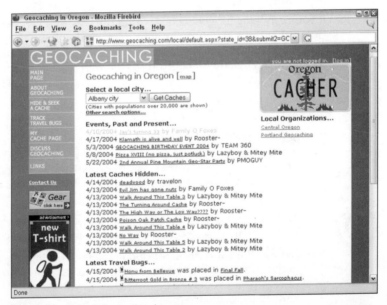

Figure 5-2: Search for caches by state.

If an asterisk follows a state or country name, one or more new caches have been added to the database for that state or country within the past seven days.

Detailed search techniques

Sometimes you might want to perform a more specific, detailed search, such as displaying only certain types of geocaches or perhaps caches that are located near a known set of latitude and longitude coordinates.

At the bottom of the basic search commands is the <u>advanced search</u> link. When you click this link, you're taken to the advanced search page (as shown in Figure 5-3). This page has the basic search commands as well as some enhanced ones that allow you to narrow down your search.

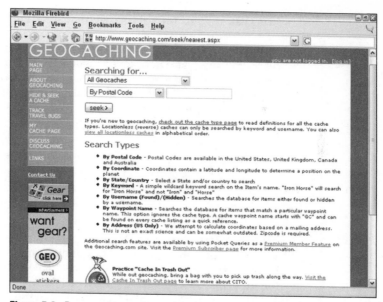

Figure 5-3: Run an advanced search here.

The following list explains the various search options:

Searching for type

The first option lets you search for different types of geocaches. The drop-down list box's default setting is to search for all types of caches. Select a cache type from the list, such as virtual cache or multicache, to display caches of only that type.

WEST ROUTT LIBRARY DISTRICT
HAYDEN PUBLIC LIBRARY

This option is used in conjunction with the other search parameters that I talk about next.

Specifying search parameters

Below the search-by-type drop-down list box is another drop-down list box that contains different search parameters — for example, by postal code, country, or coordinates.

When you select one of these parameters from the drop-down list box, the screen changes, and new entry options appear that are associated with the search parameter you select. For example, if you select By Coordinate, text entry boxes are shown, where you can enter the latitude and longitude.

After you enter the search parameters, click the Seek button to see whether any geocaches meet your search criteria. If they do, they'll be displayed in a list, which I describe in the following section.

The following list explains the parameters that are available:

- **Searching by postal code:** The By Postal Code parameter allows to you search for geocaches by postal code in the United States, the United Kingdom, Canada, and Australia. If the postal code can't be found in the database, an error message is displayed.

- **Searching by latitude and longitude:** In the By Coordinate parameter, you can enter the latitude and longitude to see whether any geocaches are near the location coordinate. When you select this parameter, a drop-down list box is displayed for specifying how you'll enter the coordinates (degrees and decimal minutes, degrees and minutes and seconds, or decimal degrees).

- **Searching by state/country:** The By State/Country parameter displays a Country drop-down list box and a State/Province drop-down list box. Select the country in which you'd like to search for geocaches. If state or province information associated with the country is available, it appears in the State/ Province drop-down list box. For example, if you select Canada, the provinces of Alberta, British Columbia, Manitoba, and so on would appear.

- **Searching by keyword:** The keyword search looks for a word that appears in the name of the geocache. For example, if you're looking for a geocache that has the word *fish* in its name, geocaches with *fish, fishing, fisherman, whitefish,* and so on would be shown.

✔ **Searching by username:** If you know someone's geocaching *alias* (their Geocaching.com account name; see the sidebar "Geocaching aliases"), you can search for caches they've either found (By Username [Found]) or hidden (By Username [Hidden]).

✔ **Searching by waypoint name:** Each geocache that's entered into the database has a unique waypoint name associated with it. If you enter the coordinates in your GPS receiver for the cache you're looking for, you can use this name with the waypoint. (To read what waypoints are and how to use them, read Chapter 3.) The waypoint names all start with *GC* (as in geocaching). If you know a cache waypoint name, this is where you can search for it.

You can also access most of the advanced search options by clicking the <u>Seek a Cache</u> link at the bottom of the Geocaching.com home page. As an added bonus, you can specify the postal code search radius — such as *show me all the caches within 20 miles of 98002.*

Looking at the Search Results

If your basic or advanced geocache search has been successful, a list of caches that meet your search criteria is displayed. You can read through the list and select a single cache to get information on. In this section, I walk you through how to use the list of geocaches and also how to get detailed information about a single cache. You'll use the detailed information as your pirate treasure map in tracking down the cache.

Viewing the list of geocaches

If geocaches are present in the Geocaching.com database that match your search parameters, a list of caches is displayed (see Figure 5-4). The result list contains the following information, sorted by how far away the cache is from the search criteria that you entered.

✔ **Icons:** Each listing bears an icon showing the type of cache. (Read the earlier section, "Defining the Types of Geocaches," for the lowdown on identifying these icons.) If a Travel Bug is present in the cache, a Travel Bug icon is also shown.

If you have a Geocaching.com account (basic or premium) and are logged in, a check mark will appear to the left of the icon for any caches that you've found and logged online. I talk more about logging your caches in Chapter 7.

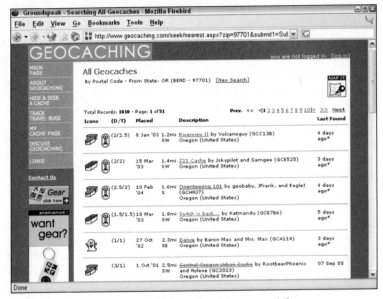

Figure 5-4: A fruitful search yields lots of caches to search for.

✔ **D/T:** D/T stands for *Difficulty* (how hard to find) and *Terrain* (how rugged the terrain is). Each has its own rating, ranging from 1 (easy) to 5 (hardest).

If you're just getting started geocaching, I recommend taking some baby steps first and initially selecting easy-to-find and easy terrain caches. This will give you a chance to learn the geocaching ropes and get some successful finds under your belt before you tackle the more challenging caches. Still, there's no reason why you can't try your hand at some of the 5/5 caches at first. Just expect a little bit of frustration . . . and perhaps exhaustion.

✔ **Placed:** This is the day, month, and year when the cache was originally placed.

✔ **Description:** The description contains

- The **distance and direction** the geocache is from the search parameter you entered

- The cache's **official descriptive name** (which you can click to get detailed information about a cache, which I talk about in the following section)

- The cache's **waypoint name** (such as GC73E2)

- The **alias** of whoever placed the cache

- The **country and state or province** (if applicable) where the cache is located

If the geocache name has a line through it, the cache is no longer available. This might be temporary or permanent; more information can be found on the cache's detailed information page.

✔ **Last Found:** This is the last time when someone located the cache and logged the find online.

If you have an account on Geocaching.com (basic or premium) and are logged in, a check box is displayed to the right of the Last Found item. If you mark the check box and click the Download Waypoints button, information about any geocaches that have been checked is downloaded to your PC. (*Hint:* You won't see this button if you're not logged in.) You can upload waypoints to your GPS receiver or use the downloaded data with geocaching software that I describe in Chapter 13. There's more information on downloading at the bottom of the geocache list page.

In addition to information about geocaches, the cache list page also has several navigation commands, including

✔ **Page scrolling:** Above the list of caches, Total Records shows you the number of geocaches that are within 100 miles (by default). Up to 20 caches are displayed on a page. You can click the page-scrolling commands that appear above the Last Found column to jump to other pages.

✔ **Mapping:** In the upper-right portion of the page is a MAP IT button. Clicking the button displays an interactive street map showing geocaches that appear in the list (as shown in Figure 5-5). You need to have a Geocaching.com account (basic or premium) and be logged in for many of the map features to work.

✔ **Detailed geocache information:** The official descriptive name of each geocache has a link to a detailed information page for the cache. I describe the information that you can get from the page in the next section.

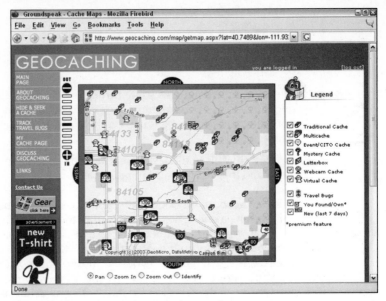

Figure 5-5: Get an interactive map of geocaches.

Getting information about a geocache

As you look through the list of geocaches, one will catch your eye sooner or later, and you'll want to get more information about the cache. Click the cache's name to display a page with detailed information. An example page is shown in Figure 5-6 and the upcoming Figure 5-7. (Because there's so much information that you'll need to scroll through the page, I included two figures that show all the information.)

The detailed geocache information is essential because you'll be using it to help you locate a cache after you set out on foot. Take a look at the types of information that appear on the page.

Geocache name

This is the official name of the geocache — it usually has something to do with the area where it's hidden, who hid it, or perhaps some clever play on words. ***Bonus:*** If you hide a cache, you get to name it. To the left of the name is an icon that shows you what type of cache it is.

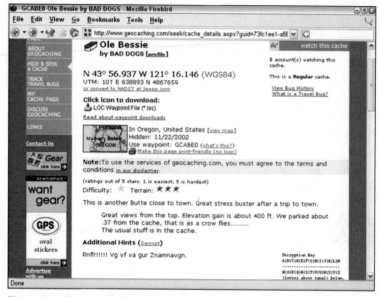

Figure 5-6: Each geocache has an information page.

Who placed the geocache

This is the cache hider's alias/Geocaching.com username. If you're logged in to the site, you can click the profile link to learn more about the cache hider.

Geocache coordinates

These tell you where the cache is located in latitude and longitude and UTM coordinates; these coordinates use the WGS 84 datum, so be sure your GPS receiver is set to this datum. (Read all about UTM and WGS in Chapter 3.)

You can click the or convert to NAD27 at Jeeep.com link and jump to the Jeeep.com (www.jeeep.com) site, where the coordinates will be automatically converted to the NAD 27 datum. (For more about the importance of datums, check out Chapter 3.)

Download coordinates

Click the download icon to download the geocache's waypoint information to your PC. You can then upload the coordinates to your GPS receiver or use them with geocaching programs. A link under the icon provides more information about downloading.

Where and when the geocache was hidden

This shows the country and state or province (if applicable) where the geocache is hidden. An overview map shows the general location of the cache. The date the cache was hidden is also shown.

Geocache waypoint name

All caches in the Geocaching.com database have a unique waypoint name: They begin with *GC,* followed by the numeric order the cache was added to the database. When you manually enter the coordinates into your GPS receiver, you can use this as the waypoint point.

Click the <u>Make this page print-friendly (no logs)</u> link to open a new window with essential information about the geocache that you can print and take with you on your hunt.

Difficulty

The difficulty rating is how hard the cache placer thinks the cache will be to find — 1 is easiest, and 5 is the most difficult. Whoever places the cache decides the difficulty level and bases the rating on how clever she thinks her hiding job was.

Terrain

The terrain rating is how difficult the terrain is. 1 is flat, easy, and level; 5 could be very steep and rocky with lots of underbrush and generally miserable to get to. As with the difficulty rating, it's up to the cache hider to rate the terrain.

Unfortunately, the difficulty and terrain ratings can be pretty subjective at times, and I've stumbled around some pretty rugged terrain for hours on a couple of caches that were supposedly rated as easy. This is another reason to read through the logged comments, described next, to get a better sense of what other geocachers experienced while searching for the cache.

General description of the geocache

Cache descriptions range from a couple of sentences to lengthy stories and history lessons about the cache location. Clues often appear in the description, so be sure to pay attention. Some cache hiders go beyond words in their descriptions and include digital photos of the cache area or elaborate artwork that's related to the cache.

Hints

The cache placer can optionally add hints to help a geocacher narrow his search. The hints are typically a brief sentence or a couple of words that appear in code; I discuss using hints and how to decode them in detail in Chapter 6.

Find

Under the Find heading (the top of Figure 5-7) are a series of links to other nearby caches, benchmarks (see Chapter 9 for how to search for benchmarks), *placenames* (prominent geographic or cultural features), and caches that have been hidden and found by the geocacher who placed the cache. Click one of the links to display its associated information list.

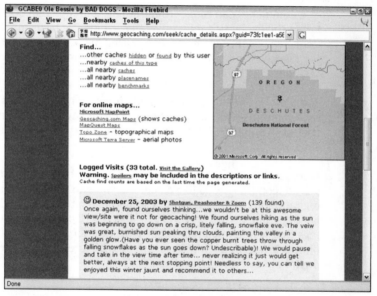

Figure 5-7: More of a geocache's information page.

Map location of the geocache

At the top of the information page is a small state map that gives you a general idea of where the cache is located. A larger map with more detail appears as you scroll down the page. You can click the large map and go to the MapQuest Web site, where you can zoom in on the cache site. I show you how to do this in Chapter 6.

There is also an online map section that contains links to Web sites that provide topographic maps, aerial photos, and other maps of the area where the cache is located. Click a link, and a new window opens up with a map. (*Note:* Most of these maps are useful only for geocaches located in the U.S.)

Logged Visits

The last part of the page contains log information related to the geocache. The number of times the cache has been found and logged online is shown as well as comments from each of the cache finders. (Only the most recent comments appear on a page, but you can read all the comments by scrolling to the bottom of the information page and clicking the <u>View them all on one page</u> link.)

The comments can range from a single sentence that someone found the cache to a mini-novel describing the trials and tribulations a geocacher went through during his or her search. Some of the logged comments are very well written and make entertaining reading.

Some of the logged visit comments might contain *spoilers* — hints that might make it easier to find the cache. Although most cachers try not to spoil the fun for others, sometimes a clue accidentally slips in.

Words aren't the only thing contained in cache logs. Any time you see an icon that looks like a camera, you can click it to display a digital photo of the cache that someone posted along with his or her log comments. There's also a <u>Visit the Gallery</u> link above cache logs that will take you to a page with thumbnail images of all the photos associated with the cache. Just be forewarned: Some of the digital photos can also act as spoilers.

Chapter 6

Searching for a Geocache

· ·

In This Chapter

▶ Choosing geocaching equipment and gear

▶ Using online maps to plan driving routes to geocaches

▶ Searching for geocaches on foot

▶ Honing your search

· ·

*A*fter you have your pirate treasure map (the online geocache description from the Geocaching.com Web site that I describe in Chapter 5), the next step is to go out and find the booty.

This is where the fun starts, especially because finding the cache might prove more challenging than you think. Remember, your GPS receiver will get you only within 10–30 feet of the cache location — perhaps even farther away if you have poor satellite coverage or the cache hider's coordinates are a little off. After your GPS unit gets you to the general vicinity of the geocache, you need to start using your eyes and your brain, which at times might be more reliable than your GPS receiver.

In this chapter, I cover the basics of searching for a geocache. I discuss the gear and equipment that you should consider bringing with you while geocaching, how to use online street maps to get close to a geocache, and how to start your search on foot. Finally, I give you some tips and hints that should increase your chances of finding a hidden geocache.

Deciding What Gear to Bring Geocaching

Indiana Jones would never set out an adventure without his trusty fedora and whip, and there are a number of items you should consider bringing with you when you're out on your own geocaching adventures.

In Chapter 1, I mention that the two things you absolutely need to go geocaching are the location coordinates of a cache and a GPS receiver. That's the bare-bones minimum, but most geocachers bring a little more equipment with them on their searches.

You can divide commonly carried geocaching gear into four general categories. (Some items overlap in the categories a bit.)

- **Cache-related:** This is the basic collection of gear that you need to locate a geocache, log your find, and trade for goodies that you discover in the cache.

- **Food and shelter:** No matter how short a planned geocaching trip is, you should follow the Boy Scout motto and be prepared. You need to have gear that protects you from the elements and keeps up your energy and hydration levels.

- **Electronic devices:** Because geocaching is a high-tech sport, you'll sometimes encounter geocachers using electronic devices such as PDAs, digital cameras, and handheld radios in addition to GPS receivers.

- **Safety equipment:** Continuing with the Boy Scout theme, don't forget safety-related gear like first aid kits, cellphones, batteries, and other handy items to have on hand in case of an emergency.

For each of these categories, see what specific types of gear geocachers bring with them on their hunts. A typical collection of geocaching equipment is shown in Figure 6-1.

Cache-related

Cache-related pieces of equipment are things that you need to find a geocache and also things that you'll use after you find the cache.

GPS receiver

Because geocaching relies on GPS receivers for finding caches, this is an essential piece of equipment to own and bring with you. If you don't have a GPS receiver, see Chapter 2 for advice on selecting one.

Before you leave home, enter the coordinates in your GPS receiver (as a waypoint) for the cache you'll be searching for. Because entering waypoints differs from model to model, check your user manual for specific instructions on how to enter and name a waypoint on your GPS receiver. If you don't know what a waypoint is, be sure to read Chapter 3.

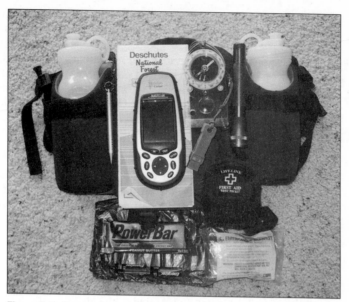

Figure 6-1: Common geocaching gear.

You can use the waypoint name on the Geocaching.com cache information page as the name of the waypoint. (It will start with the letters *GC,* for geocaching.) This six-character waypoint name is compatible with all GPS receivers. Be sure to double-check that the coordinates you entered are correct. An accidental typo while manually entering coordinates in a GPS receiver is a common error that can cause hours of frustration as you unsuccessfully search for a cache in the wrong location.

You can download a geocache's coordinates to your PC and then upload the waypoint directly to your GPS receiver. Doing so helps eliminate errors caused by typos in manually entering location coordinates. I talk about downloading coordinates in Chapter 5.

Before heading out on a geocaching trip, I always turn on my GPS receiver to check how much battery life I've got left. There's nothing more frustrating than getting close to a cache and having your batteries die — and of course, not bringing spare batteries with you at the time.

Geocache information

The Geocaching.com Web site has all the information that you need to find a cache, including the location coordinates, description, maps, and hints. Chapter 5 shows you how to access this information.

Print a copy of the cache description Web page so you can bring all the information you need with you to find the cache.

If you use an inkjet printer, its color ink smears and runs the minute that a drop of water hits a printed page. Valuable information that you printed about a geocache can be lost in a matter of moments during an unexpected rain shower. One-gallon-size, resealable plastic food storage bags enclose an 8.5 x 11" sheet of paper perfectly and also protect printed cache information and maps from the elements.

If your printer is out of ink or you're being frugal, at the very least, scribble down the geocache coordinates and any other information you think might be useful in locating the cache. Don't rely on your memory, no matter how good it is.

Map and compass

Although a fair number of geocachers use only their GPS receiver to get them to a cache, a good local map of the area can be extremely helpful. A GPS receiver can lead you in a straight line directly to a cache, but it's probably not going to tell you about the river, deep canyon, or cliffs between you and your destination. Even GPS receivers that display topographic maps often won't show detail that could help or hinder you on your way to a cache. Additionally, a map and compass serve as a backup just in case something goes wrong with your GPS receiver. (Just make sure you know how to use your map and compass. If you don't, please spend some time reading Chapter 4.)

Even if your GPS receiver has a built-in electronic compass, I still recommend that you bring a small handheld compass with you. These compasses don't need batteries, they aren't as fragile as a GPS receiver, and they don't take up much room.

Something to leave in the cache

When you locate a cache, you'll find all sorts of treasures that other people have left. Don't expect diamonds, gold bullion, or Super Bowl tickets, though. (You're far more likely to find baseball cards, costume jewelry, or corporate marketing giveaways.) Just remember that one man's trash is another man's treasure — or, to quote Captain Jack Sparrow, "Not all treasure is silver and gold, mate." The best things to leave in a cache are unique, out-of-the-ordinary items (perhaps foreign coins, fossils, exotic matchbooks, or anything that has a high cool factor). And please, avoid leaving *McToys,* which is geocaching lingo for plastic junk that you reasonably expect to find with a fast-food kid meal. One of the ethics of geocaching is to try to always trade up — leave something better than you took.

Pen or pencil and paper

Carry a small pad of paper and a pen or pencil for taking notes about your route or things you see on the way. Some geocachers keep an ongoing journal of their adventures; you never know — you might turn into a geocaching Hemingway.

For a field notebook, I like the Rite in the Rain products (www. riteintherain.com). Just about every surveyor, forester, or scientist who spends much time outdoors uses them. The specially treated paper is waterproof and won't turn into mush when it gets wet. I carry either a small, stubby pencil (old-school, but very reliable) or a more modern pressurized pen like a Space Pen brand (www.spacepen.com).

Bringing your own pen or pencil is also handy when you encounter a geocache with a logbook pen that has been left out in the cold too long and doesn't work anymore. It's a bummer when you find some elusive cache, the pen doesn't work, and you can't sign the logbook.

Small pack

Put all your gear in a small daypack while geocaching — stuffing your pockets full of stuff just doesn't cut it. Any small-volume pack (under 800 cubic inches, such as a daypack or school bookpack) should do the trick. I personally like packs that have a built-in hydration system (such as those made by CamelBak; www.camelbak.com) or are a fanny pack design that can carry gear as well as one or two water bottles.

Food and shelter

Food and shelter items are things that keep you comfy and happy while you're out geocaching, no matter what the conditions are like. Here are some suggestions.

Food and water

If you're out looking for multiple caches, you can easily spend the better part of a day searching, so be prepared with enough food and water. (The warmer the weather, the more water you should bring.) Some geocachers plan a picnic lunch or dinner around their outings, especially in scenic areas.

Consider tossing a couple of energy bars, such as PowerBars or Clif Bars, into your geocaching pack. They're lightweight and provide a fair amount of calories if your energy starts to run down. Most savvy outdoors-folks carry a little bit of emergency food with them, just in case. One way to ensure that the emergency food doesn't get munched on as a snack is to choose something edible — but unpalatable enough — that you'd eat it only in an emergency.

For tap water, you can carry it in a hydration pack or bicycle-type water bottle. Better yet, just stop at the grocery store and pick up a couple of convenient bottled waters.

No matter how pristine a stream looks, avoid the temptation to take a drink of the cool, fresh water. Bacteria, viruses, and protozoa that you can't see are often present, no matter how clean the water looks. Unless it's a survival situation, always boil, filter, or chemically treat water. A bottle of water purification tablets, such as Portable Aqua, are very lightweight and don't take up much room in your pack.

Appropriate clothes and footwear

One of the nice things about geocaching is that you don't need to worry about being in style with the latest New York or Paris fashions. Wear clothes that are comfortable and weather-appropriate and that you don't mind getting dirty. Even if it's the middle of summer, bring along a lightweight jacket in case of an unexpected rain shower or drop in the temperature.

If you're geocaching in cold or wet weather, avoid wearing cotton, such as jeans, a T-shirt, and a sweatshirt. Cotton has very poor heat-retention properties when it gets wet and contributes to *hypothermia* — a lowering of the body's core temperature — which can be quite dangerous. There's an old backcountry saying that *Cotton kills;* if you're lost and wandering around in the cold and wet, it certainly can.

Also, make sure that you're wearing sturdy and comfortable footwear if the cache is outside an urban area. High heels and wingtip loafers generally aren't recommended. I personally like lightweight hiking boots or shoes designed for trail running.

Along with appropriate footwear for rough terrain, a good walking stick or a set of trekking poles can make life much easier going down hills and negotiating uneven surfaces. Of the many different brands of trekking poles on the market, I like those manufactured by LEKI (www.leki.com). As a bonus, a stick or a pole is useful for poking around in rock cracks looking for a cache, just in case there's a creepy-crawly inside.

Shelter

If you've selected the right type of clothes based on the weather (check the forecast before you head out the door), they should provide enough shelter from the elements. You should also consider bringing something along that provides a little more shelter just in case you need to spend a night out. I'm not recommending that you lug a big tent around with you, though. I'm a big fan of simple, light, and cheap, such as these two options:

- ✔ **Yard waste bag:** These thick, plastic trash bags are light and fold up fairly compact. You can punch holes for your head and arm to make a rain poncho or crawl inside if you're forced to hunker down for the night. You can also use a waste bag to haul out any trash that you find while caching.

- ✔ **Space blanket:** These silver-colored sheets of Mylar and aluminum are designed to reflect your body heat back toward you when you're wrapped up in one. (They're called space blankets because NASA originally created them for space missions.) The lightweight models fold down to the size of a deck of playing cards. Larger versions are designed like sleeping bags so you can crawl inside. Space blankets are available at sporting goods stores and cost under $5 for the lightweight versions to around $25 for the heavier (and larger) tarp and *bivvy sack* (a bag you put over your sleeping bag to protect you from the elements) models.

Don't forget the sunscreen, which I personally consider a form of shelter for my skin. Dealing with a nasty sunburn takes a lot of the fun out of a successful day of geocaching, and sunscreen is cheap insurance against the long-term health affects of ultraviolet radiation. Get SPF 15 and above. Along with sunscreen, don't forget some insect repellant if you'll be caching in areas with mosquitoes and flies.

Electronic devices

In addition to their GPS receiver, a number of geocachers also tote other electronic devices with them on their searches for caches.

Digital cameras

Although definitely not a required piece of gear, geocachers often carry a digital camera to record their adventures or for posting pictures on the Geocaching.com or a personal Web site. If you're hiding a geocache, you might want to use digital photos as part of your clues.

PDAs

A fair number of geocachers bring a Palm or Pocket PC PDA with them that contains information about the geocaches they're looking for. (I list several PDA programs in Chapter 13 that store and display geocache information downloaded from the Geocaching. com Web site.) If you have a PDA, it's certainly handier than writing notes on paper. Also, because you're using data downloaded directly from the source, it eliminates possible mistakes that sometimes happen when you hand-transcribe information.

PDAs aren't waterproof and can be fairly fragile. If you're going to take one geocaching with you, I suggest that you carry it in some form of a protective carrier. I like the hard-shell cases made by OtterBox (www.otterbox.com) and the soft, waterproof padded pouches made by Voyageur (http://voyageur-gear.com).

FRS Radios

FRS (Family Radio Service) radios have grown extremely popular over the last several years — in Europe, the radios are known as PMR (Private Mobile Radio). The small, inexpensive radios have a range of up to about a mile (longer under the right line-of-sight conditions) and are great if you're going geocaching with other people. A pair of FRS radios ranges from $25 to under $100 depending on features.

GMRS (General Mobile Radio Service) radios are similar to FRS radios but use different frequencies, have a greater range, require an FCC license, and are slightly more expensive. There are hybrid radios that work with both FRS and GMRS frequencies.

You can use whichever channel you'd like to communicate while cache hunting, but keep in mind that the geocaching community has standardized on Channel 2 for the primary FRS and PMR channel and the alternate Channels 12 for FRS and 8 for PMR.

FRS and GMRS radios aren't cellphones. You can't call 911 on these radios to get help.

For more information on FRS and GMRS radios, check out the FRS Ultimate Resource Web site at www.ultimatefrs.com.

Spare batteries

I always bring along spare batteries for any device that uses them, including my GPS receiver and my flashlight. If you're really safety-conscious, bring along your cellphone, too. With the exception of the cellphone, all my electronic devices use the same type of batteries (in my case, AA, although it's also possible for everything to use AAA batteries, depending on the products). That way, I carry only one type of spare batteries with me. And in a pinch, I can swap batteries among the FRS radio, flashlight, and GPS receiver.

Safety equipment

Once a Boy Scout, always a Boy Scout, and that *Be Prepared* motto definitely struck a chord with me. That's where safety-related equipment for geocaching comes in. It's gear that you should have with you in case of an emergency. Ideally, you'll never have to use it, but if you do, you'll be glad it's around.

First aid supplies

Geocaching isn't a very dangerous sport unless you try to find caches that are purposely put in risky places. If you're out tromping around in the woods, however, there's always a chance of getting hurt. Carrying a first aid kit allows you to treat yourself or someone else in your party who gets injured.

Your first aid kit should be able to deal with blisters and small cuts, scratches, and other common boo-boos as well as more life-threatening conditions such as excessive bleeding.

When it comes to first aid kits, you have two options:

- ✔ **Prepackaged:** These kits are stocked with first aid items and come in a fabric or plastic case. Expect to pay around $10–$30 for a small, lightweight, well-stocked kit. (Advanced kits cost more.) Adventure Medical Kits sells some of the best, prepackaged first aid kits, and you can check out their products at www.adventuremedicalkits.com. Sporting goods stores typically carry first aid kits well suited for geocaching.

- ✔ **Do-it-yourself:** Instead of buying a prepackaged kit, you provide your own container and then stock it with supplies from the home medicine cabinet or a trip to the drugstore. Depending on what you're carrying, the do-it-yourself route is often cheaper than buying a premade kit. You can base the contents of your homemade first aid kit on a prepackaged kit or check out suggestions in any number of outdoors-oriented medical books. (I personally like *Medicine for Mountaineering & Other Wilderness Activities,* edited by James Wilkerson.)

Packing your own kit is essential if you have special medical needs, such as if you're allergic to bee/insect stings.

Having a first aid kit and not knowing how to use it is a little like carrying around a map and a compass and having no clue how to use them if you get lost. Although many prepackaged first aid kits have small how-to booklets, I highly recommend taking a Red Cross (www.redcross.org) or similar first aid class to get some hands-on experience.

If you take prescription medicine, I suggest bringing some with you in case for some reason you get delayed and can't make it home to take your scheduled medication.

Flashlight

This is a must-have for looking in cracks and crevices where a cache might be hidden — and also in case you run out of daylight. I personally like the newest generation of flashlights that use LED bulbs. The bulbs take a lot of abuse without breaking, and they're power-stingy, which means that your flashlight runs considerably longer than those using conventional bulbs. For outdoor use, I recommend a lightweight LED headlamp (yup, on your head) like the Petzl Tikka (www.petzl.com/petzl/Accueil) or the Princeton Tec Aurora (www.princetontech.com) (priced between $25–$30). These lights weigh only a few ounces and provide hands-free operation. They're not as bright as conventional bulbs but still work quite well — if you want the extra brightness, consider a hybrid LED and conventional bulb model.

Whistle

One safety-related item that's often overlooked is a good, loud whistle. Whistles are great signaling devices because the sound carries over much further distances than the human voice — and it's much more efficient and effective than shouting. In addition to getting someone's attention when you're in trouble (the universal distress signal is three sounds in a row, such as whistle blasts or gunshots, by the way), whistles are great for group geocaching outings. If you're spread out all over the countryside looking for a cache, your group can use whistle blasts to communicate with one another (such as two whistles meaning, "I've found the cache"). I recommend a Fox40 Classic whistle (www.fox40whistle.com). It's by far the loudest small whistle you can buy, is priced under $6, and is available in most sporting goods stores.

Cellphone

You probably already have a cellphone, so bring it along (preferably with the battery fully charged). Just a quick note of advice, though, from my search-and-rescue experiences: I've found at times that people think of their cellphones as a for-certain insurance policy against trouble. Just remember that phones break,

The Ten Essentials

If you spend any time in the outdoors, sooner or later, you'll hear someone talking about the Ten Essentials, which is a list of gear that was developed by The Mountaineers (www.mountaineers.org), a large Seattle-based outdoor recreation group. The list includes essential items that should be carried by anyone venturing out into the backcountry. Different versions of the list have been produced over the years (with various items added and subtracted), but the current version is pretty comprehensive and makes a lot of sense. You'll notice some items that I discuss elsewhere in this chapter. It includes

1. Navigation (map and compass)

2. Sun protection

3. Insulation (extra clothing)

4. Illumination (flashlight/headlamp)

5. First aid supplies

6. Fire

7. Repair kit and tools

8. Nutrition (extra food)

9. Hydration (extra water)

10. Emergency shelter

batteries go dead, and you might have really bad cell coverage out in the middle of nowhere (like anyplace outside an urban area or highway corridor). Although a cellphone is great to have along, be prepared to take care of yourself! (*Note:* The price of satellite phones, which don't have the coverage limitations of cellphones, is rapidly dropping.)

That's the basic gear that people use for geocaching. The whole key with gear lists is to find out what works best for you. You'll probably end up carrying too much stuff at first, so after you've geocached for a while, go through your pack and see what you're not using so you can lighten up your load. Just don't toss out the emergency gear just because you haven't used it.

Although most geocaches are located in pretty tame, civilized areas (usually 100 feet or so off a main trail or road), I advise letting someone know where you're going, when you'll be back, and what to do if you're late. Twisted ankles and broken-down cars seem to happen a lot in areas that don't have good cellphone service. It's also not a bad idea to use the buddy system when you go geocaching so there are two or more people. That's not to say you should never go geocaching by yourself — only if you do, be prepared.

Getting Close to the Geocache

With most geocaches, you'll end up using your car or truck (on a road) to get as close to the cache as you can and then head off on foot to find the cache. Before you hop in your car, you should plan the route you're going to take to get to the vicinity of the cache. That's what this section is all about.

Sometimes, a series of caches is located close together — typically separated by at least a tenth of a mile, per Geocaching.com rules. Because you're already in the neighborhood, consider trying to find several caches instead of just going for one. Check out the cache information page, as I talk about in Chapter 5, for any nearby caches and how far away they are.

Sometimes, the cache descriptions give you exact instructions where to start from, such as a specific parking lot or *trailhead* (an established point where a trail starts). The more challenging caches give you only the coordinates, and it's up to you to decide from where you'll start your search on foot and how best to get there. One of the pleasures of geocaching is that it's usually not a race (although a few timed competitions are starting to crop up here and there), and you can take as long as you want to reach the cache site, stopping to smell the roses and enjoy interesting sights.

The best way to figure out a good route for getting close to a geocache located in the United States is to use the link to the MapQuest map Web site on a cache description page. After you log in at the Geocaching.com site, you'll need a basic or premium account. Here's how:

1. **Select a cache you're interested in searching for at the Geocaching.com Web site and display its information page.**

   I describe how to do this in detail in Chapter 5.

2. **Scroll down the page until you see the general vicinity map of the geocache.**

   A pushpin icon identifies the cache's location (an example is shown in Figure 6-2).

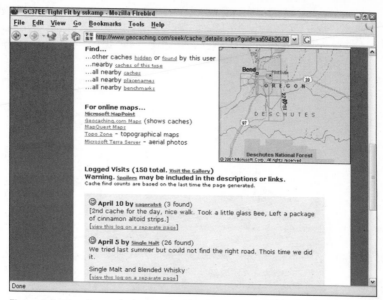

Figure 6-2: Use the cache's map at Geocaching.com to plan your route.

3. **Click anywhere on the map.**

   A new window opens, displaying a map of the geocache area at the MapQuest (www.mapquest.com) Web site (as shown in Figure 6-3).

4. **Underneath the Get Directions to Above Location From heading, enter the address of where you'll be starting your geocache search (such as your home address).**

5. **Click the Get Directions button.**

   A list of driving directions to the cache vicinity is displayed, with turn-by-turn street maneuvers, the total distance, and the estimated time it will take to get there.

   The MapQuest database primarily contains improved and established roads. There might be dirt or unimproved roads not shown on the map that might get you closer to the cache. Also, MapQuest won't tell you the best places to park, such as a turnoff, wide shoulder, or parking area. Watch out for traffic!

6. **You can also use MapQuest's map zoom-in and zoom-out features to help you plan your route.**

   A zoomed-in version of a map showing more street detail and the geocache marked with a star are shown in Figure 6-4.

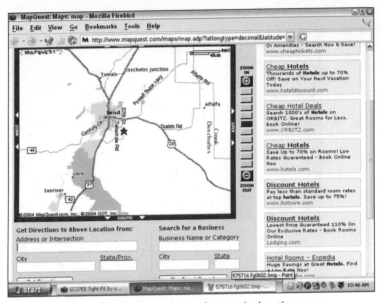

Figure 6-3: Link to MapQuest street map of geocache location.

7. **Print out the map and/or the driving directions to the cache area, and you're ready to start your search.**

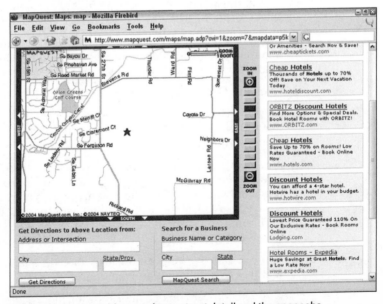

Figure 6-4: A zoomed-in map shows street detail and the geocache.

The trouble with Muggles

In geocaching jargon, a *Muggle* is someone who doesn't geocache. This comes from the Harry Potter stories, in which a Muggle is an ordinary person who isn't a wizard or witch.

At some point when you're out geocaching, you'll run into Muggles. The trouble with Muggles is they have no idea what the sport of geocaching is all about. If they see you find a cache, they might get into the cache after you leave — to see what you were up to. In the process, the contents of the cache or the entire cache itself might be taken by an uneducated or malicious Muggle.

Because you probably don't have an invisibility cloak, if Muggles are around, be stealthy with your searching. In fact, you might want to stop your search for a cache until the Muggles leave the area.

There's a good chance the Muggles will be wondering what you're doing. If they ask you, you can tell them about the sport and the Geocaching.com Web site. Some geocachers have printed up small business cards with the address of the Geocaching.com site in an effort to educate Muggles.

The other tack in dealing with Muggles is to not let on what you're up to. One of the more clever techniques I've heard of is holding your GPS receiver up to your ear and pretending it's a cellphone as a Muggle approaches. Then carry on a staged conversation, indignantly telling an imaginary friend he's over an hour late, asking where he is, and then reeling off a set of directions on how to get to your current location so you both can start your hiking trip. The polite Muggle won't want to interrupt your phone conversation, eavesdropping long enough to think he or she knows what's going on, and will then leave. You can use variations of this form of wizardry if you're so inclined.

Starting Your Search

It's finally time to start searching for that geocache, so gather up your equipment, including your GPS receiver, map and compass, food and water, and the other essential items I mention earlier in this chapter. Then use the maps and driving directions drive (bonus points if you walk or bike) to the general vicinity of the geocache.

Find a suitable place to park and start your search for the cache. Here's what to do:

1. **Turn on your GPS receiver and get a satellite lock. Ideally!**

If not, move to a different spot until your GPS receiver acquires enough satellites to tell you your current position.

Your GPS receiver needs a clear view of the sky with no obstructions to work best.

2. **Save a waypoint for your starting point.**

Getting back to your car can sometimes be a challenge after finding a remote cache, and saving a waypoint that marks your car's location can make life much easier (and get you home in time for dinner). Your GPS manual contains details for setting waypoints for your particular brand and model.

3. **Double-check to make sure that you have the coordinates, cache description, hints, and the rest of your geocaching equipment with you.**

The pack I talk about earlier in the chapter will come in handy now. From personal experience, I can tell you it's never any fun arriving at a cache and remembering that you left vital clues described in the cache description printout that's now a couple of miles away in your car.

4. **Activate the cache's waypoint.**

Activating a waypoint tells the receiver to locate that spot and calculate the distance and direction from your current position to the waypoint's location. On many GPS receivers, this is as easy as clicking a Find or GO TO button and selecting a waypoint from a list displayed on the receiver's screen. Your GPS unit will let you know how far away the cache is and what direction you need to head to get there. You're on your way!

5. **Follow the direction arrow, road map display, or compass ring on your GPS receiver toward the cache's waypoint.**

Different GPS receivers use different ways of leading you to a waypoint.

6. **When your receiver says you're within 30 feet or so of the cache, move around and find the place that reports the closest distance to the cache.**

Begin your search at that spot. This is where the real fun starts because you now shift from relying on technology to using your powers of observation and common sense. A cache could be inside a cave, tucked in a tree hollow, hiding behind a rock outcropping, or concealed under a pile of brush. Some caches are easy to find, and others are devilishly difficult.

Geocaching for weight loss and health

You've probably heard about 10-step recovery programs, but how about a 10,000-step program? This one isn't for addiction recovery but for getting yourself in better shape.

When it comes to weight loss, the simple rule is that you need to expend more calories than you take in. Diets just don't cut it; you need to watch what you eat but also get enough activity every day to burn all those calories you had for breakfast, lunch, dinner, and snacks. In addition to taking the pounds off, that additional amount of activity improves your overall level of fitness in the process.

That's where the 10,000 steps come in. The goal is to walk 10,000 steps each day. That doesn't necessarily mean all at once but totaled throughout the course of the day. Going grocery shopping, walking to a bus stop, and taking the stairs at work all count toward your step goal. You keep track of the number of steps you take with a small electronic device — a *pedometer* — that you clip on to your belt or waistband. A pedometer, which costs $10–$30, counts your steps so you can see how close you are to your 10,000-step goal. (Find a good description of the 10,000-step program at www.pbs.org/americaswalking/health/health20percentboost.html.)

What's all this have to do with geocaching? Geocaching is a great, low-impact way to tally up those steps you need to meet your weekly goals. The sport gives you a great excuse to get out and go for a walk; as an added bonus, you get to find (or hide) all sorts of cool and fun caches while you're getting in shape.

A local map can come in handy as you move toward the cache because you can use it to figure out what the terrain is like and whether any rivers, cliffs, or mountains lie between you and the cache.

Don't feel compelled to always head in the direction your GPS unit tells you to go. It might make more sense to walk around a pile of rocks or downed trees than to go over them. After you get around an obstacle, you can always check your receiver to get on the right course again.

Watch your step! As you head toward the cache, don't get so caught up in staring at your GPS receiver that you fall off a cliff or trip over a tree root.

Watch the scenery, too. Sometimes the journey is the reward.

Geocaching can sometimes look like pretty suspicious. If you're approached by a law enforcement officer while searching for a cache, keep your hands visible, don't make any sudden movements, be polite, follow all the officer's commands, tell the officer what you are doing, and offer to show your him or her your GPS receiver and cache information. You never know — you might bring a new convert to the sport.

Search Strategies as You Near the Cache

Searching for a geocache is both an art and a science. As you start looking around for a cache, you can do a few things to help improve your odds of finding it:

- ✔ **Determine the accuracy of your GPS receiver.** Check the Estimated Position Error (EPE) to see how accurate your GPS receiver currently is, based on the satellite coverage. (Refer to your GPS receiver user manual for information on how to check EPE.) If the EPE value is high, you should consider expanding your search area a bit.

  EPE is only an estimate of GPS receiver accuracy. It doesn't tell you precisely how far away from a cache you might be. The general rule is that the bigger the EPE number, the less accuracy there potentially is.

- ✔ **Follow a magnetic compass.** When you're within 30–100 feet of the geocache waypoint and your GPS receiver is showing a consistent bearing to the cache (tree cover and poor satellite coverage can cause the distance and direction numbers to jump around), use a magnetic compass to guide yourself toward the cache location. As you slow down, unless your GPS receiver has an electronic compass, the direction that your receiver reports on how to get to the waypoint becomes less precise — that means you can easily veer off-course. Handheld magnetic compasses or electronic compasses built into the GPS unit don't rely on satellite signals and won't have this problem.

- ✔ **Think about the container.** Knowing what kind of container the cache is stored in can be a big help in identifying and eliminating possible hiding spots. Sometimes the cache description lists the container type (ammo can, plastic ware, bucket, or whatever), which can narrow your search based on the size and shape of the container. For example, you shouldn't be looking for an ammo can in a 3-inch-wide crack in a large rock. Of course, if you were looking for a microcache, that would be another story.

Focus more on scanning for the shape of a container versus the color. Clever cache hiders will camouflage-paint their containers so they blend in with the surroundings. Just because a cache description says the container is an ammo can, don't expect it to be olive drab. The more geocaching you do, the more you'll discover what are natural and unnatural shapes in nature.

✔ **Think about the terrain.** Look at the surrounding environment to get a general idea of where a cache might be hidden. What natural (or man-made) features make a good hiding place? Some common hiding places include

- Stumps

- Downed trees

- Natural depressions covered up with branches

- Thickets

- Caves and cracks

Microcaches can be a big challenge to your observation skills and persistence. I discuss some of the more creative and unique hiding places for traditional and tiny caches in Chapter 8.

Unlike pirate booty hiding, geocaching has a rule against burying cache containers, so you shouldn't be burrowing holes like a gopher.

Be on the lookout for UPR or URP, which are Unnatural Piles of Rock or Unnatural Rock Piles. Although burying geocaches in the ground is a no-no, tucking them in piles of stacked rocks is acceptable.

✔ **Split up the work.** If you're geocaching with other folks, assign areas for people to check. Although you don't need to precisely measure and grid-off squares, divvying up an area to search is faster and more efficient than randomly wandering around.

✔ **Think like a cache hider.** If you were going to hide a cache, where would you hide it? Sometimes trusting your intuition can be more effective than trying to apply logic. First check the ordinary and obvious hiding places and then start looking in the unordinary spots.

There's an old safety saying in wildland firefighting that goes like this: "Look up, look down, look all around." The same advice applies to geocaching. I've seen caches tucked up in trees and birdhouses, affixed under picnic tables, and even submerged in shallow water. Geocaching is an excellent way to improve your overall awareness and observation skills.

Grid searches

In search and rescue, a *grid search* consists of lining up a group of people and walking together in a straight line. The terrain and vegetation dictate how far apart the searchers are spaced. If you want to get really formal, the two people at each end of the line both follow a preset compass course to ensure that a straight line is followed. After a section of ground is covered, the same technique is applied to an area that hasn't been searched. This time- and resource-intensive, detailed way of searching is typically used for finding evidence in criminal cases (not locating lost people).

You can apply the basic fundamentals of a grid search to geocaching if you're out with a group, especially if you encounter a stubborn cache that you can't seem to find.

One of the biggest detriments to finding a cache is that geocachers usually don't have a search plan, either when they're solo caching or while they're out with others. There's often a lot of random searching, checking here and there for a cache, without any coordination. This often results in a cache DNF (Did Not Find).

I recommend that you come up with a systematic approach to searching, either by yourself or with others. Walk back and forth in a zigzag pattern to cover an area, employ some variation of a grid search, and have someone check high and someone else check low. Figure out some system that works best for you and increases your efficiency and effectiveness in finding caches. You'll need to do some experimenting and have some practical experience, but I guarantee that if you start using a search methodology, you'll soon acquire a reputation as a geocaching guru.

Chapter 7

Discovering a Geocache

. . . .

In This Chapter

▶ Opening a cache

▶ Signing the cache logbook

▶ Trading for cache goodies

▶ Leaving the cache

▶ Logging your find online

▶ When you can't find a cache

. . . .

T he primary goal of geocaching is finding a hidden cache. That's simple enough (sometimes) and sounds good on paper, but what happens when you actually discover a cache? Exactly what do you do? In this chapter, I answer that question. You'll read about signing the cache's logbook, exchanging goodies, covering up your tracks so the cache isn't obvious to find after your visit, and how to log your find on the Geocaching.com site. I also discuss what happens when you get skunked and can't find a cache. Don't worry; this happens to the best of geocachers.

What to Do When You Find a Geocache

Maybe you immediately stumbled on the geocache that you were looking for — or perhaps it took you a couple of painstaking hours, searching high and low to find a particularly devilishly hidden cache. It really doesn't matter in the end, though, because you succeeded and found the cache (such as one shown in Figure 7-1).

Congratulations! Savor the moment. There's definitely a sense of accomplishment when you discover a cache, and a little bit of child-like wonder as you open up the container to see the treasures inside.

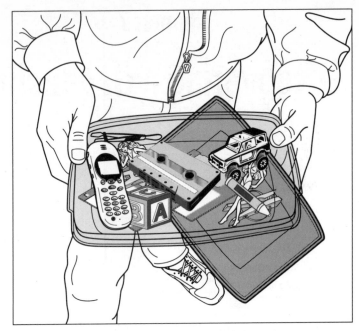

Figure 7-1: A found geocache in a plastic container.

Here are some of the things that you should do when you find a cache.

Opening the cache

When you find a cache, you're probably going to immediately want to open it to see what's inside. But before you do, take a moment and observe how the cache was placed and hidden. When you leave, the cache should appear as it did when you found it. I talk more about this in the upcoming section, "Heading home."

After you take a mental snapshot of how the cache was placed, you can open it. If water or dirt is on the lid, brush it off so it doesn't get inside the container when you open it.

Surplus military ammunition containers, fondly referred to as *ammo cans* or *boxes,* are popular geocaching containers. The metal cans are rugged and fairly waterproof. If you've never handled an ammo can before, you might spend a few minutes puzzling over how to open it. Here's how:

1. **Find the latching mechanism on the narrow side of the ammo can (see Figure 7-2).**

Figure 7-2: Ammo can latching mechanism.

Latch –
pull up
to open

2. **Pull up the bottom of the latch.**

   The latches are usually tight, so you'll have to use some muscle. Be careful, though, because a tight lid can spring open and really whack your fingers good.

3. **After the latch is released, push it up and away from the can.**

4. **Grab the handle on the top and pull up on the hinged lid to open the ammo can.**

   It might be a little snug, so again, you'll need to use some elbow grease. If it's really tight, use two hands with one hand on the lid handle and the other on the wire handle below the latch mechanism.

To shut an ammo can, do the reverse, first placing the top of the latch under a metal lip on the side of the can and then pushing down hard on the bottom of the latch.

Signing the logbook

Inside the cache container, you'll find a logbook. If the cache hider was on the ball, the logbook will be in a resealable, plastic food storage bag just in case the cache container somehow gets water inside. The *logbook* is a record of everyone who has found the cache. It's typically a small, spiral-bound notebook (such as the one shown in Figure 7-3) and has a couple of pens and pencils with it for signing in.

I always like to flip through the logbook pages. It's fun to read about other geocachers' adventures and how long ago the cache was last visited. The more you geocache in a local area, the more names you'll start to recognize of fellow geocachers who have already visited a cache you just found.

After you've read the logbook, go to the last page and write your own entry. You should jot down the current date (the time is optional), a few sentences or paragraphs about your experiences finding the cache, what goodies you took and/or added, and then sign your geocaching alias. Be sure to mention any pets or fellow geocachers who accompanied you.

10-7-01 / 11:20 AM

Tough find!! I Like it.

Figure 7-3: Read and sign the geocache logbook.

IWIDNF

IWIDNF stands for *I Wish I Did Not Find.* When you're out geocaching, you might stumble onto all sorts of things that you really wish you hadn't. Geocachers have run across meth labs, marijuana plots, discarded underwear, stolen cars, and amorous lovers in various states of undress. IWIDNFs have even included dead bodies, including a skeleton, which solved a decade-old mystery.

In February, 2004, two University of South Carolina students were out geocaching, looking for one of the many caches hidden in the Aiken-Augusta, South Carolina area. While trudging through heavy brush, they came upon a human skull and other bones. They noted the GPS coordinates and immediately hiked out of the area to contact the authorities.

A subsequent investigation revealed that the remains belonged to a man who disappeared in 1992 and had committed suicide deep in the woods, not wanting his body to be found.

If you do encounter an IWIDNF that could be part of a crime scene, first ensure your own safety in case bad guys might still be around. Enter a waypoint for the location, don't touch anything, leave, and then call the local law enforcement agency. If you think it's an emergency, dial 911. (Yet another good reason to bring a cellphone with you on your outings.)

Some geocachers have rubber stamps made up with their alias that they stamp a logbook with. Others leave business card-size geocaching cards or add custom-made stickers with their alias and a personal logo to logbook pages.

Leaving and trading goodies

One of the guiding principles of geocaching is "take something, leave something." A geocache hider places a number of goodies in a container when a new cache is first started. As people find the cache, they exchange goodies that catch their eye with trade items they've brought with them on the search.

A *signature item* is a unique item that a geocacher leaves in a cache that's his or her way of saying, "I was here." It's sort of like the Lone Ranger and his trademark silver bullet. Signature items can be anything from a printed business card to a handmade clay sculpture. (To give you some ideas, the Michigan Geocaching Organization has a database of photos of signature items on its Web site at http://mi-geocaching.org/sigitemdb.)

If you take something from a cache, be sure to leave something. If you forgot your trade items, just sign the logbook. A number of geocachers just do this anyway and don't exchange goodies. To them, finding the cache is the exciting and rewarding part of the sport — they're not really interested in the contents of a cache.

If the treasures inside a cache all seem to be related, such as all *Star Wars* trinkets or different kinds of toy frogs, you've likely stumbled on a *theme cache.* If you don't have a trade item that goes with the theme, just sign the logbook and don't leave anything.

As you find more geocaches, you'll get a better idea of what kind of goodies people leave in caches — it can be just about anything that will fit in a cache container. There's always a lot of discussion within the geocaching community about what is appropriate and not appropriate to leave in a cache. Here are some quick guidelines:

- ✓ **Don't leave food in a cache.** Food can attract animals as well as get smelly and messy, and plastic cache containers have been chewed through by critters eager to get at a tasty snack.

- ✓ **Never put anything illegal, dangerous, or possibly offensive in a cache.** Geocaching has turned into a family sport, so be responsible.

- ✓ **Always exchange something of at least equal value for whatever you take.** For example, don't purloin a cool antique coin and replace it with a cheap McToy.

- ✓ **Try to trade up.** *Trading up* means leaving something in the cache that's better than what you take. Many times, caches start out with cool stuff but soon end up filled with junk (broken toys, beat-up golf balls, cheap party favors, and so on). Some self-righteous geocachers even take it upon themselves to remove anything from a cache that doesn't meet their personal quality bar. If you can, always trade up to make the finds more interesting for everyone.

- ✓ **Put yourself in the shoes of the next cache visitor.** Would they find whatever item you just left interesting, intriguing, useful, or fun?

If the cache contains a *Travel Bug* (a to-be-taken-and-moved item that has a metal dog tag attached to it with a logo of a bug and a serial number), feel free to take the Travel Bug *but only* if you will remember to turn it loose in another cache that you find. Travel Bugs are meant for traveling. Go to www.geocaching.com and click the Track Travel Bugs link for detailed information on logging your Travel Bug find online and what to do next.

Heading home

After you sign the logbook and trade goodies (if you decided to), hit the road and head home — or perhaps try to find another nearby cache. Before leaving the cache, though, here is a checklist of things to do:

- ✔ **Make sure that the cache container is sealed.** There's nothing worse than encountering a soggy, waterlogged cache because the previous finder didn't seal the lid tightly.

- ✔ **Put the cache container back where you found it.** Make sure that it's in the same place and is hidden just as well as it was before you found it. It's not polite to relocate a cache to where you think is a better location.

- ✔ **Check the area for any of your equipment that's on the ground.** You really didn't mean to leave your cellphone, GPS receiver, or compass as part of the cache — did you?

- ✔ **Cover your tracks.** I've been to some caches where I didn't even need to use my GPS receiver because there was a well-worn path right up to the cache hiding spot from so many geocachers who had previously found it. Do your best to tread lightly on the land and don't leave too many signs of your visit.

- ✔ **Use the track-back feature of your GPS receiver to follow your exact path back to your car.** Or better yet, activate the waypoint that you set for your car when you started (but take a different route back to see some new sights).

Logging your find online

Most geocachers share their experiences with others by reporting their find online at the Geocaching.com site. When you get back to your computer (if you're a member of Geocaching.com), you can log your find on the Web site so the whole world knows you found the cache. *Note:* This is completely optional, and some geocachers prefer operating in stealth mode, keeping their discoveries and adventures to themselves.

Here's how to log your find online:

1. **Go to the information page for the geocache you found and click the Log Your Visit button at the top of the page.**

   Read Chapter 5 to read how to display and use a cache's information page.

A new page is displayed, where you can log your find (an example is shown in Figure 7-4).

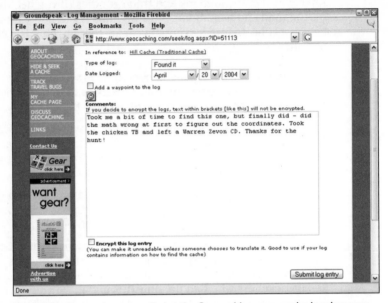

Figure 7-4: Boast about your find at the Geocaching.com cache logging page.

2. **Fill in the requested information and click the Submit Log Entry button.**

It's as simple as that. Take a look at the types of information that you'll need to provide so you know what to expect.

Type of log

This drop-down list box contains different types of log entries, including

- ✔ **Found it:** You found the cache; good for you. The cache will be added to the list of caches you've found, which is tracked by the Geocaching.com site. A smiley face icon appears next to this type of log entry in the comments on a cache information page.

- ✔ **Didn't find it:** You looked for the cache but didn't find it. Bummer. That's okay; go ahead and log it anyway. A frowny face icon is associated with this type of log entry.

- ✔ **Write note:** You want to add a note to the online cache logs. (When you view a cache log, notes have a notebook sheet of paper icon next to them.) If you write a note, it's not logged as a find. Notes are used when you drop off a Travel Bug in a cache you've previously found or for making a comment about a cache, such as it needs maintenance.

✔ **Needs archived:** Select this item if you've found a serious problem with the cache, such as it's missing or has been destroyed. An *archived* cache is currently not active; however, the cache still remains in the database, and you can view its information page to learn why it was archived.

There are several other log entry types for specialized types of caches. For example, a Webcam cache will have a Web Cam Photo Taken entry instead of Found It. CITO (Cache In, Trash Out) events will include Will Attend and Attended items in the drop-down list box.

Add a waypoint to the log

Sometimes when you find a cache, the coordinates that you get from your GPS receiver don't match the coordinates listed on the cache information page. If two coordinates really seem to differ a lot, check this box and enter your coordinates, which will then be listed in the cache's log comments. (You did first check that you had the correct datum set on your GPS receiver, didn't you?)

Date logged

In the appropriate drop-down list boxes, enter the month, day, and year when you discovered the cache. You can log a cache discovery days or weeks after when you actually found it. However, I'd recommend logging your find soon after you discover a cache so you don't forget about it.

Comments

This text entry box is for entering comments about your search and (ideally) subsequent discovery of a cache. Let your creative juices flow if you want. You can be terse or wordy. Just be careful about entering information that might be a *spoiler* (way-too-obvious hints or commentary) and ruin the fun for someone reading the logs who hasn't found the cache yet. If you're just dying to add spoiler information, see the following section.

Encrypt this log entry

When this box is checked, the log entry is encrypted, using the same algorithm used to encrypt hints. If your log comments contain any information on how to find the cache, please use this option. Any words that appear between brackets in the comments — for example, [A fun cache] — won't be encrypted, so you can mix readable and encrypted text together.

After you post a cache log, a preview page is displayed where you can edit or delete your log entry. In the upper-right corner is the <u>upload image</u> link. Click this link to upload graphics images, such as digital photos, that you have stored on your PC. The maximum size of an image is around 90K.

When You Can't Find a Geocache

So despite all your best efforts, you couldn't find the cache. Maybe you wandered around in circles for a couple of hours, or perhaps the weather got downright miserable, and you called it a day. It's okay; it happens to everyone, and it definitely isn't the end of the world.

If you're still in the hunt but are starting to get frustrated, take a deep breath and try the following:

- ✓ **Double-check the coordinates.** You did enter them correctly, didn't you? And the datums match with the coordinates and your GPS receiver, don't they?

- ✓ **Check the satellite coverage.** What kind of satellite reception are you getting in your search area? If the coverage is poor, maybe the cache hider didn't get an accurate set of coordinates when he saved the cache's location. This means that you won't be able to rely on your GPS receiver as much as normal to get you near the cache.

- ✓ **Review the logs.** If you brought printed copies of the logged visits with you, you can read comments from people who have previously found the cache. Although most geocachers try to avoid including spoilers in their comments, sometimes enough information leaks through that can help you narrow your search.

- ✓ **Use a hint.** Most cache information pages have a short hint, but you have to work for it because it's encrypted. The reason for the spy stuff is so the hint doesn't spoil the fun for another geocacher who doesn't want to use the hint as part of his search. Fortunately, the hint uses a simple substitution code (for example, A = N, B = O, C = P, and so on), so you don't need to work for the NSA to be able to break it. The decoding key is on the right side of the page, and it's pretty easy to figure it out by hand.

Geocaching stats

Just like any sport, geocaching has statistics. In this case, *stats* refer to the number of caches that you've found and hidden. When you sign up for a free or premium account at Geocaching.com (see Chapter 5), you can log the caches you've found as well as add caches that you've hidden. The site's extensive database tracks your finds and hides and displays them on a user profile page. Other members can check out your stats, and the number of caches that you've found appears next to your alias when you log your comments about a cache you've visited. Some geocachers are competitive and are in to racking up as many cache finds as possible. Others are more blasé about the whole numbers thing and couldn't care less. Like so many other aspects of geocaching, it's up to you how you want to play the game.

How you go about finding the cache is up to you. Some purists will use only the coordinates and basic description of the cache, never using the hints or the comments. Other cachers immediately decrypt the hint and read all the comments before they head out the door on a search. It's your decision.

Logging a DNF

In geocaching jargon, a DNF means *Did Not Find.* Don't worry; it's not a big deal, and you shouldn't be shy about logging a DNF online for a cache you couldn't locate. If a cache owner hasn't visited the site in a while, a number of logged DNFs could indicate that the cache has been moved or stolen. Unfortunately, cache vandalism and thievery happen: Perhaps the cache you were looking for might have been removed, and the Geocaching.com database hasn't been updated yet.

Try, try again

There's no shame in a DNF; it happens to everyone — and if someone brags about finding every cache he's searched for on the first try, don't trust him. Talk to those who have been geocaching for awhile, and they'll tell you DNF stories about taking two, three, or more visits to an area to find an elusive geocache — especially frustrating are the ones that everyone else seems to be able to easily find except you.

If you have a DNF, go back to the cache location another day and try again. Geocaching is supposed to be fun, so don't take it too seriously if you can't locate a cache. Consider bringing someone else along with you next time: Two heads are always better than one, and a different set of eyes might find something you overlooked. Quite often, when you find the cache, you'll be slapping the side of your head, trying to figure out how you missed it the first time around. Treat every find and DNF as a learning experience that makes you a better geocacher.

Geocaching etiquette

For the most part, there aren't a whole lot of rules when it comes to geocaching. It mostly boils down to respecting other geocachers and the land that you play on. Here are a few etiquette points to consider when you're out geocaching:

✓ **Always respect private property.** Need I say more?

✓ **Always trade up or replace an item in the cache with something of equal value.** Don't be a Scrooge; what's the fun in that?

✓ **Be environmentally conscious when searching for and hiding caches.** Tread lightly on the land. Check out the Leave No Trace site at www.lnt.org for more information.

✓ **Geocaching is a pretty dog-friendly sport.** Keep it that way by having Fido tethered in leash-only areas. No matter how good your dog is, have a leash ready in case other people or animals are around. And for geocaching in urban areas, don't forget a plastic bag.

✓ **Cache In, Trash Out (CITO).** If you see any litter on your way to or from a cache, get some additional exercise with a deep-knee bend, pick it up, and pack it out.

✓ **Say thank you, please.** After you visit a cache, send a quick e-mail, thank-you message to the geocacher that placed the cache or acknowledge him or her in your cache comments when you log your find.

Chapter 8

Hiding Geocaches

· ·

In This Chapter

▶ Selecting a geocache type to hide

▶ Deciding on the right cache container

▶ Selecting a location to hide the cache

▶ Recording cache coordinates

▶ Stocking the cache

▶ Submitting a cache to the Geocaching.com database

▶ Maintaining the cache

· ·

*I*f you've been geocaching for a while, one day, you'll probably get the urge to hide a cache of your own. To many geocachers, hiding caches is just as fun as — if not more enjoyable than — finding caches. It's like making a movie or staging a play. You have an idea, spend some time planning, turn the idea into reality, and then sit back and see what people have to say about your work.

In this chapter, I show you how to create and hide a cache of your own. It's not that difficult and is relatively inexpensive — you can spend $10 or less to set up their cache, which is some pretty cheap entertainment these days. Hiding a cache is also a great way to give something back to the sport. All those individual caches that have been placed do their part in keeping the sport alive and growing.

Adding your own geocache to the growing list of caches throughout the world involves selecting the type of cache and an appropriate container, stocking the cache, finding a good hiding place, submitting the cache to include in the Geocaching.com database, and then maintaining the cache.

 Don't rush out and hide a geocache until you've spent some time finding caches. Searching for other caches will give you a good idea of how other people place caches and give you some ideas for creating and hiding your own. In addition to this chapter, check out the

Geocaching.com site for some FAQ (Frequently Asked Questions) lists as well as a complete set of guidelines for placing and hiding caches.

Deciding What Type of Geocache to Create

The first step in setting up your own geocache is to decide what type of cache you want to hide. Cache types include traditional caches, microcaches, multicaches, and others. (Read Chapter 5 for a refresher on the different types of geocaches.)

Just like when you first start searching for geocaches, for hiding caches, I suggest you begin with a single, relatively straightforward, traditional cache. I'm sure that you have some great ideas for creative and challenging caches, but save them for a little later. To some people, hiding geocaches can be a like a kid getting a bunny rabbit for Easter. It's fun at first, but the reality of caring and feeding causes the novelty to wear off pretty quick. Beginning with a basic cache gives you a good idea of what's involved in cache management — and I don't mean the high finance, investment type. Starting out simple with a single cache lets you test the waters. If you like everything that's involved in hiding caches, you can hide more, making them more complicated as time goes on.

If you don't want to maintain a cache, be sure to archive it. (I talk more about *archiving* — letting other geocachers know that your cache is no longer active — later in the section, "Physical maintenance"). It's not fair to other geocachers to neglect your caches (or your Easter bunny).

Selecting a Container

Obviously, you need something to put your geocache in. The only real requirement for a cache container is that it needs to be waterproof although sometimes cachers use plastic bags inside a nonwaterproof container, which is a little less than optimal. The size of the container determines where you'll be able to hide the cache and how full you'll be able to fill it with trading trinkets. Any container that you can think of has probably been used for geocaching, including

- Plastic buckets with lids
- Breath mint tins

- ✔ Plastic margarine tubs
- ✔ 35mm film canisters
- ✔ Pill bottles
- ✔ Plastic Army decontamination kit boxes
- ✔ PVC piping (with end caps)

The best cache containers seal tightly and have snug-fitting lids.

You've probably got a suitable geocaching container lying around the house or garage. Just for the record, the two most popular types of cache containers are ammo cans and household plastic storage containers.

Ammo cans

Military surplus, steel ammunition (ammo) cans work great because they're sturdy and waterproof. They typically come in two sizes, based on the machine gun ammunition they once held. (The two types are shown in Figure 8-1.)

- ✔ **.50 caliber:** A large ammo can that's suitable for housing bigger trinkets.
- ✔ **.30 caliber:** A narrower ammo can. It doesn't hold as many goodies but is good for geocaches in confined spaces.

Depending on the terrain and vegetation, the olive-drab color makes ammo cans difficult to spot. You can typically get ammo cans for around $5 or less from local or online Army surplus stores.

Household plastic storage containers

Plastic storage containers are also popular choices but aren't quite as rugged as ammo cans. And they have the downside that some-times a geocacher won't reseal the lid very well. Plastic containers are cheaper and more available than ammo cans, though, and you can easily match a size to go with any cache.

Some cache hiders spray paint their cache containers to make them blend better with the surroundings. Figure 8-2 shows an ammo can that was painted the same color as the local rock formation and even had stones glued to the outside to aid in the camouflage. Here's a great how-to link for painting your ammo can: http://fp1.centurytel.net/Criminal_Page/new_page_4.htm.

Figure 8-1: Large and small ammo cans are favorites for geocaches.

Figure 8-2: Paint an ammo can to blend with its surroundings.

Selecting a Location

Just like in real estate or retail sales, location is everything when it comes to placing a geocache. After you select a container, figure out where to put it — or sometimes you find a perfect hiding place and then select an appropriate container to go with it. The location of your cache usually defines its success and popularity. Take a look at some hiding place considerations.

Where to hide your cache

Start out by doing some initial research to find a good, general area to hide your cache. For many geocachers, visiting a new place with some unique feature, incredible scenery, or just a plain gorgeous view is every bit as important as finding the cache. Keep this in mind as you use maps, travel guides, or fond memories from your own explorations to help you select a good cache location.

An important part of your homework is learning where caches are and are not permitted. The majority of the geocaching community tends to be very aware that the continued growth and success of the sport depend on good relationships with landowners and managers.

If you want to place a cache on private property, always first ask the owner's permission. Because geocaching is so new, many people don't know what it is, so take the time to explain how the sport works.

Most geocaches are placed on federal, state, county, or municipal public land. However, just because it's public doesn't necessarily mean that placing a geocache is permitted.

Always try to verify that the agency that manages the land allows geocaching. You can contact the agency directly, try a Google search to see whether its geocaching policies are published on the Web, or talk with other geocachers in your area to get their experiences in dealing with different agencies. For example, the U.S. Bureau of Land Management (BLM) recognizes geocaching as a recreational activity and tends to be friendly toward cache hiders who want to locate a cache in places other than wilderness or wilderness study areas. The U.S. National Park Service, on the other hand, prohibits placing geocaches on the land that it manages; if you're caught hiding a cache on such land, it's a federal offense. Yipes!

Post-9/11 geocaching

In November, 2001, outside the small town of Dorris, California, a police bomb squad exploded a suspicious object near a railroad tunnel. The United States was on alert for possible terrorist attacks against its transportation infrastructure. The suspicious object wasn't a bomb but turned out to be a geocache. The FBI got involved with the investigation, and a geocacher who went by the handle of Hillwilly was charged with terrorism, criminal trespass, and criminal vandalism for placing the cache on railroad property — which (by the way) extends within 150 feet of the rails. The terrorism charges were later dropped, but the judge upheld the other charges, and Hillwilly ended up with a one-year suspended jail sentence and paying over $2,000 in fines. Ouch!

There have been other incidents where geocaches stored in obviously military-looking ammo cans have been thought to contain explosives or drugs and were seized by law enforcement officers. A few geocachers have proposed cutting holes in the sides of ammo cans and gluing pieces of Lexan (a thick, clear polycarbonate material) to the inside of the ammo can to make a window so the suspicious or cautious can see the contents. Some agencies are starting to require see-through containers for any geocaches placed on lands that they manage.

Always be sure to clearly label your container as a geocache. And never, *ever* place a cache in a location that could get you into trouble. Remember, when it comes to certain things, the authorities tend not to have a very good sense of humor.

Many of the problems that geocachers have had with public land managers stem from a lack of education on the government employee's part about geocaching. It's worthwhile to educate land managers about the sport so they clearly understand the impacts and can make informed and wise decisions on whether to allow geocaching. Although some people in the geocaching community ardently believe they should have a Constitutional right to hide and find caches, a little more middle-of-the-road approach is useful when dealing with land managers.

Where not to hide your cache

There are definitely some places you don't want to hide your cache. To be listed in the Geocaching.com database, your cache needs to meet certain, common-sense criteria. Generally a cache can't be

- ✔ **Buried:** Covering it with branches, leaves, or rocks is okay, but no digging, please.

✔ **Placed in environmentally sensitive areas:** This includes areas with endangered plants and animals as well as archaeological and historic sites. Some things that can clue you in to an area possibly being environmentally sensitive include

- Waterholes.

- Wetlands.

- Guano- (bat or bird excrement) stained rock outcrops.

- Areas where soil and vegetation will be significantly impacted by trampling.

- Any place where human activity will distress wildlife. (If a large bird is screaming at you, that's a big hint.)

Land management agencies might not publicly identify sensitive environmental areas on the Internet or on paper maps because it's an open invitation to poachers and vandals (who tend to ruin things for the rest of us). However, usually by applying common sense and observing your surroundings, you can tell whether an area is sensitive, regardless of whether it's marked as such or not.

✔ **Placed in national parks or designated wilderness areas:** This is a no-no. Sorry; them's the rules.

✔ **Placed within 150 feet of railroad tracks:** Umm, this is for safety reasons as well as some legal ones discussed in the "Post-9/11 geocaching" sidebar.

✔ **Placed anywhere that might cause concerns about possible terrorist activities:** Use your post-9/11 brain. No-no areas include near airports, tunnels, bridges, military facilities, municipal water supplies, and government buildings.

✔ **Placed within one-tenth of a mile of another cache:** This is a rule for adding a cache to the Geocaching.com database as well as simple geocaching etiquette.

The geocaching community tends to police itself fairly well. If you try to bend the rules and put a cache where it shouldn't be, someone will probably let the Geocaching.com administrators know about it, and the cache will be removed from the database.

Hiding for seekers

After you select a good general location to put the geocache (forest, park, beach, and so forth), look around to find the perfect place to hide the cache. The simple rule for a hiding place is that the cache shouldn't be easily visible to a passerby who's not looking for the cache. Use your creativity to find a challenging hiding place: in a tree hollow, underneath bushes, wedged in rocks, and so on. Remember: The more experience you have finding caches, the more ideas you'll have for good hiding places of your own.

TIP

When you hide the cache, always watch out for *Muggles* (non-geocachers) in the area. Be stealthy so your cache isn't discovered before you get a chance to submit it to the Geocaching.com database.

Getting sneaky

Some geocachers take delight in making their caches as difficult to find as possible. In fact, some of their camouflage jobs would make the military jealous. Here are some of the more creative and challenging places geocaches have been found:

- Birdhouses
- Fake bricks
- Fake water faucets
- Hollowed-out logs
- Hollowed-out pine cones (as shown here — see the film canister?)

A plastic film container

- On the back of leaves (microcaches, obviously)
- Plastic rocks designed for hiding house keys
- Soda pop cans
- Rubber cow pies and other practical-joke animal dung
- Rubber rats

If you get really sneaky and create a difficult and challenging-to-find cache, just be sure to give people a clue about what they'll be up against in the cache description.

Recording the location

After you locate that perfect, secret hiding spot, you need to determine the cache's location coordinates as precisely as possible. (Remember to use the WGS 84 datum; see Chapter 3 for more on this.) This can be challenging because of less-than-perfect satellite coverage. You might find the location's coordinates changing on your GPS receiver every few seconds. Many GPS units have an averaging feature that compares coordinates at a single spot over a period of time and then averages the result. If your receiver does do averaging, get it as close to the cache as possible, let it sit for five or ten minutes, and then copy down the cache coordinates and enter them as a waypoint.

A manual approach to averaging is to set a waypoint for the cache location, walk away, and then come back and set another waypoint. Repeat this until you have 6–12 waypoints; then examine the list of waypoints, and pick the one that looks the most accurate (generally, the value in the middle of the list).

During certain times of the day, you might have better satellite coverage than others. This is because of the number of satellites that are in view and the position of a single satellite relative to your GPS receiver and the other satellites in the constellation. If you want to get really precise with recording your cache coordinates, select a time of the day with optimal satellite coverage. Trimble Navigation, one of the largest manufacturers of commercial and professional GPS receivers, has a free Windows program called Planning, designed for surveyors who need to know when the best time is to use GPS surveying instruments. To download Planning, go to `www.trimble.com/planningsoftware_ts.asp? Nav=Collection-8425`.

Stocking a Geocache

Finding an empty geocaching container is a big letdown to a cache hunter, so you'll need to stock the cache with a few items.

Logbook and writing utensil

At the very minimum, your cache should contain a logbook and a pen or pencil so other cachers can write about their discovery. *Hint:* Pencils work better in cold climates (the ink in most pens can freeze); mechanical pencils are the best because they don't need sharpening. The logbook is usually a spiral notebook with the name of the cache written on the cover. Some cache hiders paste their personal logo or some other graphic to the notebook cover. As the cache founder, you should write some profound thoughts about the cache on the first page.

Identifying information

The cache should have some information that identifies it as a geo-cache, describes what geocaching is, and provides instructions to the finder. (It's not uncommon for Muggles to stumble upon a cache.) The Geocaching.com site has an information sheet in a number of different languages that you can print out and place in your cache; laminating this sheet is a good idea. Be sure to record the cache's name and its coordinates.

You can also purchase vinyl stickers in different sizes that identify a geocache. (An example is shown in Figure 8-3.) These stickers are available from a number of different sources and are priced under $2. Do a Google search for *"geocaching sticker"* to find an online retailer.

Figure 8-3: Geocache identification sticker.

Goodies

You'll also want to stock your geocache with some goodies for people to exchange. These should be unique and interesting items. Because geocaching is a family sport, initially put a mix of things in it that appeal to both adults and children. You don't need to fill up the container like a stocking at Christmas. Many caches start out with 6–12 small items. If you want, you can add a Travel Bug. (Click the Track Travel Bugs item on the Geocaching.com home page to get detailed information about Travel Bugs.)

A *geocoin* is a specially minted coin with a serial number that's designed to move from cache to cache and be tracked like a Travel Bug. People get pretty excited about encountering geocoins because they're so unique. Do a Google search for *geocoin* to see examples of different coins and get information on how to order them from different sources. Depending on the quantity, they cost $4–$7.

Food; offensive, illegal, and dangerous items; and anything of a commercial, political, or religious nature are no-no's to place in a cache.

Even though your cache container might be waterproof, always put your logbook and cache goodies in resealable, plastic storage bags. This prevents your cache from turning into a soggy mush when someone inevitably forgets to seal the container's lid.

Some cache hiders put a disposable camera in their cache and ask finders to snap pictures of themselves. The cache owner returns to the cache when all the exposures are shot, develops the photos, and then places them online for everyone to see.

Submitting a Geocache

After you successfully hide the stocked geocache, it's time for a little advertising. It doesn't do much good if people don't know about your cache after you place it. The Geocaching.com Web site currently maintains the largest database of geocaches in the world and is where most people go to find information about caches. You need to have a free or premium account at the site to be able to post your cache, so if you don't have an account yet, go to the site and sign up. (I promise that it's quick and painless. Read about how to sign up for these accounts in Chapter 5.)

After you log onto the site, submitting a cache is just a matter of filling out an online form about your new cache. The form is rather long, and you need to scroll down a couple of times to enter all the information. Take a look at the types of information that you'll need to enter to get your cache listed in the database. (I'll walk you through all the entry fields in Figures 8-4, 8-5, and 8-6.)

Cache type

This is the type of cache that you've hidden. Drop-down list options include

- Traditional cache
- Multicache

- Mystery/puzzle cache
- Webcam
- Letterbox (Hybrid)
- Virtual
- Geocaching event (Event cache)
- Cache In, Trash Out event

These cache types are described at the beginning of Chapter 5.

Cache size

How big is the cache? Obviously, this is based on the cache container size. The drop-down list options include

- **Micro:** A small container cache, such as a 35mm film canister
- **Regular:** An ammo can or conventionally sized cache
- **Large:** A big container cache, such as a five-gallon or larger bucket
- **Virtual:** A cache without a container
- **Other:** Some off-the-wall cache that doesn't meet any of the above options that is explained in the description you later provide

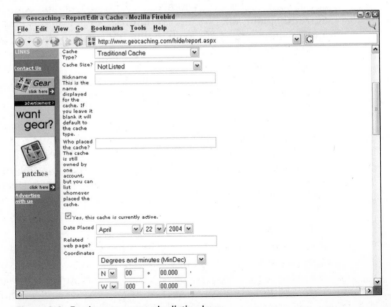

Figure 8-4: Begin your geocache listing here.

Nickname

This is the official name of the cache. Think up something cool. It often relates to some feature near the cache location or something that caught your attention or imagination when you were placing the cache.

Who placed the cache?

This is you. The Geocaching.com user account you are logged in under appears by default.

Active cache

Because it's a new cache, it's active, so make sure this check box is marked.

Date placed

Use the drop-down list boxes to enter the date you placed the cache.

Related Web page

If you have a separate Web page you created that's related to the cache, this is the place to enter its address.

Coordinates

Use the drop-down list and text entry boxes to enter the coordinates you recorded for the cache. You can select decimal degrees; degrees and decimal minutes; or degrees, minutes, and seconds. (If you don't know the difference between these coordinate formats, be sure to read Chapter 3.)

Location

Use these drop-down list boxes (top of Figure 8-5) to enter the country and state or province (if applicable).

Difficulty rating

This is how difficult you think it will be for someone to find the cache. 1 is the easiest; 5 is the hardest. Compare your cache with the ratings of similar caches you've found to see whether your rating is in the ballpark.

Terrain rating

The terrain rating ranks how difficult the travel will be to get to your cache. 1 is the easiest; 5 is the hardest. Again, compare your cache with the ratings of caches you've found with similar terrain to see whether your rating is close.

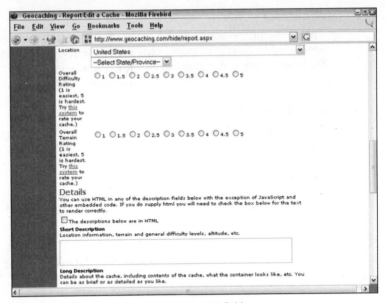

Figure 8-5: More geocache submission entry fields.

 If you're having trouble trying to determine the difficulty and terrain ratings, click the <u>this system</u> link to take you to geocacher ClayJar's online terrain and difficulty calculator (www.clayjar. com/gcrs).

HTML

You can use HTML (Web page formatting codes) to pretty up the appearance of a cache description. Select this check box if you plan on inserting HTML code in your descriptions.

 Here's a link to a great tutorial on using HTML: www.xsnrg.com/ geocachingwa/tutorial.asp. And here you can find an abbreviated cheat sheet for HTML formatting codes: http://nozen.com/ geo/html.htm.

Short description

This is a couple of sentences or a short paragraph that has general information about the cache as well as the terrain and difficulty levels.

Long description

This is detailed information about the cache, such as the items that were originally placed inside, what kind of container is being used, details on accessing the cache, and instructions for multi-caches and puzzle caches.

Hints/spoiler info

You can optionally provide hints for cache finders. Anything you enter in this text box (top of Figure 8-6) will be encrypted (unless it is enclosed in brackets), and a searcher needs to decrypt the text if he or she wants to read it. It's good form to leave a short hint. How much of a hint is up to you.

Note to reviewer

This is any other information about the cache that you think might be pertinent to the volunteers who review the cache to approve it for including in the database. This could be a statement about having gotten permission from a landowner, a description of a virtual cache item, or the final coordinates for a multicache.

Legal stuff

Select the check boxes if you've read the guidelines for listing a cache and if you agree to the terms of service. (There are links to both of these items.) Both check boxes must be marked to submit a cache.

Most of the information that you enter when you submit a cache is displayed in the cache information page. Review some other caches in the Geocaching.com database to get a better idea of the types of information that other cachers are including with their caches.

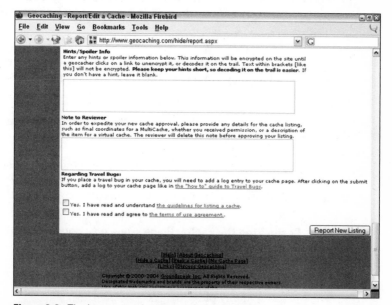

Figure 8-6: The last geocache submission entry fields.

After you enter all the cache information, submit the form. Regional and local volunteers (fondly referred to as *approvers*) will check things like whether all the information needed is present, the coordinates are generally correct, and the cache meets the general submission guidelines. The approval process can take up to a couple of days but is usually shorter. If you're approved, your cache is added to the database. If you're not approved, you'll be informed why, and you can either address the problem and resubmit or discuss the issue over e-mail with the approver.

Keep in mind that volunteers don't physically visit the cache — that would require thousands of people all over the world with a considerable amount of free time on their hands.

Maintaining a Geocache

After you hide your cache and it appears in the database, your work isn't finished yet. You need to keep track of what's happening with your cache, both in the physical and virtual worlds.

Physical maintenance

Although you might think otherwise, caches aren't entirely self-sufficient, and they need some care and nurturing. You shouldn't place a cache and then ignore it. In fact, plan on visiting your cache

- ✔ Every so often just to check on its condition.
- ✔ As soon as possible after receiving an online log comment or e-mail message that says the cache is missing or in a state of disrepair.

When you visit your cache, some of the common maintenance tasks include

- ✔ **Replacing the logbook:** You need a new logbook when the old one starts to fill up. Don't forget to bring some spare pencils and plastic bags in case they're missing or aren't in the best of shape.
- ✔ **Restocking the cache:** Place some new goodies in the cache if people are taking more than they're leaving.

✔ **Adding a Travel Bug:** Popping a Travel Bug you found in
another cache into your cache drives visits from bug lovers.

✔ **Swapping the cache container for a new one:** Sometimes the
original container becomes damaged, stolen, or just isn't
working out (for example, it's too small, and the trade items
are overflowing).

Duct tape holds the world together, and it's worth bringing a roll
with you when you're visiting your cache to make temporary field
repairs on cracked plastic containers, punctured plastic bags, or
peeling geocache identification labels.

During your visits, check that the area around the cache isn't being
extremely impacted by people searching for the cache. If the site
is being disturbed (such as several well-established foot trails that
weren't there when you first placed the cache), consider relocating
the cache. If you decide to temporarily or permanently remove a
cache, be sure to post an online log entry to let other geocachers
know when they look up information about the cache.

Archiving means making a cache inactive in the Geocaching.com
database. Any time you relocate a cache, you should archive the
original cache and then submit a new one. If you permanently
remove a cache, you should always archive it. (Abandoned caches
are often called *geolitter.*) You can archive and edit caches that
you've hidden by logging onto the Geocaching.com site and clicking
the MY CACHE PAGE button on the home page. This displays lists
of caches you've found and hidden as well as account profile information. You can also contact the volunteer who originally approved
your cache (his or her e-mail contact is listed at the bottom of the
cache information page) and request to temporarily archive a
cache. Just remember to reactivate it!

Online maintenance

In addition to physically checking the cache, you should also check
your cache online and read the comments posted from people who
have visited the cache. These comments can alert you when it's time
to make a maintenance visit to the cache. Patience, Grasshopper!
Sometimes, it can take a while for someone to first find your cache
and post about it.

If you click the Watch This Cache button at the top of a geocache
information page, you'll be notified when someone logs comments
about that cache. As a cache placer, this is a great way to keep a
virtual eye on your hidden caches. You can watch up to 100 caches
(unlimited if you have a premium subscription).

As the owner of a cache, after you log on with your Geocaching.com account, you can delete any log entries for caches that you own. It's up to you to police log comments associated with your caches, and you should delete any comments that you think are inappropriate.

If The Man calls

In the early days of geocaching, most government agencies didn't know that the sport even existed. That's changed, and many land managers now know about the Geocaching.com Web site and check it on a regular basis to see whether there are any geocaches on land they're responsible for.

If you hide a cache where it's not supposed to be (either unintentionally or on purpose), some land managers might contact you through e-mail, using your Geocaching.com alias, requesting that you relocate the cache. An example of this recently happened in central Oregon, where several geocaches were inadvertently placed near the nesting grounds of a threatened bird species. A government employee, who also happened to be a geocacher, discovered the nests and then contacted the cache owners, asking them to archive their caches until after nesting season and then relocate them. (Immediately removing the caches would have disturbed the already nesting birds.)

If an agency representative does contact you, be respectful, find out the issues that he or she has with your cache location, and ask for suggestions for a more acceptable spot. (From a communication standpoint, phone or in-person conversations are always better than e-mail.) Remember that the future of the sport depends on geocachers, property owners, and land managers all working together.

Part III
Advanced Geocaching

The 5th Wave   By Rich Tennant

"Wait, it's not a problem! The trailhead to the antidote cache is only 3 miles from here!"

In this part . . .

After you become savvy with geocaching, you might want to take a couple of steps beyond the basics. That's what the chapters in this part are all about. In Chapter 9, I introduce you to the sport of benchmark hunting. It's like geocaching in a way, but you search for permanent survey markers (typically small brass or aluminum disks driven into the ground or in rock formations). Locating benchmarks can sometimes be even more challenging than finding a geocache.

For Chapter 10, I take you into the world of organized geocaching. For such a young sport, quite a number of geocaching clubs have popped up in a short amount of time. I show you how to find geocaching clubs and organizations in your area, and I also talk about some of the benefits of joining them. In addition to clubs, I discuss organized geocaching competitions that are starting to sprout up here and there, that pit geocachers against each other and the clock. I close out this part with Chapter 11, describing how GPS and geocaching can be used for education. Pay attention to this chapter if you're a teacher or know one. There are some cool ways to incorporate geocaching into classroom curriculums, and I'll give you the lowdown and all sorts of pointers to places on the Internet where you can download lesson plans and course material.

Chapter 9

Searching for Benchmarks

· ·

In This Chapter

▶ Understanding control points and benchmarks

▶ Researching benchmark locations

▶ Understanding benchmark datasheet information

▶ Searching for benchmarks

▶ Logging your benchmark finds

· ·

*1*f you get hooked on geocaching, you'll also want to give benchmark hunting a try. *Benchmarks* are permanent markers installed by a government agency in large rocks, concrete, and other immovable objects. They serve as *control points* — known locations — for surveyors, engineers, and mapmakers. Because the precise location of many benchmarks are known, you can use your GPS receiver to find them, just like you'd search for a geocache.

Searching for benchmarks is a great way to hone your GPS and search skills because unlike caches, benchmarks aren't hidden and are much more difficult for vandals to spirit away. Benchmark hunting is also an alternative to traditional geocaching if you're more into the search and really don't care about trinkets stashed in an ammo can. And for you history buffs: Because most benchmarks are stamped with the date they were installed, it's pretty cool to find something out in the middle of nowhere that has been keeping silent watch for 50, 75, or even over 100 years.

In this chapter, I clue you in to the different types of benchmarks, show you how to look up their location coordinates (the Geocaching.com Web site offers a free database of benchmarks that you can query), give you some practical tips on searching for a benchmark, and tell you what to do when you find one.

Control points in the United States are generically called benchmarks. In other parts of the world, they have different names. For example, in Great Britain, they're called *trigpoints*. The Geocaching. com database currently contains information on only NGS (National

Geodetic Survey) benchmarks located within the United States. This is because the complete collection of NGS benchmark data is publicly available in an electronically accessible format. Geocaching.com might expand its database to include other benchmarks as international interest grows and additional data becomes available.

Understanding Benchmarks

In 1807, President Thomas Jefferson established the United States Coast Survey, which was the first U.S. government agency tasked with mapping and surveying land. An essential part of performing any type of a survey is to establish *control points* — known locations with very-precisely recorded coordinates. By using a series of control points as references and measuring the distance and angles between the points, you can complete very exacting surveys and create very accurate maps. One of the duties of the U.S. Coast Survey, now known as the NGS, was to establish a series of control points throughout the U.S. for surveying and mapping purposes. (If you're into history like this, be sure to check out Andro Linklater's book *Measuring America,* www.measuringamerica.com.)

The word *geodetic* comes from *geodesy,* which is the science of measuring and monitoring the size and shape of the Earth and the location of points on its surface. To read more about geodesy, visit http://oceanservice.noaa.gov/education/geodesy/welcome.html.

Of the different types of control points, the ones to be most interested in are

 ✔ **Vertical:** These mark the exact *elevation* of a point.

 ✔ **Horizontal:** These mark the precise *location coordinates* of a point.

Control points can take a number of different forms, including round brass or aluminum disks (an example is shown in Figure 9-1), bolts, or rods. A prominent, fixed feature — such as a water tower, radio antenna, or building — is a *landmark.*

Technically, the term *benchmark* applies only to a vertical (elevation) control point. However, most people outside the geodesy business (including the Geocaching.com Web site) refer to both vertical and horizontal control points as benchmarks. I'll do the same.

Other benchmarks

The NGS isn't the only government agency that places benchmarks in the United States. States, counties, and cities also use control points. Although no one has put together a single Web-based database of these other benchmarks as of yet, `http://surveymarks.planetzhanna.com/localcontroldata.shtml` has a variety of links organized by state where you can find information about the locations of different types of benchmarks.

Control points aren't exclusive to the United States; they're found all over the world. If you're outside the U.S., you'll need to do a bit of search engine research to see whether any Web sites are dedicated to survey markers that country. A few international sites are on the 'Net, such as `www.trigpointinguk.com`, which is devoted to finding trigpoints in Great Britain.

If you'd like to place your own benchmarks or just want some cool souvenirs, check out Berntsen Survey Markers at `www.berntsten.com`.

Figure 9-1: A metal disk benchmark.

Employees of the NGS, and its predecessor agency, the Coast and Geodetic Survey, traveled throughout the U.S. plotting the locations of landmarks and installing control points, recording the precise location of each. Hundreds of thousands of these control points are in existence, with their locations part of the public record and available to anyone with an Internet connection. What is especially impressive is the level of precision that horizontal benchmark coordinates have, especially considering that they were installed long before GPS technology was available. By using *transits* (small telescopes mounted on a tripod used for measuring horizontal and vertical angles during a survey), measuring rods, and chains, surveyors and engineers were able to achieve measurement errors of less than 1 inch in 90 miles.

Benchmarks and control points come in all different sizes, shapes, and types. For an excellent collection of photos and descriptions of various benchmarks, check out www.dustyjacket.com/benchmarks.html.

Identifying Benchmarks in Your Area

If you want to give benchmark hunting a try, the first step is to identify where benchmarks in an area are located. You can research the locations of benchmarks in the United States two different ways:

- ✔ **Use the Geocaching.com Web site** (www.geocaching.com; the same site you use for listing geocache locations).
- ✔ **Use the National Geodetic Survey Web site** (www.ngs.noaa.gov/cgi-bin/datasheet.prl).

If you start to get serious about benchmark hunting, I recommend that you pick up a copy of Maptech's Terrain Navigator Pro. In addition to providing electronic topographic maps for an entire state, the program also plots NGS benchmarks on maps that you can click to display detailed information. To find out more about the program, which is priced around $300 per state, visit www.maptech.com.

Benchmarks from Geocaching.com

The Geocaching.com site has an extensive database of NGS control points that's quick and easy to search.

The Geocaching.com home page has a <u>Check out benchmark</u> link that will take you to the benchmark search page, or you can go directly to it via your Web browser at www.geocaching.com/mark.

The benchmark page has two search options:

- ✔ **By Postal Code:** Enter the ZIP code for the area you're interested in searching for benchmarks.

  The Geocaching.com database currently lists only U.S. benchmarks.

- ✔ **By Point ID (PID):** All benchmarks have a unique permanent identifier number associated with them. This number is usually stamped on metal disk benchmarks.

Click the Other search options link to go to a page where you can search by state, benchmark designation, or latitude and longitude coordinates.

After you enter your search parameter and click GO, a list of benchmarks is displayed, such as the one shown in Figure 9-2.

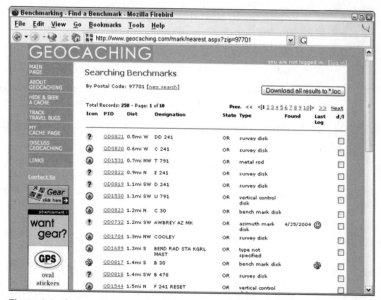

Figure 9-2: Geocaching.com results of a benchmark search.

The list has the following information:

- ✔ **Icon:** An icon that looks like a metal survey disk provides general information about the state of the benchmark. For example, an icon with an exclamation mark in the center means that someone has found and logged that particular benchmark. A legend with the meanings of the different icons appears at the bottom of the page.

- **PID:** This is the permanent identifier number assigned to the benchmark by the NGS.

- **Dist:** This is the approximate distance and direction that the benchmark is from the search ZIP code or coordinates you entered.

- **Designation:** Here you find a description of a benchmark, using standardized NGS abbreviations and codes. This information isn't critical for benchmark hunting — and in fact, can get pretty darn confusing because of the numerous abbreviations and codes. If there's some plain-English description in the designation (such as the name of a place or road), make use of it. If there isn't, feel free to ignore the description. However, if you really get into benchmarks and want to know all about designations, a complete and painfully detailed guide to benchmark designations can be viewed at www.ngs.noaa.gov/FGCS/ BlueBook/pdf/Annex_D.pdf.

Note: You need to have Adobe Reader installed on your computer to read this document. To download and install Reader (for free), go to www.adobe.com/products/acrobat/ readstep2.html.

- **State:** This is the state where the benchmark is located.

- **Type:** This lists the type of benchmark, such as horizontal control survey disk, vertical control disk, or metal rod.

- **Found:** This is the date a Geocaching.com user last found the benchmark.

- **Last Log:** Here you see an icon associated with a log entry the last Geocaching.com user made about the benchmark. A smiley face means the benchmark was located. A frowny face means that the benchmark was searched for but wasn't found, and a broken disk icon means someone looked for the benchmark and assumed or discovered it to be destroyed.

Each benchmark has a check box at the far right. You can download waypoint information for all checked benchmarks to your PC by clicking the Download Waypoint File command at the bottom of the page.

To get information about the location of a benchmark, click its PID link. A new window opens, with detailed information about the benchmark. An example is shown in Figure 9-3.

The information page contains latitude and longitude coordinates for the benchmark, its type, a general map of its location — and more importantly (scroll down to the bottom of the page), a very detailed description of its location. The directions to the bench-mark are so exact that in most cases, you don't even need a GPS receiver to zero in on the benchmark location.

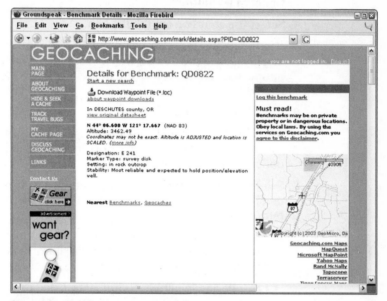

Figure 9-3: Detailed benchmark information page.

 If you click the <u>view original datasheet</u> link, a separate window opens that shows all the NGS data associated with the benchmark. Some of this is pretty detailed or technical, so don't get intimidated. You definitely don't need this level of in-depth information to search for benchmarks. However, if you turn into a real benchmark geek, you'll probably want to check it out. Better yet, read the next section on how to get detailed datasheet information right from the source.

Benchmarks from the National Geodetic Survey

In addition to using Geocaching.com, you can get benchmark infor-mation directly from the National Geodetic Survey Web site at `www.ngs.noaa.gov/cgi-bin/datasheet.prl`. Here's how, but keep in mind that using this method isn't as easy or intuitive as using Geocaching.com:

1. **Click the DATASHEETS button.**

2. **Click the <u>COUNTY</u> link.**

You can also search by the benchmark PID, USGS topographic quad map name, and other search options.

3. **Select a state from the list box and then click the Get County List button.**

4. **Select the county from the list box.**

5. **(Optional) You can also select the type of control point to display. Leave the default Any Horz. And/or Vert. Control option selected as well as the default setting for Stability Desired.**

6. **Click the Get Marks button.**

   A scrollable list of all the benchmarks is displayed, as shown in Figure 9-4. You can resort by the PID and other options that appear above the list.

7. **Select the benchmark for which you want to view detailed information and then click the Get Datasheets button.**

   A scrollable datasheet with complete information about the benchmark appears. An example is shown in Figure 9-5. Pertinent information includes

   • Latitude and longitude coordinates, listed on the same line as the map datum. (Read Chapter 3 for more on datums.)

   • The type of benchmark and how it is placed.

   • Historical information about the benchmark.

   • A text description of the benchmark location.

I prefer using the Geocaching.com site for doing general benchmark research because its user interface is considerably better than the NGS site. Geocaching.com uses the same NGS benchmark information in its database although the NGS benchmark datasheets might be more up-to-date in certain cases.

I use the NGS site if I want to take advantage of its advanced search features or plot benchmarks on a digital map. BMGPX is a free Windows program that converts the location coordinates found in NGS benchmark datasheets into the *GPX* data format (GPS Exchange, which is a file format that allows mapping and GPS programs to easily share data). You can then import the benchmark location data to a map program to overlay the locations of the benchmarks. BMGPX is available at www.parkrrrr.com.

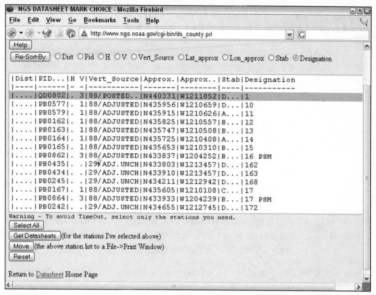

Figure 9-4: NGS benchmark selection page.

```
DATASHEETS - Mozilla Firebird
File  Edit  View  Go  Bookmarks  Tools  Help
      http://www.ngs.noaa.gov/cgi-bin/ds_county.prl

QD0822;                North        East   Units   Estimated Accuracy
QD0822;SPC OR S    -   271,730.    1,436,400.   MT  (+/- 180 meters Scaled)
QD0822
QD0822                    SUPERSEDED SURVEY CONTROL
QD0822
QD0822  NGVD 29 (??/??/92) 1054.210  (m)        3458.69   (f) ADJ UNCH   1 2
QD0822
QD0822.Superseded values are not recommended for survey control.
QD0822.NGS no longer adjusts projects to the NAD 27 or NGVD 29 datums.
QD0822.See file dsdata.txt to determine how the superseded data were derived.
QD0822
QD0822_U.S. NATIONAL GRID SPATIAL ADDRESS: 10TFP364855(NAD 83)
QD0822_MARKER: DD = SURVEY DISK
QD0822_SETTING: 66 = SET IN ROCK OUTCROP
QD0822_STAMPING: E 241 1941
QD0822_STABILITY: A = MOST RELIABLE AND EXPECTED TO HOLD
QD0822+STABILITY: POSITION/ELEVATION WELL
QD0822
QD0822  HISTORY     - Date     Condition        Report By
QD0822  HISTORY     - 1941     MONUMENTED       ORDT
QD0822  HISTORY     - 1974     GOOD             NGS
QD0822  HISTORY     - 19880721 MARK NOT FOUND   NGS
QD0822
QD0822                     STATION DESCRIPTION
QD0822
QD0822'DESCRIBED BY NATIONAL GEODETIC SURVEY 1974
QD0822'3.5 MI N FROM BEND.
QD0822'REACHED FROM THE JUNCTION OF U. S. HIGHWAYS 20, AND 97, WHICH IS 2.5
QD0822'MILES NORTH OF BEND, GO NORTH ON U.S. HIGHWAY 97 FOR 1.0 MILE TO THE
QD0822'ENTRANCE TO THE KOA CAMPGROUNDS, AND THE BENCH MARK ON THE LEFT, 0.05
QD0822'MILE NORTH OF COOLEY ROAD, 56 FEET WEST OF THE CENTER OF U.S. HIGHWAY
QD0822'97, 36 FEET NORTH OF THE CENTER OF THE DRIVEWAY TO THE KOA
```

Figure 9-5: Detailed information about a benchmark on an NGS datasheet.

Finding Benchmarks

After you discover where a benchmark is located based on the NGS data, it's time to go find it. But before you head out the door, though, note these important distinctions between geocaching and benchmark hunting. With benchmark searches, there are

- ✔ **No GPS receivers required:** Information about most benchmarks was recorded in the pre-GPS days, and the descriptions on how to get to the locations are often detailed enough that you don't need a GPS receiver. (It's still not a bad idea to bring your receiver with you with the benchmark coordinates entered as a waypoint.)

- ✔ **No logbooks to sign:** However, you can still log your finds online at the Geocaching.com Web site if you want, just like when you find a geocache.

- ✔ **No goodies to exchange:** Please don't try to take a benchmark with you as a souvenir; doing so is a federal offense.

- ✔ **No cache containers:** Benchmarks, especially the common, metal disk variety, are weatherproof and are usually encased in concrete.

- ✔ **No concealed hiding places:** Benchmarks were placed so someone who knew their location could find them. However, that doesn't mean there's a big neon sign with an arrow pointing to their location.

Finding a benchmark can sometimes be just as challenging as locating a geocache for a number of reasons, including

- ✔ **Color:** The color of the benchmark, especially if it's a metal disk, might blend in with the surroundings.

- ✔ **Hidden:** Vegetation or soil might obscure the benchmark.

- ✔ **Gone:** The benchmark might have been taken or destroyed since the last verified NGS visit.

- ✔ **On private land:** Unlike geocaches, which tend to be on public land, a number of benchmarks are located on private property. (Please respect property owners.)

- ✔ **Oops:** The coordinates might be in error. This is particularly true with vertical control points, which were used for recording elevations and didn't need the high level of precision coordinates found with horizontal control points. Also, there's always human error, and sometimes the surveyor just made a boo-boo.

Waiting for recovery

In benchmark-speak, a *recovery* happens when the location of a benchmark has been verified. In a datasheet, if you see that a benchmark has been recovered, the existence of the benchmark has been confirmed — it doesn't mean the benchmark has been removed by the NGS.

Not all benchmarks are located in the middle of nowhere. Some are in urban areas or next to highways or other busy roads. Be careful not to get run over in your excitement to log a new benchmark find.

Starting your benchmark search

Starting your search for a benchmark is pretty straightforward. Here are the steps that you'll take:

1. **Print a copy of the directions from the benchmark datasheet. Also gather any maps that might be helpful in locating a benchmark.**

   Some benchmarks are identified on topographic maps with the letters *BM*.

2. **Enter the benchmark's location as a waypoint in your GPS receiver.**

   Check out Chapter 3 for more on waypoints if you don't know what they are.

3. **Drive as close to the benchmark as you can get.**

   You can use some of the techniques for getting close to a geocache that are described in Chapter 6.

4. **Activate the benchmark's waypoint and use your GPS receiver to guide you to the benchmark location.**

   You did set a waypoint for where your car was parked so you can find your way back to it, didn't you?

5. **As you head toward the benchmark location, use the printed directions in conjunction with your GPS receiver to help you zero in on the location.**

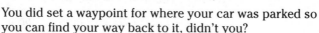

6. **Keep your eyes open for the benchmark.**

   Review Web sites that have photos of found benchmarks so you know what you're looking for the first couple of times out. Geocaching.com has a photo gallery devoted to benchmarks that's a good resource.

As you search, pay close attention to the benchmark description and directions. Whoever first placed the benchmark will have provided detailed information on exactly where the benchmark is located: for example, "The disk is set in bedrock flush with the ground. It is 24 feet north of the edge of pavement on Highway 20 and 140 feet west of the centerline of Cooley Road." (Just remember that the original or recovery description likely won't account for any recent development, like new subdivisions, road widening, or land clearing.)

 Watch for a light bluish color that catches your eye. The elements will sometimes tarnish older brass survey disks, leaving a blue patina on the surface that makes them easy to spot.

Documenting a found benchmark

Finding a benchmark is a cool experience because of the history that's associated with the marker. Benchmark searchers have located benchmarks that were *monumented* (survey-speak for when the benchmark was first placed) over 100 years ago.

After you find a benchmark, here's what you should do:

1. **If you brought a camera with you, take a digital photo of the benchmark and the area around it.**

2. **If you've got a GPS receiver with you, record the benchmark's coordinates.**

   Use the same techniques for recording the location of a geocache you've hidden as described in Chapter 8.

3. **Log your find in the Geocaching.com database.**

   At the top of a benchmark information page is a <u>Log this benchmark</u> link. If you have a Geocaching.com account and are logged in (read about this in Chapter 5), click this link and enter the requested information to record your find. You can also add digital photos of your finds to the gallery.

4. **Check the most current NGS datasheet to determine the last time someone officially visited the benchmark.**

   If it's been more than a year, the NGS would be interested in hearing from you to know that the benchmark is still there and what condition it's in to update its records. Check out the benchmark section in the Geocaching.com forums (`http://forums.groundspeak.com/gc`). There's a permanent thread at the top of the forum with information about submitting your find to the NGS with the name and e-mail address of a government employee whom you can contact.

The Geocaching.com forum that's devoted to benchmarking hunting has lots of excellent, firsthand information. There's also an extensive FAQ on the bottom of the Geocaching.com benchmark search page.

Earth Science Corps

If you live in the United States and are into benchmark hunting or geocaching, you might be interested in joining the USGS Earth Science Corps.

Volunteers update USGS topographic maps to ensure that they are accurate. This involves walking and driving around and using your GPS receiver to record map information. There are over 54,000 USGS topographic quadrangle maps that cover the United States, and there's a good chance that a map nearby where you live might need to have a volunteer assigned to update it.

For more information and to request a volunteer application kit, visit `http://mapping.usgs.gov/www/html/escorps.html`.

Chapter 10

Organized Geocaching Clubs and Competitions

In This Chapter

▶ Discovering geocaching clubs

▶ Finding a local club

▶ Tracking geocaching stats

▶ Competing in organized geocaching events

*A*s the popularity of geocaching continues to grow, geocaching clubs and organizations are springing up everywhere. These clubs provide an outlet for like-minded people to get together and participate in and learn more about their sport.

In this chapter, I talk about some of the benefits of getting involved with a geocaching club and how to find one in your area. I also give you the lowdown on organized caching competitions, in which you race against the clock or other geocachers.

Geocaching Clubs

As any sport, hobby, or pastime becomes popular, people who enjoy it are drawn together and eventually form clubs. The same thing has happened with geocaching, and for such a relatively young sport, a large number of clubs have appeared in a very short amount of time.

Because geocaching relies on the Internet, you'll find most clubs pretty electronic communications-savvy. Club Web sites, online forums, e-mail lists, and the use of instant messaging are all very common.

Why join a club?

Maybe you just started geocaching or perhaps you've been at it for a while. Why should you consider joining a geocaching club? Here are a number of good reasons:

- ✔ **Learn the ropes.** If you're new to geocaching and using GPS receivers, clubs are a good way to get up to speed. You'll find geocachers of all levels and abilities eager to share their experiences and skills, either in person or online.

- ✔ **Find out about local restrictions for placing caches.** Clubs provide a great source of intelligence for anyone interested in hiding caches. You can learn which public lands allow hiding caches and which ones have restrictions on them. This can save you a lot of time researching these issues yourself.

- ✔ **Participate in group events.** Most clubs sponsor events that combine geocaching with picnics and other outdoor activities. The events tend to be family-oriented, with some open only to club members and other events open to the general public. Many clubs also do volunteer public service work, such as litter cleanups and park and trail maintenance.

- ✔ **Hang out with like-minded people.** In addition to getting out in the fresh air to geocache, most clubs have regular scheduled meetings indoors over coffee or pizza to discuss geocaching and other related and unrelated topics.

Geocaching teams

Another organized form of geocaching involves teams, which are groups of people who geocache together. They might all live in the same area and go hunting caches in a group. (If so, they'll often have a team name and an account for logging their finds in the Geocaching.com database.) Or, the team's members might not live anywhere near one another but work together as a virtual team to find particularly challenging geocaches. A classic example is the notorious Blood & Guts cache located somewhere in the Eastern United States; so far, only a few people have been able to locate it. To find the cache, you must solve a series of puzzles. Virtual teams comprising geocachers from all over the world have been formed to try to unravel the clues needed to discover the locations of some of these hard-to-find geocaches. Team members exchange e-mail and online information so that members who live near the cache site can zero in on its location. Most of these teams have gotten together in the regional forums at Geocaching.com.

Like so many other aspects of geocaching, joining a club is a personal preference. If you like to socialize with people, clubs present a great opportunity for meeting new friends. If you're not a people-person, that's okay, too. You can still glean a lot of information about the local geocaching scene by visiting club Web sites and forums.

Finding a local club

You can use the Internet several different ways to find a local or regional geocaching club. Take a look at some of the options.

Geocaching.com event calendar

One of your first stops for locating a club should be Geocaching.com (`www.geocaching.com`). The Web site has a calendar of geocaching events — *event caches,* which are database entries that have information about upcoming activities and events. Geocaching clubs and organizations put on most of these events, and the listings provide contact and other information that you can use to find a club. To display the event calendar, click the View the event calendar link on the Geocaching.com home page (or go to `www.geocaching.com/calendar` in your Web browser). See a sample result in Figure 10-1.

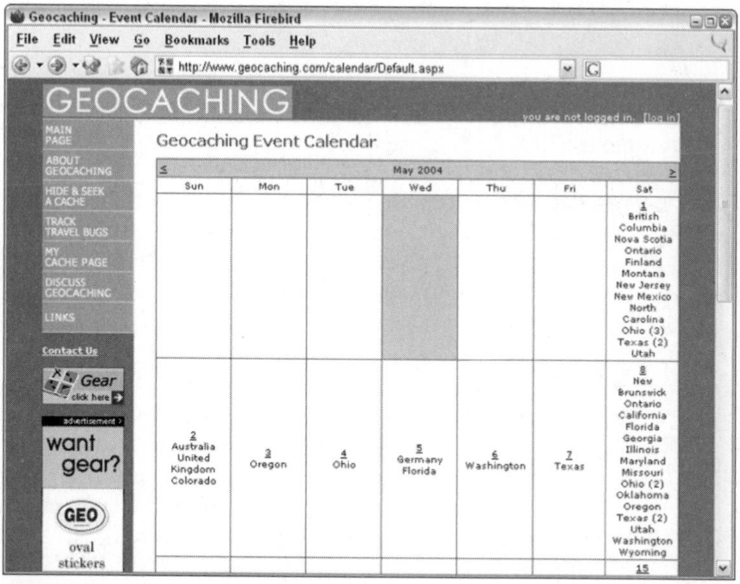

Figure 10-1: Find event caches here.

The current month is shown. A list of the countries and U.S. states where the geocaching events are planned to take place is displayed. Click the day of the month to view all the events that are scheduled for that date, as shown in Figure 10-2.

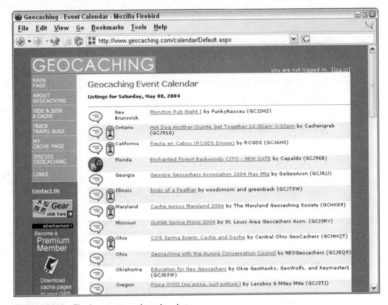

Figure 10-2: Find event caches by date.

Click the name of an event to find out more about it, like the date, time, and location. An example event cache page is shown in Figure 10-3.

You can also display recent and current events listed by state or country. From the Geocaching.com home page, perform a search by state or country. (See Chapter 5 for details on how to perform these types of searches.) A list of events, as well as recently hidden caches, is displayed.

Internet listings and search engines

Many geocaching groups have Web sites and provide up-to-date information on local geocaching happenings. Table 10-1 has a list of United States geocaching clubs by state with their Web site addresses. You can also try doing a Google search for your state or city along with the word *"geocaching"* to find clubs that might not appear on the list.

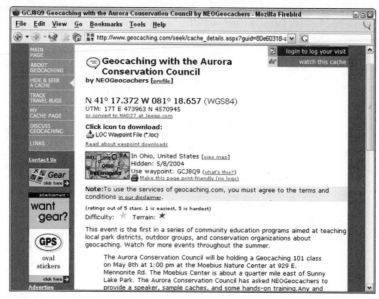

Figure 10-3: Find specific event cache information.

Table 10-1	U.S. Geocaching Clubs and Web Sites
State	*Club/Web Address*
Alabama	Alabama Geocachers Association: www.alacache.com Huntsville Area Geocachers: www.hsvgeocache.us/main/index.php
Alaska	Alaska Geocaching: www.alaskageocaching.com
Arizona	Arizona Geocaching: www.azgeocaching.com
Arkansas	Arkansas State Parks: www.arkansasstateparks.com/things/geocache Ozark Mountain Geocachers: http://groups.yahoo.com/group/ozmtngeocachers Missouri, Arkansas Geocachers Association: http://groups.yahoo.com/group/ARK-MO-Geocachers
California	Southern California Geocachers: www.scgeocachers.org

(continued)

Table 10-1 *(continued)*

State	Club/Web Address
Colorado	Colorado Geocaching Association: www.coloradogeocaching.com
Florida	Florida Geocachers: www.floridacachers.com Florida Cachers: www.cacheflorida.com
Georgia	Georgia Geocachers Association: www.ggaonline.org
Hawaii	GPS Hawaii: www.lightfantastic.org/gps
Idaho	Idaho Geocachers: http://idahogeocachers.org
Illinois	Chicagoland Geocachers: www.chicagogeocaching.com Great Plains Geocaching: www.gpgeocaching.com Chicago Geocachers: www.chicagogeocachers.com Illinois Central Area Cache Hunting Enthusiasts: http://icash.sub-genius.com
Indiana	Indiana Geocaching: www.indianageocaching.com Ohio, Kentucky and Indiana Cachers: www.OKIC.org
Iowa	Great Plains Geocaching: www.gpgeocaching.com
Kansas	Great Plains Geocaching: www.gpgeocaching.com
Kentucky	Geocachers of Central Kentucky: www.geocky.org Ohio, Kentucky and Indiana Cachers: www.OKIC.org
Louisiana	Louisiana Geocaching: www.lageocaching.com
Maryland	Maryland Geocaching Society: www.mdgps.net
Michigan	Michigan Geocaching Organization: www.mi-geocaching.org
Minnesota	Great Plains Geocaching: www.gpgeocaching.com Minnesota Geocaching Association: www.mngca.org
Mississippi	Mississippi Geocachers Association: www.msga.net
Missouri	Ozark Mountain Geocachers: http://groups.yahoo.com/group/ozmtngeocachers St. Louis Area Geocachers Association: www.geostl.com Missouri, Arkansas Geocachers Association: http://groups.yahoo.com/group/ARK-MO-Geocachers

State	Club/Web Address
Nebraska	Great Plains Geocaching: www.gpgeocaching.com
Nevada	Nevada Geocaching: www.nevadageocaching.com
New York	New York Geocaching Organization: www.ny-geocaching.org
North Carolina	North Carolina Geocachers Association: www.ncgeocachers.com Triangle Geocachers: http://groups.yahoo.com/group/TriangleGeocachers
North Dakota	Great Plains Geocaching: www.gpgeocaching.com
Ohio	NE Ohio Geocachers: www.geocities.com/neogeocachers Ohio, Kentucky and Indiana Cachers: www.OKIC.org
Oklahoma	Great Plains Geocaching: www.gpgeocaching.com Oklahoma Geocachers: http://geocaching.donewise.com Tulsa Area Geocachers: www.members.cox.net/geocache
Oregon	Central Oregon Geocaching: www.cogeo.org Portland Geocaching: www.pdxgeocaching.com Oregon Geocaching: www.oregongeocaching.org Emerald Valley Cachers: http://gotcache.com
South Dakota	Great Plains Geocaching: www.gpgeocaching.com
Tennessee	Geocachers of Southeast Tennessee: www.geoset.org Middle Tennessee Geocachers: http://pub64.ezboard.com/bmiddletennesseegeocachers
Texas	Great Plains Geocaching: www.gpgeocaching.com Southeast Texas Geocachers: www.houstoncachers.org Texas Geocaching Association: www.texasgeocaching.com Texas Geocaching: www.txga.net
Utah	Utah Geo-Club: www.cachunuts.com Utah Geocachers: www.utahgeocachers.com

(continued)

Table 10-1 *(continued)*

State	Club/Web Address
Virginia	Geocaching Hampton Roads Virginia: http://groups.yahoo.com/group/Geocaching-HamptonRoadsVA
Washington	**Washington State Geocaching Association:** http://geocachingwa.org
Wisconsin	**Great Plains Geocaching:** www.gpgeocaching.com **Wisconsin Geocaching Association:** www.wi-geocaching.com

Geocaching.com forums

Geocaching.com offers regional discussion forums organized by state and country at http://forums.groundspeak.com/gc. These forums are a great way to see what's happening with the geocaching scene in your part of the world and are a way to hook up with other geocachers in your area. (Anyone can browse through the forums, but you need a free account to post messages. Read Chapter 5 to see how to set up an account.)

Competitive Geocaching

It seems that sooner or later, any recreational activity eventually develops a competitive aspect, and geocaching is no exception. Although the roots of geocaching are grounded in the personal challenge of finding a hidden cache, competing against others has found its way into the sport. Don't worry, though. This simply adds another element to geocaching, and you'll always have a choice of getting involved in competition or simply enjoying the fun of the sport.

If you have a competitive nature, take a quick look at several areas of geocaching that you might be interested in.

Geocaching stats

To some people, geocaching stats (as in statistics) are a way of measuring their own and others' ability and credibility within the sport. Geocaching.com's account profile pages make it easy to track how many caches you've found and hidden, and some cachers take these numbers pretty seriously.

If geocaching stats are important to you, that's great. Just don't get carried away with inflated feelings of grandeur at your cache numbers. Remember, a whole lot of cachers could not care less about stats but are into the sport for the challenge, enjoyment, and quality of the experience — all of which are pretty hard to assign meaningful numbers.

If you're a competitive type and insist on comparing your geocache finds and hides against others, check out this Web page, which maintains a leader board based on Geocaching.com stats: `http://zinnware.com/HighAdv/Geocaching/most_caches_found.html`. For the record, at this point in time, CCCooperAgency is leading with over 5,000 finds, and King Boreas has hidden over 400 caches. That's a lot of caches.

Organized competitions

Keeping track of stats has been around since the early days of geocaching, but more recently, organized caching competitions have started to crop up. These events pit geocachers against one another and the clock, with awards and prizes.

Many geocaching events are modeled after traditional orienteering competitions and include courses. (*Orienteering* is a sport in which you use a map and compass to locate flags.) A *course* is a single race. There are usually several courses during an event, each with a varied level of difficulty. One course might be more suited for beginning geocachers, while another would be appropriate for cachers with intermediate to advanced skills.

A series of geocaches or tags with coordinates is hidden on the course. The competitors are given the coordinates and must find as many caches or tags as possible within a certain amount of time. (Sometimes the tag directs competitors to the next tag location, like a multicache.) The participants might be given punch cards to validate each find; each cache or tag has a unique paper punch used to punch the card.

That's basically how a competition works although you can find all sorts of different variations. Individuals or teams compete against one another, often in separate divisions, such as classes divided by age group.

Competitive geocaching is currently in its infancy. Although I don't foresee professional cachers with multimillion-dollar contracts and product endorsements, I do think competitive events will become more widespread and popular.

If you're interested in trying your hand at competitive caching, check the Geocaching.com events listings that I describe earlier in this chapter for any upcoming races.

You've heard of football, baseball, basketball, and bowling leagues, but how about one for geocaching? The Cache League pits organized geocaching teams against one another for prizes. The team members don't even need to all be in the same place because points are accumulated by individual team member finds. The league got started in the spring of 2004; find out more about it at www.cacheleague.com.

Speed caching

You don't need to enter an organized geocaching competition to get the adrenaline rush associated with racing against others. Athletically inclined geocachers can try speed caching.

Speed caching simply involves finding one or more caches as fast as you can. From some set starting point, you hit the stopwatch button on your watch; using your GPS receiver as a guide, you then run or jog toward the cache location. (The route you select is up to you.) When you find the cache, press the stopwatch button again and record your time.

The added pressure of the clock ticking away helps you hone your GPS and navigation skills under stress. (Plus you get a pretty good workout in the process.) You can either speed cache by yourself as an individual form of exercise or tell your friends your times and challenge them to find a cache faster than you did.

Chapter 11

GPS and Geocaching in Education

In This Chapter

▶ Discovering the benefits of GPS in education

▶ Reviewing examples of GPS and geocaching in the classroom

▶ Adding GPS and geocaching to course materials

▶ Acquiring GPS receivers for classroom use

▶ Accessing GPS educational resources on the Internet

*U*sing GPS receivers and heading out on geocaching trips is a lot of fun. In addition to the recreational aspects, the whiz-bang location technology and high-tech, treasure hunt capabilities offer some intriguing and cool educational possibilities. Creative teachers who think outside the box are starting to recognize that GPS can be used in the classroom to enhance learning in a number of different subjects.

That's what this chapter is all about. I want to introduce you to some ideas on using GPS and geocaching in the classroom or for home schooling. I discuss how GPS can be used when teaching various subjects, give you some pointers on incorporating GPS and geocaching into a curriculum, and provide you with all sorts of Internet resources where you can get lesson plans and student and instructor materials devoted to using GPS for education. (I even clue you in on some excellent forums where you can discuss GPS topics with other educators.)

My goal with this chapter is to get you thinking about how GPS and geocaching can be used in the classroom. If you're interested in using GPS in one of your courses, you'll find all the information and pointers to resources you need to get started.

GPS in the Schools

In many cases, GPS has snuck in through the back door of school systems. An educator who has experience with a GPS receiver (such as a geocacher or outdoor recreator) decides to incorporate GPS into his or her class.

As the price of GPS receivers continues to drop and they become easier to use and more common, teachers and students in primary and secondary schools will have greater access to GPS receivers as educational tools.

Some of the benefits that GPS receivers offer include

- ✔ **Providing technology training:** Students gain technology skills that can be used in the instruction of traditional subjects such as math, history, and geography.

- ✔ **Giving students practical hands-on and real world applications:** Understanding that math and geography have applications in addition to standard textbook theory can motivate students in these areas.

- ✔ **Capturing student attention:** Students are interested in the unique and different. (**Bonus:** You get them outside.)

- ✔ **Decreasing new course material development time:** A growing number of lesson plans and resources related to GPS are available on the Internet.

- ✔ **Providing value for your resource dollar:** GPS receivers are relatively inexpensive compared with other high-tech hardware. (You can purchase four or five low-end GPS receivers for the price of a single, low-end PC.) Additionally, receivers don't become obsolete as quickly as other computer technologies.

Take a look at some examples of how GPS and geocaching can be used in teaching different types of subjects. (This isn't meant to be an exhaustive list, and its main purpose is to get some ideas of your own percolating.)

Geography

Because the purpose behind GPS purpose is to provide accurate location data, you probably guessed that GPS and geography go hand-in-hand. You have lots of topical possibilities for using GPS in a geography class.

✔ **Latitude and longitude:** With a GPS receiver, you can clearly show students the basics of latitude and longitude by having them watch the coordinates change as they walk in a straight line. (A football field is a perfect spot for kids to get a handle on the distances associated with latitude and longitude minutes and seconds.)

✔ **Coordinate systems:** Setting up geocaches gives students a better spatial understanding of latitude and longitude and teaches them practical applications of coordinate systems.

✔ **Map reading:** By using GPS receivers in conjunction with widely available, free and low-cost Geographic Information System (GIS) and digital mapping software, you can make maps come alive by taking advantage of a digital map's interactive nature.

One of my favorite Web sites for learning about world geography is the Degree Confluence Project (`www.confluence.org`). The goal of this project is to collect digital photos of all the primary latitude and longitude line intersections on Earth. This is a remarkable tool for relating to the rest of the world outside your own backyard.

History and sociology

Although it seems logical to use GPS in geography-related courses, the technology is equally at home in history and other classes that are people-oriented.

Using GPS receivers to locate old trails, city boundaries, and significant historical sites helps students better relate to the past and present. For example, the Project Alternative Learning High School in Helena, Montana received a National Geographic Educational Foundation grant, part of which involved using GPS and GIS software to confirm or correct longitude and latitude measurements originally documented by Lewis and Clark.

You can choose how ambitious you want your project to be. A relatively simple activity could involve setting up a series of virtual geocaches that takes students on a walking tour of local historic sites. When students reach the waypoints associated with the sites, they answer questions about what they find.

Ecology

One of the primary uses for GPS receivers in ecology-related classes is as data loggers. Students use a GPS receiver to record the locations of plants and animals and then plot the locations on digital maps. A good example is the 7th-grade students in Nancy Spencer's Earth Sciences class in Waitsfield, Vermont, who used GPS and GIS to investigate the role of wildlife tracking and habitat mapping in landscape conservation and stewardship.

National Geographic has hundreds of teacher-used and -approved lesson plans for many different subjects; including a number that incorporate GPS. To check out the free online lesson plans, visit `www.nationalgeographic.com/xpeditions`.

Mathematics

The technology that makes GPS work relies on mathematics, and GPS can be used to teach time, distance, and speed concepts. With a GPS receiver, students can learn about basic principles such as determining the area of a polygon. Or they can get into more complex math, such as learning how the Pythagorean theorem, inverse trigonometric functions, and equations relating to circles and spheres all are used in making the GPS system work correctly. Basic math skills can be incorporated into a multicache or mystery cache (see Chapter 5 for more about these types of caches), such as completing an equation to get the correct coordinates of the cache.

For some excellent examples of using GPS and geocaching to teach various math concepts, see David Royster's *GPS: Global Positioning Systems and Mathematics* presentation and handout at `www.math.uncc.edu/~droyster`.

Physical education

I talk about health and fitness benefits that geocaching can bring to adults in Chapter 6, and the same holds true with kids. Setting up multicaches, dividing up a PE class into teams, and having the teams find the caches as quickly as possible is one possible application. GPS receivers can also measure the distance of jogging courses and average speeds to give students an idea of how fast they are going when they run a set distance in a certain amount of time. One unique use of GPS took place in a middle school in Howland, Maine, as part of its PE and health classes. Teacher Barb Hamlin received a grant for students to use GPS receivers and mapping software to create maps of local snowmobile trails. Previous maps of the area weren't very accurate. Along with the educational aspects, the activity was also a public service project because the new maps were to be made available to local snowmobilers.

Containerless caches

When it comes to geocaching and education, caches don't always consist of ammo cans and plastic containers. *Virtual* caches (which don't have a cache container associated with them) and *locationless* caches (which also don't have containers but sort of work in reverse where you locate something and then record its coordinates) are well suited for educational caches. (Read about all the different types of caches in Chapter 5.)

Some excellent locationless caches have been developed by New York educator Anton Ninno and appear in the Geocaching.com database. Here are a few caches that should give you some ideas.

Know your birds:
http://www.geocaching.com/seek/cache_details.aspx?ID=43009

Women of Courage:
http://www.geocaching.com/seek/cache_details.aspx?ID=36018

Native American History Lesson:
http://www.geocaching.com/seek/cache_details.aspx?ID=26263

Unfortunately, the Geocaching.com staff put a moratorium on locationless caches a while back, so for the time being, you can't add new caches of this type to the database. However, that doesn't stop you from creating your own locationless caches for your students and publishing them on a school Web site so they are available to anyone with an Internet connection.

As you can see, GPS receivers can be used in teaching a number of different subjects. If a school can acquire GPS receivers for student use, it makes sense to have them available for multiple teachers and classes. Don't get locked into the idea that GPS receivers can be used only for geography classes.

Incorporating GPS in a Class

Incorporating GPS into a class takes a little bit of thought and planning. In this section, I highlight some of the issues that you'll need to address when using GPS in the classroom. I discuss some curriculum considerations, give you some ideas on how and where to get GPS receivers for your students, and talk a little about evaluating your success.

Developing the curriculum

Because this book primarily focuses on geocaching and GPS, I'm not going to get into the fine points of curriculum and course material development. (If you're an educator, I'm sure you're already have that dialed in.) Rather, I cover a few issues to think about if you're considering adding a GPS or geocaching component to an existing curriculum or developing a new one wrapped around GPS.

Is there a fit?

First off, you should determine whether GPS or geocaching fits into the subject matter that you'll be teaching. Although I'm a techno-geek at heart, I don't believe in using technology for technology's sake. Trying to shoehorn technology into a curriculum when it really doesn't make sense is not a good idea — such as if you're not comfortable with the technology (which is okay) or if it doesn't significantly contribute to the educational goals of your class.

I'm also a big believer in applying a cost/benefit model to curriculum development. Educators are usually faced with limited time and small budgets, and I'm a fan of maximizing time and money investments to get the most educational bang for your buck. That means you should carefully estimate how much time, effort, and money it will cost to add a GPS component to a curriculum and then determine what the probable return will be on your investment.

Teaching students how to use GPS receivers

If you incorporate geocaching or GPS use in the classroom, both you and your students will need to know how to use a GPS receiver. If at a quick glance, you can't tell the difference between a cell-phone and a GPS receiver (although some of them do look the same) and have never used a receiver before, don't worry. You can find some excellent lesson plans and instructional materials that other educators have already developed that can bring you and your students up to speed. I list a number of different Internet resources at the end of this chapter that you can consult and download files from.

Adding geocaching to subject matter

If you already have course material developed for one of the subject you teach, you can add geocaching-related activities to engage students and reinforce topics you'll be covering.

For an example of incorporating geocaching into a 6th-grade Social Studies class, check out some of activities that Mike Seavert (a teacher at Whitnall Middle School in Greenfield, Wisconsin) came up with at www.whitnall.com/teachers/6th_grade/seavert/geocaching.htm.

Reading through the ideas and activities mentioned in this chapter should start you thinking about how to set up your own educational geocaches. Skim through the rest of the book to get a better understanding of the nuances of geocaching. Here are some general steps to help you get rolling:

1. **Determine what you want to get out of a geocaching activity.**

   This could be a better understanding of latitude and longitude, tracking the progress of a Travel Bug as it moves from cache to cache, or setting up a puzzle cache that relies on historical facts to find.

2. **Identify appropriate cache locations.**

   This could be a traditional cache hidden in a container or a virtual cache with a location and no cache container. You need to record the location coordinates of the cache, which I describe how to do in Chapter 8.

3. **Set up the cache.**

   This involves getting the cache ready. It could mean selecting a cache container (if you decide to use one), inserting goodies into the container, or coming up with clues that are associated with the cache.

4. **Announce the cache so your students can use it.**

   Here are the two ways to accomplish this:

   • *Use the Geocaching.com site:* Add your educational caches to the Geocaching.com database. Students will need to know how to access the Internet and use a Web browser to get the cache information — both very good skills to have. This approach makes the educational cache available to the general public.

   • *Provide cache information to students:* Use handouts or the school's Web site. This makes the cache a little more private and more under your control.

5. **Get your students geocaching!**

   It's the moment of truth — time to see how your activity turns out.

Acquiring GPS receivers

Obviously, you're going to need GPS receivers if you want to incorporate GPS or geocaching into a curriculum or class material. In terms of cost, you can currently purchase GPS receivers for around $100 that are more than adequate for educational use. (Check out Chapter 2 for some guidance on selecting a GPS receiver.)

 You certainly don't need to purchase one GPS receiver for every student in a class. In fact, GPS receivers really work well in small group activities. Depending on your class size and budget, you can develop activities in which 2–7 students share a GPS receiver and work together as a team.

Some possible ways to acquire GPS receivers for classroom use include

- Technology-in-education grants

- Fund raising events

- Loaned units from recreational businesses (ski resorts, guide services, and other companies that might use GPS receivers)

- Education-friendly GPS retailers that might make you a great deal on GPS receivers

- GPS receivers loaned from your students' parents

 If at all possible, try to standardize the GPS receiver models you'll be purchasing and using in the classroom. Although all receivers have the same basic features, their user interfaces vary considerably from model to model and even within a brand. Using a single model is much easier to teach (and troubleshoot).

Evaluating your success

After you've used a GPS or geocaching activity in a class, at some point, take a few moments to evaluate its success. Here are some questions to ask yourself:

- Did you incorporate pre- and post-testing to measure instructional effectiveness? What were the outcomes?

- Were there any differences in grades associated with past classes that didn't use GPS as part of the course?

✔ How did your students respond to the activity?

✔ Was the activity worth the time it took to develop and implement, and will you use it again?

Regardless of the results, share the outcome with other educators. By incorporating GPS in your class, you're something of a pioneer, and sharing your experiences with others is beneficial so they can learn from your efforts. In the next section, I list some Internet resources, including a great e-mail list where you can interact with other educators who use or are interested in using GPS in the classroom.

Educational Internet Resources

If using GPS and geocaching for education interests you, you don't need to be the Lone Ranger in figuring everything out. The Internet has a wealth of resources where you can download lesson plans, interact with other educators, and come up to speed on GPS technology. Here is a list of essential resources:

✔ **NYGPS** (`http://groups.yahoo.com/group/nygps`): NYGPS is a Yahoo! Group started by New York educator Anton Ninno. Its purpose is to serve as a clearinghouse for information on GPS-related educational material. You'll find articles, lesson plans, lively discussion, and an extensive collection of resources on using GPS in the classroom. I highly recommend joining this group. Don't just rely on group e-mail messages. The collection of links and documents that Ninno has available through the group home page is remarkable.

✔ **Lane Education Service District** (`www.lane.k12.or.us/insttech/vtc/gps.html`): The Lane Education Service District (Lane County, Oregon) has an excellent GPS in education Web page. Educator Lynn Lary has given workshops and written articles that promote the use of GPS as an educational tool. This Web page contains many of Lary's resources and is a great starting place for anyone interested in including GPS and geocaching in K–12 curriculums.

✔ **Louisiana Center for Educational Studies** (`www.doe.state.la.us/lde/lcet/398.html`): The Louisiana Department of Education INTECH 2 Social Studies CD is a complete series of lesson plans and classroom materials for teaching students about GIS and GPS; including a section on geocaching. The original contents of the CD were placed on this Web site and provide a great resource for teachers.

✔ **Institute for the Application of Geospatial Technology (IAGT) at Cayuga Community College** (www.iagt.org): The IAGT is a not-for-profit organization that specializes in the application of Geographic Information Technologies (GIT) — science-speak for activities relating to GPS, GIS, and remote-sensing. Part of IAGT's mission is to help teachers incorporate GIT in their classrooms. Every year, the IAGT sponsors CORSE (Conference on Remote Sensing Education), which teaches educators about geospatial technology and how to include it in course material. In addition to sponsoring the conference, the IAGT also maintains a collection of GPS-related lesson plans and resources on its Web site.

✔ **GPS In Education Geocaching.com forum** (http://forums.groundspeak.com/gc): One of the Web discussion groups in the Geocaching.com forums is GPS In Education, which is devoted to educators and using GPS, including geocaching, in the classroom. Anyone can browse through past messages, but you need a free account to post messages.

Part IV
The Part of Tens

The 5th Wave   By Rich Tennant

"Okay, Darryl, I think it's time to admit we didn't load the onboard mapping software correctly."

In this part . . .

The foundations of geocaching are based on slick technology, and this is the techie part of the book. No, not the high-level math that makes GPS work but rather the more practical applications that anyone can use. In Chapter 12, I list ten of what I consider to be the best geocaching resources on the Internet. You'll find Web sites with how-to information, cool historical facts, and a few surprises thrown in as well. In Chapter 13, I clue you in to some of the most popular free and shareware programs that geocachers use. You'll find programs that serve as cache databases on PCs and PDAs, software that plots cache locations on aerial photos and topographic maps, and utilities that convert different format types of GPS-related data.

Chapter 12

Ten Internet Geocaching Resources

In This Chapter

▶ www.geocaching.com

▶ www.navicache.com

▶ http://brillig.com/geocaching

▶ www.gpsvisualizer.com

▶ www.todayscacher.com

▶ www.geocacher-u.com

▶ http://members.aol.com/_ht_a/marklent60544/myhomepage/ Geocaching/markwellcachemain.htm

▶ www.keenpeople.com

▶ http://members.cox.net/pkpublic/index.html

▶ www.letterboxing.org

▶ www.gpsinformation.net

*B*ecause geocaching relies so much on the Internet, it shouldn't come as too much of a surprise that a number of Web sites are devoted to the sport. In this chapter, I give you the lowdown on ten great geocaching Web sites (plus a bonus GPS site) that you should definitely check out.

Geocaching.com

www.geocaching.com

This is the primary geocaching site on the 'Net — you might have already guessed that from me talking about the site so much in this book. In addition to an extensive database of caches and FAQs about the sport, the site also has a large number of forums dedicated to different geocaching topics.

Navicache.com

www.navicache.com

This is the second-largest Web site dedicated to geocaching; but it's still quite a bit smaller than Geocaching.com in terms of caches listed. The site has many of the same features as Geocaching.com and is viewed by some geocachers as an alternative to the larger, more mainstream site. You'll note some duplication in the cache listings between the two sites, but you should always check them both when you're checking out lists of caches hidden in an area. The more caches to search for, the better.

The geocaching community is not immune to politics. Small skirmishes and large-scale battles can break out between individuals and rival Web sites. It's best just to duck your head, look at your GPS receiver, and head to a cache waypoint.

Buxley's Geocaching Waypoint

http://brillig.com/geocaching

This Web site has an extensive collection of world maps that provide a bird's-eye view of geocaches. Dots on the maps represent caches; when you click a dot, you go to the Geocaching.com information page associated with that cache. This is a great way to scout caches by area. The site also has geocaching statistics, event listings, and other information related to the sport.

GPS Visualizer

www.gpsvisualizer.com

Okay, it's not geocaching-specific, but it is a very cool and useful Web site. GPS Visualizer generates maps based on GPS data that you upload to the site. You can overlay GPS waypoints, including Geocaching.com *LOC files* (a file format that contains waypoint information), onto aerial and satellite photos and topographic and street maps to plot exactly where a cache is located. GPS Visualizer is perfect if you don't want to (or for some reason can't) install mapping programs on your PC. One of its benefits to international users is that it can create maps of areas both inside and outside the United States. GPS Visualizer is currently free although the author does ask for a small donation if you find the site useful.

Today's Cacher

www.todayscacher.com

Today's Cacher is an online magazine devoted to geocaching. The Web site debuted in the spring of 2004 and includes first-person geocaching accounts, descriptions of cool caches, editorials, and miscellaneous hints and tips. The articles are well written, informative, and entertaining. You should definitely put this site in your Web browser's bookmarks to check every month.

Geocacher University

www.geocacher-u.com

The goal of this Web site is to provide educational material to both new and experienced geocachers. The site features an excellent *Let's Go Geocaching!* brochure that you can download and print to give to people who are interested in the sport. (One geocacher claims that the brochure saved him from getting arrested when he showed it to a law enforcement officer who wondered what he was up to.)

Markwell's FAQs

http://members.aol.com/_ht_a/marklent60544/
myhomepage/Geocaching/markwellcachemain.htm

When you need information that goes beyond the Geocaching.com FAQ, this Web site is the place to visit for a comprehensive collection of facts. Markwell is a longtime geocacher out of the Chicago area who has gained a reputation as a font of knowledge as well as having a near-photographic memory for topics discussed in the Geocaching.com forums. In fact, his name has been turned into a verb on the forums and is synonymous with citing a thread (or threads) where a topic was already talked about, ending the need to discuss it again.

KeenPeople.com

www.keenpeople.com

This Web site is a friendly, open community of geocachers and outdoors enthusiasts. You'll find geocaching news, stats, and some great map and GPS resources.

The First 100 Geocaches

http://members.cox.net/pkpublic/index.html

If you're a geocache history buff, this Web site is for you. It contains a list of the 100 oldest geocaches, including who hid them, their location, and whether they're still active or not. This site is fun just to see how the sport got started only a few short years ago.

Letterboxing North America

www.letterboxing.org

Letterboxing is a forerunner of geocaching that has British roots. It involves hiding logbooks and specially made rubber stamps in waterproof boxes. The hider gives clues to a box's location (no GPS receivers are required). When a searcher finds the box, she stamps the box's logbook with her personal stamp and then stamps her personal logbook with the box's stamp. Every box and letter-boxer has unique stamps (some very much works of art), so the logbooks turn into an aesthetic historical record. Letterboxing has a certain elegance and Old World charm to it and can even be more challenging than geocaching. This Web site tells you everything you need to know to get started with letterboxing in the U.S. (It also has references to international letterboxing sites.)

GPSInformation.net

www.gpsinformation.net

Finally, because geocaching is so dependent on GPS, I've got to mention the best source of information on the Internet, GPSInformation.net. This comprehensive Web site has GPS receiver reviews, technical data, and addresses just about any question about GPS you might have. If you're in the market for a new GPS receiver or want to get the most out of your current receiver, this is the place to visit.

Chapter 13

Ten Geocaching Programs

In This Chapter

▶ GSAK

▶ GPXSonar

▶ CacheMate

▶ Watcher

▶ Plucker

▶ GPX Spinner

▶ GPX2HTML

▶ GPSBabel

▶ USAPhotoMaps

▶ TopoFusion

*W*hen it comes to computers, geocaching doesn't mean just using Internet and Web sites. You can use a number of standalone programs on your PC or PDA to assist with your geocaching hobby. In this chapter, I present ten programs that are especially useful for geocachers. All these software programs are free or are nominally priced shareware titles, so you don't need to come up with a lot of cash to use them. (Sorry, I've been waiting the entire book to include that pun.)

You can purchase GPS receiver cards to use with a Palm or Pocket PC PDA. In fact, some geocachers rely on GPS-equipped PDAs instead of conventional handheld GPS receivers. Using a PDA with an integrated GPS receiver provides some slick benefits, including the ability to use detailed topographic maps and geocaching software in the field away from your PC. However, remember that PDAs aren't waterproof, are considerably more fragile than handheld GPS receivers, and have a significantly shorter battery life than a GPS receiver. Expect to spend roughly $150–$250 for a GPS card.

Geocaching Swiss Army Knife (GSAK)

http://gsak.net

The popular Geocaching Swiss Army Knife (commonly known by its abbreviation, GSAK) lives up to its name of being one of the most multi-purpose, do-everything, geocaching programs around. This free Windows program serves as a database for caches you've found or are looking for; an interface to GPS receivers for uploading and downloading waypoints; and a utility for exporting cache location information to digital mapping programs such as DeLorme Street Atlas USA (www.delorme.com), Microsoft Streets & Trips (www.microsoft.com/streets/default.asp), and National Geographic TOPO! (http://maps.nationalgeographic.com/topo).

GPXSonar

http://gpxsonar.homeip.net/default.aspx

GPXSonar is a free program for Pocket PC PDAs for those whose goal is zero-paper geocaching. The utility manages cache data that you download from Geocaching.com. You can view cache information, log finds, generate reports, and export cache waypoints to GPS receivers.

CacheMate

www.smittyware.com/palm/cachemate

If you're a Palm PDA user, check out CacheMate, a cache information manager and database. The big advantage to programs like GPXSonar and CacheMate is that you don't need to constantly print out geocache information pages every time you go hunting for a cache. Just load cache data from Geocaching.com onto your PDA, and you're ready to go. CacheMate is priced at $7.

 If you use a database program on your PDA for keeping track of caches, instead of just loading the next cache you plan on looking for, consider loading a number of caches you haven't located yet. This allows you to be spontaneous with your geocaching adventures. When you have some free time, just grab your PDA and GPS receiver, and you can go after caches that aren't on your found list yet.

Watcher

http://clayjar.com

One of the benefits of becoming a Premium Member of Geocaching.
com (see Chapter 5) is the ability to download Pocket Queries —
information about up to 500 geocaches saved to a single GPX format
file. (*GPX* stands for GPS Exchange, which is a format that makes it
easy for mapping and GPS programs to exchange data.) Watcher is
a popular and free Windows program that manages Pocket Query
cache information. After you download a Pocket Query for selected
caches, Watcher provides you with all the cache information that
you'd normally find on the Geocaching.com site without the need
for an Internet connection. The program has a number of powerful
filtering options that display only those caches that meet your
search criteria.

Plucker

http://plkr.org

Plucker is a free offline Web browser that works with Palm OS PDAs.
That is, it can access saved HTML Web pages so you can view the
Web pages at some later time without an Internet connection. You
can use Plucker to view geocache information pages that have
been saved from Geocaching.com.

To get the HTML files into a format that Plucker understands,
Windows, Linux, and Mac OS X desktop versions of Plucker are
available (http://desktop.plkr.org) that save Web pages on
your PC and then sync them with your Palm.

Better yet are geocaching-specific programs such as GPX Spinner
(www.gpxspinner.com) and GPX2HTML (a free utility available
at http://home.comcast.net/~fizzymagic/gpx2html.html),
which create HTML files on your PC from GPX data that you can
then upload to your Palm PDA.

GPSBabel

http://gpsbabel.sourceforge.net

GPSBabel is a free, must-have utility for any GPS receiver owner
who deals with digital maps and software programs that interface
with GPS data. One of the big challenges for a GPS user is the wide

array of waypoint, route, and track log data formats. For example, trying to transfer waypoints stored in one map program to another can be extremely frustrating. As its name suggests (from the Biblical Tower of Babel), GPSBabel eliminates many of the communication problems that you encounter when you try to get two programs or different brands of GPS receivers to work with the other's GPS data. GPSBabel can convert waypoints, tracks, and routes from one format to another. Windows, Linux, and Mac versions of the program are available.

Find an online version of GPSBabel available at `http://wayhoo.com/index/a/gpsbabel`, where you can do all your conversions with a Web browser and Internet connection.

USAPhotoMaps

`http://jdmcox.com`

TerraServer-USA (`www.terraserver-usa.com`) is a cool Web site that displays aerial photos and topographic maps of the United States. USAPhotoMaps is a free, standalone Windows program that downloads TerraServer-USA images to your PC, creating scrollable maps on your hard drive that you can zoom in and out. Even better yet, the program interfaces with GPS receivers and can download a waypoint that you've created for a geocache, overlaying its location on a map or an aerial photo. Although USAPhotoMaps is free, the author asks for a small donation if you find the program useful.

TopoFusion

`www.topofusion.com`

TopoFusion is another Windows program that uses TerraServer-USA data to display aerial photos and topographic maps. In addition to being able to plot geocache waypoint locations on maps, TopoFusion also has a number of powerful features, such as creating three-dimensional maps based on terrain elevation, extensive waypoint and track point management, and the ability to link digital photos with GPS coordinates. The extensive feature list and the fast image display speed make this one of my favorite PC mapping programs. TopoFusion is priced at $40, but you can download a trial version of the software (fully functional but prints "DEMO" on parts of the map).

Index

Numerics

2-D and 3-D determinations, 25
9/11 terrorist attack, impact on
    geocaching, 148
10,000-step programs, 127

• A •

accessories (GPS receivers), 39–40
accuracy of GPS receivers, 10, 27–30
activating routes, 52
Adventure Medical Kits Web site, 119
agency representatives, handling
    contacts from, 160
agonic line, 64
Alabama Geocachers Association
    Web site, 181
Alaska Geocaching Web site, 181
aliases, user names
  choosing, 97
  online searches using, 103
  viewing, 105
almanac data, 54
altimeters (GPS receivers), 37
ammo cans
  as containers, 145–146
  opening, 132–133
antennas (GPS receivers)
  external antennas, 35
  internal, 34–35
archived caches, 17, 139, 144, 159
Arizona Geocaching Web site, 181
Arkansas State Parks Web site, 181
atlases, 73
atomic clocks, 23
autorouting feature, 38–39
azimuth, 67, 83

• B •

back bearing, 84
back-track feature (GPS receivers),
    137

base plate compasses, 65, 69
basemaps, 32
basic account (Geocaching.com), 97
batteries (GPS receivers)
  battery needs, 41
  for electronic compasses, 36–37
  extra, need for, 118–119
  Internet information about, 58
  types, 35–36
Battery University Web site, 58
Be Expert with Map and Compass
    (Kjellström), 88
bearings
  defined, 83
  taking, 64, 84–85
benchmark hunting
  challenges, 172–173
  defined, 19
  documenting findings, 174
  equipment needs, 172
  logging finds, 174–175
  search process, 173–174
benchmark page (Geocaching.com)
  contents, 167–169
  information details, 169
  searching for, 166–167
benchmarks
  defined, 163
  locating using Geocaching.com, 166
  NGS datasheets, 169–171
  photo gallery, 166
  types of, 165
  vertical control points, 164
bezel (compasses), 67
blocked signals, 29
BMGPX benchmark plotting program,
    169–171
Brunton Web site, 70
building height and receiver
    accuracy, 29
burying caches, 148
Buxley's Geocaching Waypoint Web
    site, 200

• C •

cache DNF (Did Not Find), 130
Cache In, Trash Out (CITO), 142
cache information page. *See*
  geocache information pages
cache machine, defined, 17
CacheMate program, 204
caches
  alias of placer, 105
  cache types, 101–102, 144
  containers for, 144–146
  closing and sealing, 137
  date last found, 105
  defined, 10, 11
  distance and direction indicators,
    105
  DNF (Did Not Find) caches, 141
  D/T (Difficulty/Terrain) rating,
    104, 108
  events caches, 94
  finding directions for, 122–124
  icons, 103
  impossible-to-find, troubleshooting,
    140
  information page for, 153–158
  leaving and trading trinkets,
    135–136
  letterbox hybrids, 94
  locating and choosing a cache to
    find, 91
  log caches, 96
  logging finds, 137–140
  microcaches, 96
  multicaches, 92–93
  mystery caches, 93
  official descriptive name, 105
  online searches for, 101–102
  opening, 131–133
  placement date, 104
  placing and stocking, 151
  themed, 95
  traditional, 92
  virtual and locationless, 93, 191
  waypoint name, 105
  writing descriptions of, 104–105
C/A-code (Coarse Acquisition) radio
    signals, 24, 28

calibrating electronic compasses, 37
California, geocaching clubs in, 181
camouflage painting for containers
    145
cardinal compass points, 70
cellphones, 120–122
Central Oregon Geocaching Web
    site, 183
Chicago Geocachers Web site, 182
Chicagoland Geocachers Web site, 182
citation (maps), 76, 78
CITO (Cache In, Trash Out), 142
classrooms, using GPS in, 187–188
ClayJar Web site, 156
clocks, accurate, importance of, 23
clothing needs, 116
clubs
  advantages of joining, 177–179
  listing of by state, 181–184
  online searches for, 100
clue caches, 92–93
clues, hints
  on geocache information pages,
    108–109
  for hard-to-find caches, 140
  spoilers, 18, 100
Coarse Acquisition radio signals
    (C/A-code), 24, 28
collar (maps), 76
color screens (GPS receivers), 31
Colorado Geocaching Association
    Web site, 182
compass rose (maps), 76
compasses, electronic
  as battery drain, 41
  calibrating, 37
  on GPS receivers, 36–37
  using, 126
  waypoint direction headings, 60
compasses, magnetic
  base plate, 65, 69
  bearings, 64
  declination, 63–64
  dials, 67
  and GPS receiver accuracy, 29
  holding and reading, 82–83
  how they work, 62–65

manufacturers of, 70
needle, 66
north direction, 63
optional features, 67–68
pocket compasses, 70
as a protractor, 86
recommended features, 71
sighting, 69–70
triangulation using, 87–88
usefulness of, 17, 61, 62, 114
using for last 30 feet, 128
using with maps, 81–82
competitive geocaching, 184–186
computers on satellites, 23
Consolidated Space Operations
　Center (CSOC), 24
containers
　choosing, preparing, 12, 144–146
　as clue to cache location, 128–129
　maintaining and replacing, 159
contour intervals, 79
contour lines (maps), 72, 78–81
control points, 163–166
controls, external (GPS receivers), 42
converting NAD 24 to/from WGS
　84, 107
coordinate marks (maps), 76, 77–78
coordinate systems
　choosing during setup, 57
　latitude and longitude, 16, 44–47
　teaching about, 189
　UTM (Universal Transverse
　　Mercator), 47–49
coordinates
　benchmark hunting, 163
　entering as waypoints, 58
　hiding, 12
　for new caches, recording, 151
　viewing and downloading, 107
costs
　compasses, 69–70
　of GPS receivers, 16
country
　of cache, viewing in search results,
　　105
　online searches using, 100–102
courses, setting, 83, 85

creating caches
　adding identifying information, 152
　adding treasures, Travel Bugs,
　　152–153, 159
　container options, 128–129
　logbooks and writing utensils,
　　151–152
CSOC (Consolidated Space
　Operations Center), 24
current location
　marking as waypoint, 58
　viewing on receiver screen
　　display, 55
curricula using GPS
　developing, 191–193
　evaluating effectiveness of, 193–195
customizing defaults (GPS receivers),
　56–57

• *D* •

dampened magnetic needles, 66
Dana, Peter (Geographer's Craft Web
　site), 50
datums, 49–50, 57
daypacks, 115
decimal degrees (latitude and
　longitude), 47
declination, 63–65, 83
Degree Confluence Project, 189, 19
degrees (measurement units)
　on compass dials, 67, 83
　and declination values, 64
　latitude and longitude, 45–46
dehydration prevention, 116
DeLorme Web site, 74
Department of Defense, U.S., 26. *See
　also* Global Positioning System
　(GPS)
Description column (geocaching
　page), 104
Designation column (benchmark
　page), 168
DGPS (Differential GPS), 27–28
dials (magnetic compasses), 67
Did Not Find (DNF) caches,
　18, 130, 141

Didn't find it log entries (geocache information page), 138
Differential GPS (DGPS), 27–28
difficulty ratings, 104, 108
digital cameras
  bringing on searches, 117
  documenting benchmarks using, 174
digital maps, 74–75
direction of caches, 104
directional arrows, 60
display screens (GPS receivers), 42
Distance column (benchmark page), 168
distance of caches, 104
DNF (Did Not Find) caches, 18, 130, 141
drawings, GPS, 19
drinking water safety, 116
driving directions, sources for, 122–124
D/T (Difficulty/Terrain) column (geocaching page), 104

• *E* •

Easting units (UTM), 49
ecology courses, using GPS in, 189–190
educational applications of GPS
  as benefit of geocaching, 15
  classroom uses, 187–188
  curriculum development, 191–193
  ecology courses, 189–190
  geography skills, 188–189
  history and sociology courses, 189
  Internet resources on, 195–196
electronic compasses
  as battery drain, 41
  calibrating, 37
  on GPS receivers, 36–37
  using, 126
  waypoint direction headings, 60
electronic maps
  datums, 49–50
  display screens, 31
  versus paper maps, 33
  as proprietary data, 33

routes, 51–52
waypoints and tracks, 32, 51, 52–53
elevation determinations, 25
ellipsoids, 49–50
Emerald Valley Cachers Web site, 183
emergency situations, 135
encrypting online log entries, 139
EPE (Estimated Position Error) number, 56, 128
ephemeris data
  defined, 24–25
  errors in, and receiver accuracy, 29
  initializing GPS receivers using, 54
equator, 45
errors from NAVSTAR satellites, built-in, 28
Estimated Position Error (EPE) number, 56, 128
etiquette, 142
event caches
  defined, 18, 94
  locating, 179–180
event calendar (Geocaching.com), 179–180
exercise
  as benefit of geocaching, 14, 16
  10,000-step programs, 127
external antennas (GPS receivers), 35
external controls (GPS receivers), 42

• *F* •

Family Radio Service (FRS) radios, 118
field notebooks, 115
field work, 64
Find column (geocache information page), 109
finding caches
  closing caches and leaving area, 137
  giving up, 141
  hard-to-find caches, troubleshooting, 140
  opening caches, 131–133
  removing and replacing treasures, 135–136
  signing logbooks, 133–135

first aid supply needs, 119–120
The First 100 Geocaches Web site, 202
First to Find (FTF), defined, 18
flashlights, 120
Florida Geocachers Web site, 182
food supplies, 115–116
forums (Geocaching.com), 175, 184
Found column (benchmark page), 168
Found It log entry (geocache
    information page), 138
FRS (Family Radio Service) radios, 118
FTF (First to Find), defined, 18

• *G* •

gazetteers, 73
General Mobile Radio Service (GMRS)
    radios, 118
geocache identification sticker, 152
geocache information pages
  accessing, 106
  cache coordinates, 107
  cache-hider's name/alias, 107
  carrying during searches, 113–114
  clues, 108
  date hidden, 108
  detailed descriptions, 108
  difficulty and terrain ratings, 108
  hints, 109
  links to nearby caches,
      benchmarks, 109
  logging visits and finds, 110, 137–139
  mapping location from, 109–110
  for new caches, creating, 153–158
  official descriptive name, 106
  spoilers, 110
  updating, 159–160
  waypoints, waypoint names,
      108, 139
Geocacher University Web site, 201
Geocachers of Central Kentucky Web
    site, 182
Geocachers of Southeast Tennessee
    Web site, 183
geocaches. *See* caches

geocaching
  appeal and benefits, 11–15
  competitive geocaching, 184–186
  statistics, 141
geocaching clubs
  advantages of joining, 177–179
  listing of by state, 181–184
Geocaching Hampton Roads Web
    site, 184
Geocaching Swiss Army Knife (GSAK)
    program, 204
geocaching teams, 178
Geocaching.com Web site
  account options, 96–97
  aliases, 97
  benchmark information,
      163–164, 166
  cache approval process, 158
  cache list page, 103–105
  event calendar, 179–180
  FAQ, 144
  forums, 175, 184
  GPS in Education forum, 196
  hiding coordinates on, 12
  legal disclaimers, 157
  locating caches using, 91
  logging found benchmarks in,
      174–175
  MAP IT button, 105
  navigating cache list page, 105–106
  posting photographs on, 117
  recording new caches, 153–157
  resources lists, 9
  searching, advanced techniques,
      101–103
  searching, basic techniques, 98–101
  statistical information, 141
geocoins, 18, 153
geodashing, 19
geodesy, 164
Geographer's Craft Web site
    (Dana), 50
geographic north, 63
geography skills, teaching using GPS,
    188–189
Georgia Geocachers Association Web
    site, 182

global compasses, 68
Global Positioning System (GPS). *See also* GPS receivers
  as core geocaching technology, 10
  education uses, curriculum development, 187–193
  ground stations, 24
  history, 26
  space segment (satellites), 22–24
GMRS (General Mobile Radio Service) radios, 118
Google searches, 100, 180
GPS (Global Positioning System). *See also* GPS receivers
  as core geocaching technology, 10
  education uses, curriculum development, 187–193
  ground stations, 24
  history, 26
  space segment (satellites), 22–24
GPS: Global Positioning Systems and Mathematics (Royster), 190
GPS Hawaii Web site, 182
GPS Information Web site, 42, 58
GPS receivers
  accessories, 41
  accuracy, 26–27, 29–30, 128
  acquiring for schools, 194
  almanac data, 25
  altimeters, 37
  antennas, 34–35
  autorouting feature, 38–39
  back-track feature, 137
  batteries, 35–36, 41
  carrying during searches, 112–113
  customizing defaults, 56–57
  datums, 50
  described, 22
  display screens, user interface, 31–32, 42
  electronic compasses, 36–37
  EPE (Estimated Position Error) number, 56
  ephemeris data, 25
  external controls, 42
  finding optimal satellite coverage, 151
  GPS drawings, 19

how they work, 25
importance of, 14, 16, 40
initializing, 54
latitude and longitude readings, 44–47
manufacturers, 39
mapping capabilities, 32–33, 40
memory, 33, 41
PC interface, 34, 42
plot displays, 60
routes, 51–52
satellite status page, 55–56
shells, 30–31
software and accessory programs, 39, 204–205
storage capacity, 51, 53
survey-grade receivers, 27–28
tracks, 52–53
2-D and 3-D determinations, 25
using to locate caches, 12–13, 59, 125–126
UTM (Universal Transverse Mercator), 47–49
WAAS (Wide Area Augmentation System), 37–38
waypoints, 51, 57–59
weight and size, 42
GPS Visualizer Web site, 200
GPSBabel program, 205–206
GPSInformation.net Web site, 202
GPSR/GPSr (GPS Receiver), described, 18
GPXSonar program, 204
Great Britain, benchmarks, 163
Great Plains Geocaching Web site, 182, 183, 184
grid searches, 130
ground stations, 22, 24
Groundspeak Premium Membership (Geocaching.com), 97
GSAK (Geocaching Swiss Army Knife) program, 204

• *H* •

haunted caches, 93
Hawaii, geocaching clubs in, 182
headlamps, 120

hidden caches, 100
hiding caches
  deciding on a location, 147–150
  hiding tips, 149–150
  locations to avoid, 148, 160
  recording location, 151
hints, clues
  on geocache information pages,
    108–109
  for hard-to-find caches, 140
  spoilers, 18, 100
history
  of geocaching, 10
  of Global Positioning System, 26
history courses, using GPS in, 189
hitchhiker, 18
holding compasses, 82–83
horizontal control points, 164
household plastic containers, 145
HTML (Web page formatting
    codes), 156
Huntsville Area Geocachers Web
    site, 181
hypothermia, preventing, 116

• *I* •

I Wish I Did Not Find (IWIDNF)
    situations, 135
IAGT (Institute for Application of
    Geospatial Technology), 196
Icon column (cache list page), 103
icons
  for benchmarks, 167
  for caches, 92–93
  for Travel Bugs (TBs), 95
  viewing in search results, 103
Idaho Geocachers Web site, 182
Illinois Central Area Cache Hunting
    Enthusiasts Web site, 182
Imaging resource Web site, 58
inclinometer, 68
index contour, 79
Indiana, geocaching clubs in, 182
initializing GPS receivers, 54
Institute for Application of Geospatial
    Technology (IAGT) Web site, 196

intermediate contours, 79
internal antennas (GPS receivers),
    34–35
International Date Line, 45
Internet. *See* online searches; Web
    sites
ionosphere conditions and receiver
    accuracy, 29
Iowa, geocaching clubs in, 182
IWIDNF (I Wish I Did Not Find)
    situations, 135

• *K* •

Kansas, geocaching clubs in, 182
KeenPeople.com Web site, 201
Kentucky, geocaching clubs in, 182
keyword searches, 102
kilometer, 48
Kjellström, Björn (*Be Expert with Map
    and Compass*), 88

• *L* •

landmarks. *See* waypoints
Lane Education Service District Web
    site, 195
language settings, 57
Last Found column (cache list page),
    103–105
Last Log column (benchmark page),
    168
latitude
  measuring, 44–47
  searching by, 102
  teaching about, 189
  2-D and 3-D determinations, 25
Leave No Trace Web site, 142
legal disclaimers, 157
legend (maps), 76
legs (routes), 51, 85–86
lensatic compasses, 70
letterbox hybrid caches, 94
letterboxing, 13, 94, 202
Linklater, Andro (*Measuring America*),
    164
locationless caches, 93, 191

locations, hiding places
  choosing, 147–148, 149–150
  locations to avoid, 148–149, 160
  recording, 151
lodestone (magnetite), 62
log caches, 96
Log Your Visit button (geocache
    information page), 137–138
logbooks
  adding to new caches, 151–152
  maintaining, replacing, 158
  signing, 13, 96, 115, 133–135
logging
  benchmark finds, 174–175
  cache visits and finds, 110, 137–140
  Travel Bugs, 136
Long Range Aid to Navigation
    (LORAN), 26
longitude
  measuring, 44–47
  searching by, 102
  teaching about, 189
  2-D and 3-D determinations, 25
LORAN (Long Range Aid to
    Navigation), 26
Louisiana Center for Educational
    Studies Web site, 195
Louisiana Geocaching Web site, 182

• *M* •

magnetic fields, 36
magnetic needles (magnetic
    compasses), 66
magnetic north, 63–64
magnetite (lodestone), 62
magnifying glasses, 68
mAh (milliampere-hours), 58
maintaining caches, 158–160
map reading skills, 189
Map Tools Web site, 78
mapped area, 76
mapping models (GPS receivers), 40
MapQuest Web site
  geocache locations, 75
  getting driving directions using,
    122–124

maps, electronic
  datums, 49–50
  display screens, 31
  versus paper maps, 33
  as proprietary data, 33
  routes, 51–52
  waypoints and tracks, 32, 51, 52–53
maps, online
  accessing from geocache
    information page, 109–110
  driving directions, 122–124
  uploadable, 32
  viewing locations using, 74–75
maps, paper and printed
  bringing on searches, 114
  coordinate marks, 77
  orienting to north, 83–84
  planimetric, 72–73
  printing from the Internet, 75
  scale, 75–77
  street maps, 74
  topographic, 72–73
  triangulation using, 87–88
  usefulness of, 16, 17, 61, 71–72
  USGS topo maps, 74
  using with compasses, 81–82
Maptech Terrain Navigator Pro, 166
Maptech Web site, 74
marks. *See* waypoints
Markwell's FAQs Web site, 201
Maryland Geocaching Society Web
    site, 182
mathematics courses, 190
McToys, 18, 114, 136
measurement units
  choosing during setup, 57
  degrees, 45–46, 64, 67, 83
  seconds, 46
  scale, 76–77
Measuring America (Linklater), 164
*Medicine for Mountaineering & Other
    Wilderness Activities*
    (Wilkerson), 119
memory (GPS receivers), 33, 41
metal disk benchmarks, 165
metal objects and compass use, 71
metric system, 47–49

Michigan Geocaching Organization Web site, 135
microcaches, 96
Middle Tennessee Geocachers Web site, 183
milliampere-hours (MaH), 58
Minnesota Geocaching Association Web site, 182
minutes, 46
Mississippi Geocachers Association Web site, 182
Missouri, Arkansas Geocaching Association Web site, 181, 182
monochrome LCD screen (GPS receivers), 31
The Mountaineers Web site, 121
Muggles
  defined, 18
  tips for dealing with, 125, 128
multicaches, 92–93
multipath errors, 29–30
mystery caches
  defined, 93
  searching for, by state, 100

• *N* •

NAD 27 (North American Datum 1927)
  converting from WGS 84, 50
  features, 49
naming, names
  caches, 104, 106, 155
  user names, aliases, 97, 105
  waypoints, 59, 105, 112–113
National Geodetic Survey (NGS)
  benchmarks, 19, 163–164, 166, 169–171
National Geographic education programs, 189
Navicache.com Web site, 200
navigating
  and declination, 65
  maps and compasses for, 83–88
  navigational hints, 60
  to waypoints, 59–60

NAVSTAR (Navigation Satellite Timing and Ranging) satellites
  built-in errors, 28
  data received from, 25
  history, 26
NE Ohio Geocachers Web site, 183
neatline (maps), 76
Nebraska, geocaching clubs in, 183
Needs archived option (geocache information page), 139
neocacher, defined, 18
Nevada Geocaching Web site, 183
New York Geocaching Organization Web site, 183
newsgroups, USENET, 11, 58
NGS (National Geodetic Survey)
  benchmarks, 19, 163–164, 166, 169–171
nickel metal-hydride (NiMH) batteries, 36
nicknames, for caches, 155
9/11 terrorist attack, impact on geocaching, 148
no account option (Geocaching. com), 96
North American Datum 1927 (NAD 27)
  converting from WGS 84, 50
  features, 49
North Carolina Geocachers Association Web site, 183
north (compasses), 63–64
North Dakota, geocaching clubs in, 183
Northing values (UTM), 49
notebooks, field, 115
NUDET (NUclear DETonation) sensors, 23
NYGPS Web site, 195

• *O* •

Odden's Bookmarks map link Web site, 75
offset caches, 92
Ohio, Kentucky and Indiana Cachers Web site, 182, 183

Oklahoma Geocachers Web site, 183
online maps
  accessing from geocache
    information page, 109–110
  driving directions, 122–124
  viewing locations using, 74–75
online searches
  for benchmarks, 167
  by country, 100
  by geocache type, 101–102
  locating caches, 14
  by state, 99–100
  by ZIP code, 97–99
opening caches, 131–133
organizations, geocaching, 100,
    181–184
Oregon Geocaching Web site, 183
orientation, topographic, 84
orienteering, 17, 84
origins, 10–11
outdoor recreation, 16
Ozark Mountains Geocachers Web
    site, 181, 182

• *P* •

pacing, 87
paper and printed maps
  bringing on searches, 114
  coordinate marks, 77
  orienting to north, 83–84
  planimetric, 72–73
  printing from the Internet, 75
  scale, 75–77
  street maps, 74
  topographic, 72–73
  triangulation using, 87–88
  usefulness of, 16, 17, 61, 71–72
  USGS topo maps, 74
  using with compasses, 81–82
patch antennas, 34
PC interface (GPS receivers), 34, 42
Pc-Mobile Web site, 35
P-code (Precision) radio signals, 24
PDAs (personal digital assistants), 118
pens and pencils
  adding to new caches, 151–152
  bringing on searches, 115
Persian Gulf War, use of GPS during, 28

personal digital assistants
    (PDAs), 118
physical education courses, using
    GPS in, 190
PID (Point ID, benchmarks), 167, 168
Placed column (Geocaching.com
    search results), 104
placenames (geocache information
    pages), 109
planimetric maps, 72–73
Planning Web site, 151
plasma (ionosphere), and receiver
    accuracy, 29
plastic yard bags, 117
plot displays, 60
Plucker program, 205
PMR (Private Mobile Radio), 118
pocket compasses, 70
Point ID (PID, benchmarks), 167, 168
Portland Geocaching Web site, 183
Portland, Oregon (original
    geocache), 11
postal code searches, 102
precision needs, 27–28
Precision radio signals (P-code), 24
premium account (Geocaching.
    com), 97
primary zones (UTM), 48
Private Mobile Radio (PMR), 118
private property, respecting, 142
protractor, using a compass as, 86
puzzle geocache, 93

• *Q* •

quad sheets (USGS maps), 74
quadrangles (USGS maps), 74
quadrants (magnetic compasses), 67
quadrifilar (quad) helix antenna,
    34–35

• *R* •

radio equipment needs
  Family Radio Service (FRS) radios,
    118
  General Mobile Radio service
    (GMRS) radios, 118
  Private Mobile Radio (PMR), 118

radio transmitters (satellites)
  C/A-code (Coarse Acquisition) radio
    signals, 24, 28
  P-code (Precision) radio signals, 24
reading compasses, 83
reading maps, 75–77
reradiating antennas (GPS
    receivers), 35
retirees, appeal of geocaching to, 16
reusable batteries, 36
routes, 51–52
Royster, David (*GPS: Global
    Positioning Systems and
    Mathematics*), 190
RVers, appeal of geocaching to, 16

• *S* •

SA (Selective Availability), 10, 28
safety equipment, 119–122
satellites
  accuracy, 27
  ephemeris and timing errors, 24
  equipment on, 23
  function, 22–23
  NUDET (NUclear DETonation)
    sensors, 23
  optimal coverage determinations,
    151
  satellite status page, 55
  2-D and 3-D determinations, 25
scale (maps), 75–77
schools, using GPS in, 187–188
Schriever Air Force Base (CO), 24
schwag (swag), defined, 18
screen displays (GPS receivers)
  accuracy indicator, 27
  monochrome versus color, 31
  satellite status page, 55–56
  size, 31–32
searching for caches. *See also* GPS
    receivers; online searches
  benchmark hunting, 173–174
  clothing and footwear needs, 116
  digital cameras, 117
  equipment needs, 112–115
  food and water needs, 115–116
  grid searches, 130

hard-to-find caches, 140–142
last 30 feet, 126–129
safety equipment, 119–122
search strategies, 128–130
shelter needs, 117
using the receiver, 125–126
seconds (measurement units), 46
Selective Availability (SA), 28, 10–11
shells (GPS receivers), 30–31
shelter needs, 117
sighting compasses, 69–70
signal strength indicators, 55–56
signature items, 18, 136
Silva Web site, 70
size and weight (GPS receivers), 42
social aspects of geocaching, 15
sociology courses, using GPS in, 189
South Dakota, geocaching clubs
    in, 183
Southern California Geocachers Web
    site, 181
south-pointers, 62
Southwest Texas Geocachers Web
    site, 183
space blankets, 117
speed caching, 186
spoilers, 18, 110
St. Louis Area Geocachers
    Association Web site, 182
stash hunt, 11
State column (benchmark page), 168
state-based online cache searches,
    102
statistics, personal and competitive,
    141, 184–185
stocking cache containers
  adding identifying information, 152
  adding treasures, Travel Bugs,
    152–153, 159
  logbooks and writing utensils,
    151–152
  restocking, 158
storage capacity, GPS receivers
  tracks and track logs, 53
  waypoints, 51
street maps, 74
students, appeal of geocaching to,
    187–188

sunscreen needs, 117
survey-grade GPS receivers, 28
Suunto Web site, 70
swag (schwag), defined, 18
symbols on maps, 78. *See also* icons
synchronization, importance of, 24, 25

• T •

TBs (Travel Bugs)
  adding to existing caches, 159
  adding to new caches, 152
  defined, 18, 95
  latest, searching for, 100
  removing and logging, 136
team building using geocaching, 15
teams, geocaching, 178
10,000-step programs, 127
Tennessee, geocaching clubs in, 183
terrain, as clue, 129
terrain association, 84, 103
terrain ratings, 104, 108
TerraServer-USA Web site, 75
terrorist attacks, impact on
  geocaching, 148
Texas Geocaching Association Web
  site, 183
Texas, geocaching clubs in, 183
Texas Geocaching Web site, 183
theme caches, 95, 136
time displays, 57, 60
title (maps), 76
TNLN (Took Nothing, Left Nothing),
  defined, 18
Today's Cacher Web site, 201
tools and equipment, overview,
  16–17. *See also* GPS receivers
TopoFusion program, 206
topographic maps
  contour lines (maps), 78–81
  features, 72–74
topographic orientation, 84
track logs/history, 52
tracks (GPS maps), 32, 52–53
trading up, 13, 136, 142
traditional caches, 92
trails (GPS maps), 32, 52–53

transits, 166
travel, as benefit of geocaching, 14
Travel Bugs (TBs)
  adding to existing caches, 159
  adding to new caches, 152
  defined, 18, 95
  latest, searching for, 100
  removing and logging, 136
travel time displays, 60
treasures, trinkets. *See also* Travel
  Bugs (TBs)
  bringing on searches, 114
  leaving and trading, 135–136
  trading up, 13, 136, 142
  what not to leave, 136
Triangle Geocachers Web site, 183
triangulation, 87–88
trigpoints, 163, 165
troposphere conditions and receiver
  accuracy, 29
true north, 63–64
Tulsa Area Geocachers Web site, 183
2-D and 3-D determinations, 25
Type column (benchmark page), 168

• U •

Ulmer, Dave (first geocacher), 11, 92
United States Geological Survey
  (USGS) maps
  colors on, 79
  contour lines, 78–80
  symbols on, 78–79
  uses for, 50, 74
units of measurement
  choosing during setup, 57
  degrees, 45–46, 64, 67, 83
  seconds, 46
  scale, 76–77
Universal Transverse Mercator
  (UTM), 16, 47–49
uploadable maps, 32
U.S. Department of Defense, 26. *See
  also* Global Positioning System
  (GPS)
USAPhotoMaps program, 206
USENET newsgroups, 11, 58

user interface (GPS receivers), 42
user names, aliases
  choosing, 97
  online searches using, 103
  viewing, 105
username searches, 103
USGS Earth Science Corps, 175
USGS (United States Geological
    Survey) maps
  colors on, 79
  contour lines, 78–80
  symbols on, 78–79
  uses for, 50, 74
Utah Geocachers Web site, 183
Utah Geo-Club Web site, 183
UTM (Universal Transverse
    Mercator), 16, 47–49

• *V* •

vertical control points, 164
Virginia, geocaching clubs in, 184
virtual caches, 93, 191

• *W* •

WAAS (Wide Area Augmentation
    System), 27–28, 37–38
Washington State Geocaching
    Association Web site, 184
Washington State, geocaching clubs
    in, 184
Watch the Cache button (geocache
    information page), 159–160
Watcher program, 205
water needs, 115–116
waterproofing, 153
waypoints
  adding to online cache logs, 139
  defined, 11
  entering, 57–59
  for IWIDNF (I Wish I Did Not Find)
    situations, 135
  naming and entering, 59, 105,
    112–113
  routes and legs, 51–52
  searching for caches using, 103
  selecting and navigating to, 59–60

storage capacity for, 51
versus tracks, 52
uses for, 32
using to locate caches, 126
viewing lists of, 108
weather conditions, and receiver
    accuracy, 30
Web cam caches, 94
Web page formatting codes (HTML),
    156
Web sites
  Adventure Medical Kits, 119
  Alabama Geocachers Association,
    181
  Alaska Geocaching, 181
  Arizona Geocaching, 181
  Arkansas State Parks, 181
  Battery University, 58
  benchmark information sites, 165
  benchmark photo gallery, 166
  BMGPX benchmark plotting
    program, 170
  Brunton, 70
  Buxley's Geocaching Waypoint, 200
  cache league competition, 186
  CacheMate program, 204
  camouflage painting, 145
  Central Oregon Geocaching, 183
  Chicago Geocachers, 182
  Chicagoland Geocachers, 182
  ClayJar, 156
  Colorado Geocaching Association,
    182
  compass manufacturers, 70
  coordinate calculators and
    converters, 47
  datum conversions, 107
  daypacks, 115
  declination information, 65
  Degree Confluence Project, 19, 189
  DeLorme, 74
  educational resources, 195–196
  Emerald Valley Cachers, 183
  The First 100 Geocaches, 202
  flashlights and headlamps, 120
  Florida Cachers, 182
  Florida Geocachers, 182
  FRS and GMS radios, 118

Web sites *(continued)*
  Geocacher University, 201
  Geocachers of Central Kentucky, 182
  Geocachers of Southeast Tennessee,
    183
  Geocaching Hampton Roads, 184
  Geocaching Swiss Army Knife
    (GSAK) program, 204
  Geocaching.com, 9, 12, 199
  geodashing, 19
  geodesy information, 164
  Geographer's Craft, 50
  Georgia Geocachers Association,
    182
  GPS drawing gallery, 19
  GPS Hawaii, 182
  GPS Information, 42
  GPS receiver manufacturers, 39
  GPS Visualizer, 200
  GPSBabel program, 205–206
  GPSInformation.net, 202
  GPXSonar program, 204
  Great Plains Geocaching,
    182, 183, 184
  handling topographic maps, 74
  HTML tutorial, 156
  Huntsville Area Geocachers, 181
  Idaho Geocachers, 182
  Illinois Central Area Cache Hunting
    Enthusiasts, 182
  Indiana Geocaching, 182
  Institute for Application of
    Geospatial Technology (IAGT),
    196
  KeenPeople.com, 201
  Lane Education Service District, 195
  Leave No Trace, 142
  Letterboxing, 13, 94
  Letterboxing North America, 202
  locationless caches, 191
  Louisiana Center for Educational
    Studies, 195
  Louisiana Geocaching, 182
  map sites, 74–75
  Map Tools, 78
  MapQuest, 75, 122–124
  Maptech, 74

Markwell's FAQs, 201
Maryland Geocaching Society, 182
Michigan Geocaching Organization,
  135, 182
Middle Tennessee Geocachers, 183
Minnesota Geocaching Association,
  182
Mississippi Geocachers
  Association, 182
Missouri, Arkansas Geocachers
  Association, 181, 182
The Mountaineers, 121
National Geodetic Survey (NGS),
  19,166, 169–171
National Geographic Expeditions,
  190
Navicache.com, 200
NE Ohio Geocachers, 183
Nevada Geocaching, 183
New York Geocaching Organization,
  183
North Carolina Geocachers
  Association, 183
NYGPS, 195
Odden's Bookmarks, 75
Ohio, Kentucky and Indiana
  Geocachers, 182
Oklahoma Geocachers, 183
online orienteering, 84
Oregon Geocaching, 184
Ozark Mountain Geocachers,
  181, 182
Pc-Mobile, 35
PDAs (personal digital assistants),
  118
Planning, 151
Plucker program, 205
Portland Geocaching, 183
Red Cross, 120
reradiating antennas, 35
Silva, 70
Southern California Geocachers, 181
Southwest Texas Geocachers, 183
St. Louis Area Geocachers
  Association, 182
state geocaching clubs, 181–184
Suunto, 70
10,000-step programs, 127

TerraServer-USA, 75
Texas Geocaching, 183
Texas Geocaching Association, 183
Today's Cacher, 201
TopoFusion program, 206
trekking poles, 116
Triangle Geocachers, 183
Tulsa Area Geocachers, 183
USAPhotoMaps program, 206
USGS Earth Science Corps, 175
USGS (United States Geological
    Survey) maps, 78
Utah Geocachers, 183
Utah Geo-Club, 183
Washington State Geocaching
    Association, 184
Watcher program, 205
Whitnall Middle School curriculum,
    193
Wisconsin Geocaching Association,
    184
writing materials and log books, 115
ZIP codes, 99

weight loss, as benefit of geocaching,
    127
WGS 84 (World Geodetic System 1984)
    datum, 50, 57
whistles, 120
Whitnall Middle School curriculum,
    193
Wide Area Augmentation System
    (WAAS), 27–28, 37–38
Wilkerson, James (*Medicine for
    Mountaineering & Other
    Wilderness Activities*), 119
Wisconsin Geocaching Association
    Web site, 184
World Geodetic System 1984 (WGS 84)
    datum, 50, 57

● *Z* ●

ZIP code searches, 98–99

Notes

FOR
DUMMIES®

Helping you expand your horizons and realize your potential

PERSONAL FINANCE & BUSINESS

0-7645-2431-3   0-7645-5331-3   0-7645-5307-0

Also available:

Accounting For Dummies
(0-7645-5314-3)

Business Plans Kit For
Dummies
(0-7645-5365-8)

Managing For Dummies
(1-5688-4858-7)

Mutual Funds For
Dummies
(0-7645-5329-1)

QuickBooks All-in-One
Desk Reference For
Dummies
(0-7645-1963-8)

Resumes For Dummies
(0-7645-5471-9)

Small Business Kit For
Dummies
(0-7645-5093-4)

Starting an eBay Business
For Dummies
(0-7645-1547-0)

Taxes For Dummies 2003
(0-7645-5475-1)

HOME, GARDEN, FOOD & WINE

0-7645-5295-3   0-7645-5130-2   0-7645-5250-3

Also available:

Bartending For Dummies
(0-7645-5051-9)

Christmas Cooking For
Dummies
(0-7645-5407-7)

Cookies For Dummies
(0-7645-5390-9)

Diabetes Cookbook For
Dummies
(0-7645-5230-9)

Grilling For Dummies
(0-7645-5076-4)

Home Maintenance For
Dummies
(0-7645-5215-5)

Slow Cookers For
Dummies
(0-7645-5240-6)

Wine For Dummies
(0-7645-5114-0)

FITNESS, SPORTS, HOBBIES & PETS

0-7645-5167-1   0-7645-5146-9   0-7645-5106-X

Also available:

Cats For Dummies
(0-7645-5275-9

Chess For Dummies
(0-7645-5003-9)

Dog Training For
Dummies
(0-7645-5286-4)

Labrador Retrievers For
Dummies
(0-7645-5281-3)

Martial Arts For Dummies
(0-7645-5358-5)

Piano For Dummies
(0-7645-5105-1)

Pilates For Dummies
(0-7645-5397-6)

Power Yoga For Dummies
(0-7645-5342-9)

Puppies For Dummies
(0-7645-5255-4)

Quilting For Dummies
(0-7645-5118-3)

Rock Guitar For Dummies
(0-7645-5356-9)

Weight Training For
Dummies
(0-7645-5168-X)

Available wherever books are sold.
Go to www.dummies.com or call 1-877-762-2974 to order direct

FOR DUMMIES®

A world of resources to help you grow

TRAVEL

Italy For Dummies
0-7645-5453-0

Hawaii For Dummies
0-7645-5438-7

Walt Disney World & Orlando For Dummies
0-7645-5444-1

Also available:

America's National Parks For Dummies
(0-7645-6204-5)

Caribbean For Dummies
(0-7645-5445-X)

Cruise Vacations For Dummies 2003
(0-7645-5459-X)

Europe For Dummies
(0-7645-5456-5)

Ireland For Dummies
(0-7645-6199-5)

France For Dummies
(0-7645-6292-4)

Las Vegas For Dummies
(0-7645-5448-4)

London For Dummies
(0-7645-5416-6)

Mexico's Beach Resorts For Dummies
(0-7645-6262-2)

Paris For Dummies
(0-7645-5494-8)

RV Vacations For Dummies
(0-7645-5443-3)

EDUCATION & TEST PREPARATION

Spanish For Dummies
0-7645-5194-9

Algebra For Dummies
0-7645-5325-9

U.S. History For Dummies
0-7645-5249-X

Also available:

The ACT For Dummies
(0-7645-5210-4)

Chemistry For Dummies
(0-7645-5430-1)

English Grammar For Dummies
(0-7645-5322-4)

French For Dummies
(0-7645-5193-0)

GMAT For Dummies
(0-7645-5251-1)

Inglés Para Dummies
(0-7645-5427-1)

Italian For Dummies
(0-7645-5196-5)

Research Papers For Dummies
(0-7645-5426-3)

SAT I For Dummies
(0-7645-5472-7)

U.S. History For Dummies
(0-7645-5249-X)

World History For Dummies
(0-7645-5242-2)

HEALTH, SELF-HELP & SPIRITUALITY

Diabetes For Dummies
0-7645-5154-X

Sex For Dummies
0-7645-5302-X

Parenting For Dummies
0-7645-5418-2

Also available:

The Bible For Dummies
(0-7645-5296-1)

Controlling Cholesterol For Dummies
(0-7645-5440-9)

Dating For Dummies
(0-7645-5072-1)

Dieting For Dummies
(0-7645-5126-4)

High Blood Pressure For Dummies
(0-7645-5424-7)

Judaism For Dummies
(0-7645-5299-6)

Menopause For Dummies
(0-7645-5458-1)

Nutrition For Dummies
(0-7645-5180-9)

Potty Training For Dummies
(0-7645-5417-4)

Pregnancy For Dummies
(0-7645-5074-8)

Rekindling Romance For Dummies
(0-7645-5303-8)

Religion For Dummies
(0-7645-5264-3)

Available wherever books are sold. Go to www.dummies.com or call 1-877-762-2974 to order direct

FOR DUMMIES

A world of resources to help you grow

HOME & BUSINESS COMPUTER BASICS

0-7645-0838-5

0-7645-1663-9

0-7645-1548-9

Also available:

Excel 2002 All-in-One Desk Reference For Dummies
(0-7645-1794-5)

Office XP 9-in-1 Desk Reference For Dummies
(0-7645-0819-9)

PCs All-in-One Desk Reference For Dummies
(0-7645-0791-5)

Troubleshooting Your PC For Dummies
(0-7645-1669-8)

Upgrading & Fixing PCs For Dummies
(0-7645-1665-5)

Windows XP For Dummies
(0-7645-0893-8)

Windows XP For Dummies Quick Reference
(0-7645-0897-0)

Word 2002 For Dummies
(0-7645-0839-3)

INTERNET & DIGITAL MEDIA

0-7645-0894-6

0-7645-1642-6

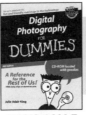

0-7645-1664-7

Also available:

CD and DVD Recording For Dummies
(0-7645-1627-2)

Digital Photography All-in-One Desk Reference For Dummies
(0-7645-1800-3)

eBay For Dummies
(0-7645-1642-6)

Genealogy Online For Dummies
(0-7645-0807-5)

Internet All-in-One Desk Reference For Dummies
(0-7645-1659-0)

Internet For Dummies Quick Reference
(0-7645-1645-0)

Internet Privacy For Dummies
(0-7645-0846-6)

Paint Shop Pro For Dummies
(0-7645-2440-2)

Photo Retouching & Restoration For Dummies
(0-7645-1662-0)

Photoshop Elements For Dummies
(0-7645-1675-2)

Scanners For Dummies
(0-7645-0783-4)

Get smart! Visit www.dummies.com

- **Find listings of even more Dummies titles**
- **Browse online articles, excerpts, and how-to's**
- **Sign up for daily or weekly e-mail tips**
- **Check out Dummies fitness videos and other products**
- **Order from our online bookstore**

Available wherever books are sold. Go to www.dummies.com or call 1-877-762-2974 to order direct

FOR DUMMIES

Helping you expand your horizons and realize your potential

GRAPHICS & WEB SITE DEVELOPMENT

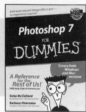

Photoshop 7 For Dummies
0-7645-1651-5

Creating Web Pages For Dummies
0-7645-1643-4

Macromedia Flash MX For Dummies
0-7645-0895-4

Also available:

Adobe Acrobat 5 PDF For Dummies
(0-7645-1652-3)

ASP.NET For Dummies
(0-7645-0866-0)

ColdFusion MX For Dummies
(0-7645-1672-8)

Dreamweaver MX For Dummies
(0-7645-1630-2)

FrontPage 2002 For Dummies
(0-7645-0821-0)

HTML 4 For Dummies
(0-7645-0723-0)

Illustrator 10 For Dummies
(0-7645-3636-2)

PowerPoint 2002 For Dummies
(0-7645-0817-2)

Web Design For Dummies
(0-7645-0823-7)

PROGRAMMING & DATABASES

C++ For Dummies
0-7645-0746-X

Visual Studio .NET All-in-One Desk Reference For Dummies
0-7645-1626-4

XML For Dummies
0-7645-1657-4

Also available:

Access 2002 For Dummies
(0-7645-0818-0)

Beginning Programming For Dummies
(0-7645-0835-0)

Crystal Reports 9 For Dummies
(0-7645-1641-8)

Java & XML For Dummies
(0-7645-1658-2)

Java 2 For Dummies
(0-7645-0765-6)

JavaScript For Dummies
(0-7645-0633-1)

Oracle9i For Dummies
(0-7645-0880-6)

Perl For Dummies
(0-7645-0776-1)

PHP and MySQL For Dummies
(0-7645-1650-7)

SQL For Dummies
(0-7645-0737-0)

Visual Basic .NET For Dummies
(0-7645-0867-9)

LINUX, NETWORKING & CERTIFICATION

Red Hat Linux 7.3 For Dummies
0-7645-1545-4

TCP/IP For Dummies
0-7645-1760-0

Networking For Dummies
0-7645-0772-9

Also available:

A+ Certification For Dummies
(0-7645-0812-1)

CCNP All-in-One Certification For Dummies
(0-7645-1648-5)

Cisco Networking For Dummies
(0-7645-1668-X)

CISSP For Dummies
(0-7645-1670-1)

CIW Foundations For Dummies
(0-7645-1635-3)

Firewalls For Dummies
(0-7645-0884-9)

Home Networking For Dummies
(0-7645-0857-1)

Red Hat Linux All-in-One Desk Reference For Dummies
(0-7645-2442-9)

UNIX For Dummies
(0-7645-0419-3)

Available wherever books are sold.
Go to www.dummies.com or call 1-877-762-2974 to order direct